WHAT REALLY HAPPENED: THE DEATH OF HITLER

WHAT REALLY HAPPENED

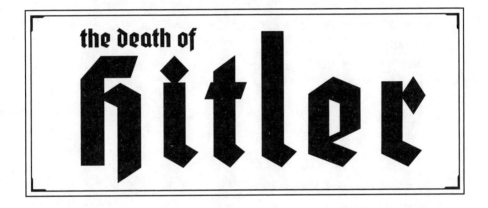

the death of

hitler

ROBERT J. HUTCHINSON

REGNERY
HISTORY

Regnery History™ is a trademark of Salem Communications Holding Corporation
Regnery® is a registered trademark of Salem Communications Holding Corporation

ISBN: 978-1-62157-888-8
eISBN: 978-1-62157-889-5
Library of Congress Control Number: 2020932917

Published in the United States by
Regnery History, an imprint of
Regnery Publishing
A Division of Salem Media Group
300 New Jersey Ave NW
Washington, DC 20001
www.Regnery.com

Manufactured in the United States of America

10 9 8 7 6 5 4 3 2 1

Books are available in quantity for promotional or premium use. For information on discounts and terms, please visit our website: www.Regnery.com.

For Kelly, Tim, Barney, Barry, and Kathleen

Rebellion against tyrants is obedience to God.

—Benjamin Franklin

CONTENTS

INTRODUCTION

The announcement, although longed for by much of the civilized world, was still a surprise when it came.

At 10:25 p.m. on May 1, 1945, German radio ceased the music it was playing, Bruckner's Seventh Symphony. A stern announcer's voice came on the air:

"It is reported from the Führer's headquarters that our Führer Adolf Hitler, fighting to the last breath against Bolshevism, fell for Germany this afternoon in his operational headquarters in the Reich Chancellery," the announcer intoned in German. "On April 30, the Führer appointed Grand Admiral Dönitz his successor."[1]

A moment later, the voice of Grand-Admiral Karl Dönitz, commander-in-chief of German forces in the north, came over the radio waves:

"German men and women, soldiers of the armed forces: Our Führer, Adolf Hitler, has fallen," Dönitz declared. "In the deepest sorrow and respect the German people bow. At an early date he had recognized the frightful danger of Bolshevism and dedicated his existence to this struggle. At the end of his struggle, of his unswerving straight road of life, stands his hero's death in the capital of the German Reich. His life has

Based on Nazi radio reports, newspapers around the world featured enormous headlines stating that Hitler was dead, including this May 2, 1945, edition of the U.S. Army newspaper *The Stars and Stripes. Wikimedia Commons*

been one single service for Germany. His activity in the fight against the Bolshevik storm flood concerned not only Europe but the entire civilized world."

Then Dönitz repeated what the announcer had said—that he was now the acting head of state. Dönitz asked for the German people's confidence as he strove to save Germany from destruction by "the advancing Bolshevist enemy." He promised his listeners that "if we do all that is in our power, God will not forsake us after so much suffering and sacrifice."

The next day papers across the world broadcast the stunning news with banner headlines.

"Der Führer Gefallen," reported the *Hamburger Zeitung*.[2] "Hitler Dead," the U.S. Army newspaper, *The Stars and Stripes*, blared in giant type that took up half the page.

Other papers mirrored the message, with a few noting that there was no actual evidence for this news aside from the claims of the Nazis themselves.

From the very first reports of Hitler's death, there was skepticism. The Nazis hadn't invented fake news, but they had certainly perfected it, and some newspapers were understandably hesitant to accept the reports at face value.

"I still find it difficult to believe that Hitler is really dead," the Associated Press's Berlin correspondent Louis Lochner wrote. "Hitler couldn't afford to accept unconditional surrender, so what may prove to be the legend of his meeting a hero's death had to be staged. I still cannot escape the feeling that Hitler is some place where nobody expects him to be."

The problem was that no one in the West could investigate what really happened for quite some time.

Western Allied forces did not enter Berlin for almost two full months after Germany formally surrendered on May 8, 1945.

While the conquest of the city had been assigned to Soviet Russia at the Yalta Conference the previous February, U.S. and British commanders had wanted to push ahead anyway. British Field Marshal Bernard Montgomery's 21st Army Group was within striking distance of the city from the west, and there were plans for the U.S. Army's 17th Airborne Division, 82d Airborne Division, and 101st Airborne Division to seize the key Berlin airfields of Tempelhof, Rangdor, and Gatow.

But other Allied military leaders, including General Dwight Eisenhower, supreme commander of Allied forces in Europe, feared that Nazi forces might try to take up a redoubt in the heavily defended German Alps where they could delay the end of the war by months, perhaps even years. One of the biggest rumors of World War II was that the Nazis had built a vast, virtually impregnable underground fortress hidden in the Alps. But that wasn't the only reason American forces held off from seizing Berlin. Another American general, Omar Bradley, warned that it might cost a hundred thousand casualties to capture the capital in the face of desperate German resistance.

As a result, Eisenhower ordered Western Allied forces not to cross the Elbe and Mulde Rivers to the west of Berlin. Instead, the Western Allies would concentrate on southern Germany and on cutting off any resistance there, making sure German troops did not head into the mountains. The United States would let Stalin have Berlin.

For seven weeks, U.S. and British military forces stood outside the German capital as the 1st Belorussian Front of the Soviet Red Army, under the command of Marshal Georgy Zhukov, destroyed and looted much of the city.

What the German population had feared the most, the vengeance of the Soviet military, is precisely what it got. There were widespread reports of summary executions and rapes of German women.[3] Thousands of German women committed suicide rather than endure that fate. There were accounts of men shooting their wives and all of their children. Some women deliberately slashed their faces with razors to avoid attracting the attention of Soviet soldiers.

The British were furious. They had wanted to capture Berlin and were already thinking about what the postwar map of Europe would look like. Eisenhower, a soldier and not a statesman, wanted the war to end as quickly as possible and with as few Allied casualties as possible. He was regarded as dangerously naïve by British leaders such as Winston Churchill.

When the Western forces finally did enter Berlin on the Fourth of July, 1945, to take control of their respective sectors, one of the great mysteries they faced was this: What happened to Adolf Hitler?

People today, accustomed to movie reconstructions of Hitler's final days in the so-called Führerbunker, as in the 2004 German film *Downfall*, don't realize that these reconstructions took decades to gradually piece together. Many of the witnesses to the final days in the Führerbunker were dead, missing, or being held prisoner in Soviet military camps, kept away from both journalists and Western intelligence investigators. Some were able to tell their versions of what happened only a decade or more after the war had ended. A few never told the full stories of what they knew until the 1990s or even the 2000s.

The truth is, in the early months and years after the war, no one in the West knew what really happened to Adolf Hitler. All investigators had to go on were the initial reports from the Nazis themselves and conflicting statements from the Soviets. And no one seemed able to produce a body...or even part of a body.

By all accounts, Soviet troops arrived at Hitler's Chancellery headquarters on May 2. At first, the Soviets said they had found no remains of Adolf Hitler at all. He appeared to have vanished. However, just a few days later, Russian sources contradicted this initial report and said that Hitler had, in fact, been killed and his body burned. They also produced a photograph of a dead man who looked very much like Hitler with a bullet hole in his forehead, a body said to have been found inside the bombed-out bunker. Yet by the end of that summer of 1945, the Soviets had reversed themselves yet again and were now claiming that Hitler actually had escaped…aided by the Western Allies!

Where Was Hitler's Body?

In the final days of the war, Berlin was in chaos. Soviet units battled the remnants of the German army, reinforced by teenage boys and old men, in savage door-to-door combat. Top Nazi officials such as SS Chief Heinrich Himmler put on disguises and were caught trying to sneak out of the city under assumed names. Others, including Hitler's longtime secretary and confidant Martin Bormann, vanished without a trace.

Many wondered: Could the same thing have happened with Hitler?

It was well known that the German dictator had used body doubles, including a man named Gustav Weler, who occasionally took Hitler's place at ceremonial events.

Could top Nazis have faked the Führer's death, killed one of the body doubles—and spirited their leader out of the country?

While unlikely, such a scenario was not outside the realm of possibility. Even during the final Soviet assault, planes continued to fly in and out of Berlin, using the city's deserted boulevards as makeshift runways. Nazi Armaments Minister Albert Speer had flown into the city on April 23 to say a final goodbye to Hitler, Eva Braun, and his other comrades. A plane was spotted taking off from the East-West Axis Road, in the Tiergarten, as late as April 28. Could Hitler have escaped by plane?

In early July, after American forces had entered Berlin, *Time* magazine reported that Hitler's chauffeur had claimed that the Nazi leader had been shot in the head and his body burned outside the Reich Chancellery.

Yet if that were true, where were Hitler's remains? Where was Hitler's body?

To this day, it has never been found.

From the late 1940s until the mid-1960s, sensationalist tabloids such as the *Police Gazette* regularly ran stories alleging that Adolf Hitler had escaped from Germany and was living secretly in Argentina. *Pulp International*

To make matters even more confusing, in July 1945, British newspapers began reporting that a Soviet officer had claimed that a blackened body thought to have been Hitler's corpse was in reality "a very poor double."[4]

Not surprisingly, rumors about what really happened to Hitler ran wild in the years after the war.

Almost immediately, in July and August 1945, there were reports that Hitler had been sighted alive. There were literally thousands of news reports of Hitler sightings in 1945 and then throughout the rest of the 1940s.

"The Hitler mystery continues to grow daily," one newspaper report in recently declassified FBI files stated. "As most of the other Nazi bigwigs prepare to go on trial for their lives at Nuremberg, the most hunted of all the Nazis, Adolf Hitler, still is absent and unaccounted for. Is Hitler dead or alive or in hiding? If he died, as most of his confederates claim, why has his body never been identified or found?"[5]

One account said that Hitler had succumbed to a cerebral hemorrhage. Another claimed that the Nazi leader had been held prisoner by Himmler. Still others asserted that Hitler had escaped from Berlin at the last minute and made his way to South America.

The most plausible rumor was that Hitler and Eva Braun had boarded a small plane at the last minute, flown to a secret Nazi airbase in Denmark and then on to Spain, and then escaped Europe by submarine, traveling across the Atlantic to the German colony in Argentina. The idea was that, before Hitler and Braun escaped, subordinates had dressed another man's corpse in the Nazi leader's uniform and a woman's body in Eva Braun's clothes to make it appear they had died.

This rumor was buttressed by apparently accurate accounts of German submarine activity off the Argentine coast in the summer of 1945. The rumors were sufficiently credible that no less an authority than General Eisenhower himself was reported to have believed, at least for a time, that Hitler actually had escaped.

More creative stories even claimed that the doubles likely had dental work done before they were killed to fool any doctors carrying out autopsies on their bodies.

The Official Story

In September 1945, the Western Allies launched an investigation to determine the truth. British intelligence decided to get to the bottom of conflicting Soviet accounts and possible disinformation to find out what really happened in the Führerbunker in late April. A young British Army major, Hugh Trevor-Roper, who in civilian life was a professional historian at Oxford, was assigned to investigate the matter.

Trevor-Roper spent only two months on his initial investigation and was only able to interview about seven German eyewitnesses. Many of the key witnesses of events in the final days in the bunker had been taken away to Soviet prison camps.

Nevertheless, Trevor-Roper's account of what happened to Hitler, published in his 1947 book *The Last Days of Hitler,* became the consensus view among mainstream historians and remains so to this day. (Trevor-Roper's credibility took a beating in the 1980s, however, when he vouched for the authenticity of one of history's great hoaxes, the forged documents known as *The Hitler Diaries.*)

According to Trevor-Roper and most professional historians, by the last days of April 1945 it was apparent to all, including Hitler himself, that the jig was up. The Thousand Year Reich was coming to an end after just a dozen years.

Berlin was surrounded by the Soviet Red Army. Soviet artillery units were systematically destroying the city, block by block. Hitler believed that his two most trusted lieutenants, Field Marshal Hermann Göring and Heinrich Himmler, had both betrayed him—Göring by trying to usurp his position as Führer and Himmler by negotiating with the Allies.

In the early hours of April 29, according to the official consensus, Hitler married his longtime mistress, Eva Braun, and then dictated his last will and testament to his secretary, Gertraud "Traudl" Junge. Perhaps mindful of the ignominious end of Benito Mussolini and his mistress—hanged upside down for public humiliation in Milan just two days before—Hitler stated in his will that he had no intention of suffering execution at the hands of his enemies.

"I will not fall into the hands of an enemy who requests a new spectacle, exhibited by the Jews, to divert his hysterical masses," Hitler declared in the document, which the Allies obtained after the war. "I have therefore decided to remain in Berlin, and there to choose death voluntarily at the moment when I believe the residency of the Führer and Chancellor can no longer be held."

According to the witnesses interviewed by Trevor-Roper, the next day, April 30, Hitler ate lunch with his two secretaries around two in the afternoon. He was then joined by his new wife, who wore a dark blue dress. The couple met with everyone remaining in the Führerbunker, shaking hands and bidding farewell.

Around 3:30 p.m., Hitler and Eva Braun retired to Hitler's spare personal quarters. After a brief delay, a single shot was heard. When two men finally entered the bedroom, they found Hitler lying dead on the sofa, soaked with blood. Next to him lay Braun, an unused revolver lying next to her. She apparently had died by biting down on a cyanide capsule.

The body of Hitler was wrapped in a blanket and carried, along with that of Braun, down the bunker hallway passages to a stairway leading to the emergency exit above. Outside, machine-gun fire crisscrossed nearby streets and artillery shells could be heard pounding the neighborhood.

Two or more people were observed by a guard in a nearby gun tower carrying Hitler's body, the face and chest wrapped in a blanket, while another carried the clearly visible body of Eva Braun. The men laid the two bodies side by side in a large bomb crater in the garden outside the bunker. They then poured over them 180 liters of gasoline from five Jerry cans that had been placed nearby earlier that morning.

But before the soldiers had finished the job, Russian artillery fire forced them to retreat to the safety of the bunker doorway. One of the men had to light a rag doused in gasoline and toss it from the bunker doorway over to the depression where the bodies had been placed. As the gasoline caught fire and the bodies burst into flames, the soldiers stood at attention and raised the Nazi salute. Continuing artillery fire forced them to seek refuge in the bunker, but they returned periodically to pour more gasoline upon the corpses.

After dark, when the bodies had been burning for a few hours, the soldiers returned to bury what was left of them. The soldiers moved the remains to a nearby bomb crater, filled the crater with dirt, and smoothed the dirt over. They intended to keep the burial site a secret, but the guard in the tower was still watching, and he could see the burial spot clearly. And, it would turn out, he was not the only witness.

This was where Hugh Trevor-Roper ended his account—with the burial of the bodies. The Oxford historian admitted that he was unable to determine what happened to Hitler and Eva Braun's mortal remains. Their bones, he said, "have never been found."

The Continuing Mystery Surrounding Hitler's Death

Inevitably, much of the public remained skeptical of the official story. Polls taken at the end of the war revealed that 50 percent of Americans didn't believe Adolf Hitler and Eva Braun had committed suicide in their bunker in 1945 as captured Nazi officials claimed. Instead, they believed the dictator had faked his own death and escaped, perhaps to Argentina.

This wasn't a crazy opinion. It was widely reported in the news that Joseph Stalin had told Allied leaders that Soviet forces never discovered Hitler's body and that he personally believed the Nazi leader had escaped justice. At least two German submarines crossed the Atlantic and landed on the coast of Argentina in July 1945. Plus, there were numerous reports of top Nazi officials successfully fleeing to South America, where there was a large German colony.

And as incredible as it sounds, the mystery surrounding Adolf Hitler's death only deepened over the decades. In May 1960, Israeli agents announced that they had kidnapped and spirited away to Israel none other than SS-Obersturmbannführer Adolf Eichmann, one of the chief facilitators of the Holocaust. He had been living quietly under an assumed name in a house he had built for his family at 14 Garibaldi Street in the San Fernando neighborhood of Buenos Aires. Eichmann's capture seemed to give credence to the theory—later popularized in Frederick Forsyth's 1974 novel *The Odessa File*—that there existed a secret international network dedicated to helping top Nazis escape after the war.

A few years after Eichmann was tried and executed by the Israeli government, the Soviets appeared to change their story once again. In 1964, Marshal Vasily L. Chuikov, the Soviet general who led the final assault on Berlin, claimed in his published memoirs that the Soviet Army had indeed found the "scorched body of Hitler"—despite what Stalin and other Soviet leaders had said—when they arrived at the Reich chancellery building on May 2, 1945.

"When the troops of the Eighth Guards Army broke into the courtyard of the Reich Chancellery on the morning of May 2, they found a still smoking rug, and in it the scorched body of Hitler," Chuikov wrote.[6] The general didn't say, however, what the Soviets ultimately did with Hitler's remains. Four years later, in 1968, a Russian journalist claimed he knew what had really happened. In a book published in Germany, the journalist, Lev Bezymenski, who had served as an interpreter during the Battle of Berlin, stated that the Soviets had secretly buried Hitler's body in a hidden location, along with the remains of Eva Braun and the entire family of Nazi propaganda minister Joseph Goebbels. What's more, he added that the Soviets had physical evidence of Hitler's death in their top secret archives—a portion of his skull, teeth, and jawbone.

This was an important development—yet this account, too, was widely doubted. For one thing, the Soviets adamantly refused to allow outside experts to examine any of the physical evidence they claimed to have in their possession. Soviet officials permitted Bezymenski to reproduce in his book photographs of teeth they claimed were Hitler's but refused to allow any Western scientists or investigators to see, much less examine, the dental remains for themselves. Only after the fall of the Soviet Union in the 1990s, and then again in 2003, did Russian officials permit Western journalists to take new photographs of skull and jaw fragments that the Russians claimed had been taken from Hitler's autopsy a half-century earlier.

And it wasn't until 2009, sixty-four years after Hitler's alleged death in 1945, that the Russians finally allowed scientific experts to test the physical remains, and they weren't happy with the results. University of Connecticut archaeologist and bone specialist Nick Bellantoni flew to Moscow to examine the skull fragments and perform DNA tests. His conclusions shocked the world: The skull fragment that the Russians claimed was from Hitler had actually belonged to a woman between the ages of twenty and forty, Bellatoni announced. It was not Hitler's skull after all.

This was a bombshell revelation that resulted in headlines across the world.

"Tests on skull fragment cast doubt on Adolf Hitler suicide story," *The Guardian* asserted in a headline in September 2009. The paper concluded, "In the wake of new revelations, the histories of Hitler's death may need to be rewritten—and left open-ended."[7]

"Adolf Hitler may not have shot himself dead and perhaps did not even die in his bunker, it emerged yesterday," agreed the UK's *Daily Mail* newspaper. "The story of Hitler's death will have to [be] rewritten as a mystery—and conspiracy theorists are likely to latch on to the possibility that he may not have died in the bunker at all."[8]

That claim was an understatement.

Almost immediately, a slew of books appeared asserting that Hitler not only hadn't died in the manner historians had long believed—shooting himself in the head in his underground bunker—but had actually escaped to Argentina, just as the Soviets had originally claimed. The most influential of these revisionist accounts was Gerrard Williams and Simon Dunstan's 2011 thriller, *Grey Wolf: The Escape of Adolf Hitler.*

As unbelievable as the conspiracy theories in these books appeared, it soon came to light that at least some experts had taken the claims of Hitler's escape seriously enough to investigate them: officials at the U.S. Federal Bureau of Investigation (FBI) and Central Intelligence Agency (CIA).

In 2014, President Barack Obama signed an executive order authorizing the release of all top secret FBI and some CIA documents related to Hitler's death. Researchers quickly discovered that both agencies had indeed investigated claims of Hitler's escape well into the 1950s and beyond, even dispatching field agents to Argentina. Because of this, in 2015, the History Channel launched a three-year reality TV series, *Hunting Hitler*, hosted by a former CIA case worker, that set out to investigate afresh the circumstances of Hitler's death. As the series was running, in 2017, Western scientists were finally able to perform exhaustive forensic analyses on the physical remains the Russians have in their archives.

What Really Happened?

Thus, as we can see, there has been enough obscurity and conflicting claims surrounding the death of Adolf Hitler that it seemed an appropriate subject for the recently launched What Really Happened™ series.

The goal of this series is to summarize the facts surrounding key events in history as clearly and accurately as possible, without embellishment. The series seeks to avoid theories, conspiracy or otherwise, and stick closely to what is actually known or can be reasonably proven from existing evidence. For this book, then, I wanted to tackle head-on some of the enduring questions that have surrounded Hitler's death, including...

- What did surviving Nazi eyewitnesses really say about the Führer's final days in the bunker—and could they have been lying to aid Hitler's escape?
- If Hitler didn't escape, why did the Allies not find his body?
- What about Hitler's proven use of body doubles? Could Hitler have used a body double in the bunker while he and Eva Braun flew to safety in a long-range aircraft that took off from a runway in Berlin's Tiergarten?
- How did Hitler managed to escape numerous assassination attempts when hundreds of top military leaders were plotting his death?
- Why did the FBI continue to investigate reports of Hitler's survival for more than a decade after World War II— reports that were only declassified in 2014?
- What about sensational claims in books such as *Grey Wolf* that Hitler and Eva Braun lived in an isolated chalet in the Andes—and that Hitler died in 1962?
- Why were forensic tests on crucial physical evidence only conducted in 2017, more than seventy years after World War II ended?

...to name just a few.

To probe these questions, I delved into mainstream historical accounts written by Hugh Trevor-Roper and other top historians, examined firsthand the once–Top Secret reports in FBI and CIA files released in 2014, and studied the first-person accounts of eyewitnesses who were with Hitler in his bunker during the final days of World War II.

Some of these eyewitness memoirs have become available only in the last few years as the last surviving Nazis, such as Hitler's bodyguard,

Rochus Misch, penned their autobiographies in their old age (Misch wrote his account, in German, in 2013). And as noted above, the results of physical tests, conducted in 2017, only became available in 2018.

To piece the story together, we begin with the famous attempt to assassinate Hitler that occurred on July 20, 1944, long planned by high-ranking officers in the German military but finally carried out by the young German aristocrat Claus von Stauffenberg. We begin with this and other assassination attempts because what happened later—Hitler's final orders and decision to hole up in an underground bunker in Berlin—was shaped by Hitler's perception that he had been betrayed by his own military. And a look at the July 20 assassination plot inevitably requires briefly exploring some background information on who Hitler was, how he came to power so quickly, and why he was able to captivate an entire nation to such a degree that the only way they could break free was through his death. From there, we trace the unfortunate events that prevented Stauffenberg from succeeding and explore how Hitler's survival only fed his increasingly irrational sense of his own invincibility and drove forward the final bloody events of the war. In the final months of 1944 and in early 1945, it became clear to many that Germany was an apocalyptic drama right out of Wagner's operas, a Götterdämmerung or "twilight of the gods" in which Hitler would fight to the death. The failure of the German military to kill Hitler meant there would be no negotiated peace and no pause in the carnage—that the industrialized slaughter would go on until Hitler was dead. Finally, we examine how the final climax to the story—the death of Hitler—ended up not merely shrouded in mystery but actually covered over, for more than sixty-five years, with deliberate lies and deception. As we will see, the answer to the question of what really happened to Adolf Hitler was only definitely resolved in 2018.

As part of this investigation, I took a year-long crash course in German at a local college and traveled to Berlin to see for myself the site of Hitler's bunker (now buried beneath a parking lot off Gertrude-Kolmar-Strasse), the Bendlerblock complex of offices where Colonel Stauffenberg plotted Hitler's death and was himself executed, the Reichstag, the

Wannsee Villa where the Final Solution was revealed and discussed, Plötzensee Prison where Hitler's would-be assassins were executed, Stauffenberg's house, and other sites related to the Nazi era. I also watched the twenty-two lost film interviews with Führerbunker eyewitnesses, conducted in 1948 by Nuremberg Judge Michael Musmanno but only rediscovered and released to the American public in 2015.

As with all book projects I've undertaken, I could not have finished this one without the support and patience of my wife and children. My five adult children must have viewed with alarm the growing pile of books about Nazis that suddenly appeared in my office, the endless documentaries about World War II in our Netflix and Amazon Prime feeds. I should also thank Alex Hoyt, my agent; Elizabeth Kantor, my editor; and Alex Novak, the publisher of Regnery History. As always, I would also like to thank my beautiful and research-obsessed wife, Glenn Ellen, for sticking with me for more than thirty years and enduring the craziness of the writing life. She is my inspiration in more ways than she knows.

—Robert J. Hutchinson,
Berlin, February 2020

1 | PLOTTING THE DEATH OF HITLER

At 5:30 on the morning of July 20, 1944, a young German officer sat up in his bed in the cozy three-story house he shared with his older brother at 8 Tristanstrasse in the once leafy but now desolate suburb of Wannsee in southwest Berlin. The house still stands, an eerie reminder of a long-ago crisis and the mystery of how it ended.

The young officer had only slept for four hours the night before. Yet now he was wide awake, every nerve in his body on fire.

His name was Claus Philipp Maria von Stauffenberg.

Only thirty-six years old, the father of four young children, Stauffenberg had recently been promoted to chief of staff of Nazi Germany's Reserve Army—known somewhat derisively as the Ersatzheer or Fake Army.

Just days before, Adolf Hitler had ordered the young officer to come up with a plan to provide badly needed reinforcements for the German troops who were fighting overwhelming Soviet forces on the Eastern Front. Stauffenberg had worked late into the night finalizing the report he would present personally to the Führer later that day.

Yet unbeknownst to Hitler, Stauffenberg and his associates were in reality doing everything they could to *fail* at their assigned task—without appearing to do so. The last thing they wanted was to send more young

The plot within the German Army to kill Adolf Hitler was taken over in 1944 by a young aristocrat and army officer named Claus Philipp Maria von Stauffenberg. *Wikimedia Commons*

Germans to die fighting the Soviets, thereby prolonging the war.

Stauffenberg stood up stiffly from his bed. His driver would arrive in just a few minutes, at precisely six o'clock.

Movie-star handsome—he looked a little like a young Clark Gable—Stauffenberg had a straight jaw, blue eyes, a full head of dark-brown hair, neatly parted on the left, and a bright smile.

Yet he was now also severely handicapped.

On April 7 the year before, serving with Field Marshal Erwin Rommel's Afrika Korps in Tunisia, Stauffenberg had been badly wounded during the fighting that followed the Battle of Kasserine Pass, where Rommel had been engaged in a massive counteroffensive against newly arrived British, American, and French forces.

Stauffenberg, then a lieutenant colonel, had driven alongside units of the 10th Panzer Division near the Tunisian mountain town of Mezzouna. Suddenly, Spitfire fighter bombers from the Allied Desert Air Force appeared overhead and strafed Stauffenberg's vehicle. He was nearly killed.

Despite three months in a military hospital in Munich, Stauffenberg lost his left eye (he now wore a black eye patch), his entire right hand, and the ring and pinkie fingers of his left hand.

Getting dressed in the standard-issue uniform of the Wehrmacht was therefore an ordeal. The tunic was thick gabardine material with large brass buttons and a stiff collar, and Stauffenberg had difficulty getting it on and off with only two fingers and the thumb on his left hand.

With the steely determination for which he was known, Stauffenberg had trained himself to do it.

Now he quickly washed his face, shaved, and carefully pulled on a freshly ironed tunic. Stauffenberg wanted nothing unusual to draw attention to himself. Months of careful planning were about to come to fruition. The destiny of Germany, and of the entire world, was about to be irrevocably changed.

IN THEIR OWN WORDS

"They are shooting Jews *en masse*. These crimes must not be allowed to continue."

—*Claus von Stauffenberg, August 1942*[1]

Since the previous autumn, the young German officer had taken over as de facto leader of a five-year-old conspiracy within the Wehrmacht—Germany's armed forces—to overthrow the Führer. He was determined to do what dozens of other top-ranked generals, politicians, and religious leaders had been planning for years but failed to accomplish: to kill Adolf Hitler.

In addition, the conspiracy was far more ambitious than merely an attempt on Hitler's life.

Stauffenberg and his associates were determined to save Germany from utter destruction, particularly from the marauding and revenge-minded Soviet Red Army.

Yet to do so, they not only had to kill Hitler and his top aides but also somehow neutralize the vast Nazi organization that had penetrated, like a virus, every facet of German life.

The conspirators had hit upon a brilliant way to do this: take advantage of an already existing Nazi plan, code-named Operation Valkyrie, that called for the Reserve Army bureaucracy to take control of the country in the event of an attempted coup or catastrophic breakdown of the Nazi government.

EYEWITNESS ACCOUNT

"A man of intractable will…Stauffenberg was clear and purposeful in one respect: he did not want Hitler to drag the fatally imperiled army down with him in his own destruction. A soldier to the core, the salvation of his fatherland was equivalent in Stauffenberg's mind to the salvation of the Wehrmacht."

—*Hans B. Gisevius, July 20 plot survivor*[2]

The Nazis themselves had foreseen the possibility of a coup attempt. They feared that the four million foreign workers, prisoners of war, and outright slaves inside Germany might rise up against the government.

Playing on that fear, the conspirators had persuaded Hitler to establish an elaborate parallel system of communications and operations that could be activated, in an emergency, to maintain government control.

And unbeknownst to Hitler's inner circle, anti-Nazi conspirators had partially infiltrated this alternative government apparatus at the highest levels. The key word, however, is *partially*. Some of the highest-ranking members of the Reserve Army, such as Stauffenberg, were plotting to kill Hitler; others took a wait-and-see attitude; and still others knew nothing about the plot.

General Friedrich Fromm, the head of the Reserve Army since 1937, was one example of an officer who was on the fence. The fifty-six-year-old career army officer, who knew about the conspiracy against Hitler, was an opportunist who took no active part in the plot but promised to support the conspirators if a coup succeeded.

Yet in a stroke of good luck, Stauffenberg—one of the few junior officers Hitler trusted—had recently been promoted to be Fromm's deputy. It was this role, in fact, that required him to report to Hitler regularly.

As the Nazi war machine collapsed in the face of the combined Soviet and Western Allies' advance, Hitler was continually reorganizing his military units and pretending he still had forces at their peak strength. In fact, however, the full-strength divisions that Hitler was moving around on his large military maps existed only on paper and in his own mind; in reality, he was deploying the tattered remnants of decimated units and the unfortunate teenagers and old men the Nazis dragooned into service at the end of the war.

The plan that Stauffenberg and his fellow conspirators had hatched was to kill Hitler and then blame his assassination on disloyal Nazi leaders. The conspirators would then activate the Operation Valkyrie alternative government, and the Reserve Army units under the control of the Valkyrie command center would quickly arrest all the top Nazi leaders, seize the communications centers, and declare that the Army had saved the country from anti-Hitler conspirators among Nazi Party officials.

In other words, the conspirators would use the Nazi government's own emergency plan against it.

The plotters would then immediately declare a ceasefire and negotiate with the British and American governments for a separate peace to stop the advance of Soviet forces into Europe. It was an audacious plan that could well have worked—and saved millions of lives.

A German Prince

Stauffenberg was an unlikely choice to head up such an operation. He was only thirty-six years old and a member of the most prominent family in southern Germany. His parents held the titular ranks of count and countess.

Stauffenberg's father, Alfred Klemens Philipp Friedrich Justinian, was a high official in the Kingdom of Württemberg, which, until 1918, had been a constitutional monarchy within the German Empire established in 1871. His mother, Gräfin von Üxküll-Gyllenband, came from an equally distinguished family. Born in 1907, Stauffenberg was raised in the rarefied atmosphere of a lavish country estate, Castle Stauffenberg, located amidst the rolling green meadows and lush forests of Lautlingen, just south of the university town of Tübingen. He and his two brothers, Berthold and Alexander, spent their childhood riding horses (Stauffenberg was an expert equestrian), playing classical music (he played the cello), and wandering the hills of Bavaria as part of the Wandervogel German youth movement.

Unsure of what to do with his life— he considered careers in music and architecture—Stauffenberg eventually followed the example of other sons of the aristocracy and joined the Army in 1926 at the age of nineteen. He was commissioned a lieutenant in 1930.

Like many Germans, Stauffenberg neither supported nor opposed the Nazis when they first came to power. He took a wait-and-see attitude and liked some aspects of the Nazi program. Stauffenberg supported the rearmament of Germany's military, the renewal of German national pride, the annexation of parts of Poland and the Sudetenland, and even some aspects of Nazi racial ideology. Yet Stauffenberg, who was raised and remained a Roman Catholic all his life, never joined the Nazi Party.

The young aristocrat had been a member of the circle of intellectuals attracted to the esoteric writings of the German poet Stefan George, who had called for a spiritual aristocracy— what he called a "Secret Germany"—to rebuild the nation. Although the Nazis incorporated into their propaganda some of George's concepts, including the idea of a "Thousand Year Reich," George despised the Nazis. He fled to Switzerland shortly after Hitler came to power, dying there in 1933.

That same year, Stauffenberg married a young Lutheran aristocrat named Magdalena ("Nina") von Lerchenfeld, the daughter of a Bavarian politician and a Baltic-German noblewoman. Although both their mothers were Lutherans, the young couple married in a Catholic ceremony in Bavaria, and their five children were raised Catholic.

As the years passed, whatever initial enthusiasm Stauffenberg may have felt for the Nazi promises to revitalize Germany dissipated. He became severely disillusioned.

Stauffenberg was not entirely free of the anti-Semitic bias of his age. Recent scholarship has even challenged the notion that he was an unqualified hero.[3] Yet the barbarism of the Nazis towards the Jews and other persecuted minorities—seen, for example, during the Kristallnacht attacks on Jewish synagogues in 1938—genuinely disgusted him.

As a young officer, Stauffenberg participated in the German invasion of Russia code-named Operation Barbarossa. There he learned of and was appalled by the atrocities committed by the murderous Schutzstaffel (SS) units in Poland and elsewhere, including the mass shootings of Jewish civilians in Russia. He also witnessed the atrocities committed against Russian prisoners of war. (Some historians have recently claimed that he was complicit in some of these atrocities.)[4]

Soon Stauffenberg discovered that there was strong opposition to Hitler and the Nazis within the German Army. Disaffection with the Führer in the Wehrmacht had begun as early as 1934 but intensified in 1938. Many in the top ranks of Germany's professional army regarded Hitler, who had served with distinction during World War I but only achieved the low rank of Gefreiter (lance corporal), as an arrogant, untrained military amateur who could very easily lead Germany to destruction. Yet so long as Germany's newly rearmed armies swept from victory to victory, the anti-Hitler members of the military felt powerless to take action.

At first, it seemed that Hitler could do no wrong. The lightning-fast conquests, first of Poland and then of France, convinced many Germans that Hitler was a military genius. In reality, Hitler may not have known much about military strategy and tactics, but he had an instinctive grasp of the weakness of political leaders—and exploited that weakness every chance he got.

The Flight to the Wolf's Lair

Just a few minutes after 6:00 a.m., Stauffenberg's regular chauffeur, Gefreiter (Lance Corporal) Karl Schweizer, parked outside the

The house on Tristanstrasse in the Berlin suburb of Wannsee that Stauffenberg shared with his brother. *Wikimedia Commons*[5]

house on Tristanstrasse. Stauffenberg and his older brother Berthold walked outside, passing through the brick gate that marked the entrance to the property.

The night before, following Stauffenberg's instructions, the driver had made his way to an address in nearby Potsdam, another quiet Berlin suburb. There he picked up a briefcase from a high-ranked Army official, Lieutenant Colonel Fritz von der Lancken.

Unbeknownst to Schweizer, who was not part of the conspiracy, the briefcase contained two rectangular blocks of plastic explosives, along with special acid detonators. For weeks, Stauffenberg had been carrying this briefcase of explosives with him into meetings with Hitler, waiting for an opportune moment to trigger the explosives and blow the Nazi dictator to bits.

After a frustrating series of aborted attempts, Stauffenberg believed that this moment had finally come.

Stauffenberg and his brother climbed into the staff car. They drove about a mile through the quiet, deserted streets to the home of Stauffenberg's adjutant, Lieutenant Werner Karl von Haeften, age thirty-five, who was waiting outside on the street with his own brother, Lieutenant Bernd von Haeften, a naval officer. The four men then took the thirty-minute drive to Rangsdorf Airfield, located just twenty-five miles to the southeast.

At the airfield, they were joined by Major General Hellmuth Stieff, forty-three, and his aide, Major Röll. While their brothers both remained at the airfield, Stauffenberg and Haeften joined Stieff and Röll in the waiting Junkers JU-52 transport aircraft.[6]

One of the very few officers with personal access to Hitler, Stieff had once volunteered to kill Hitler himself in an elaborate suicide mission. Just two weeks earlier, Stieff was supposed to trigger a bomb when Hitler appeared at an enormous palace near Salzburg, Austria, but he had backed out at the last minute. It was only after Stieff had repeatedly refused pleas to carry out the mission that Stauffenberg had finally made up his mind that he would have to do it himself, despite his considerable physical handicaps.

Yet this presented a serious logistical problem: As the highest-ranking officer of the Reserve Army who was part of the conspiracy, Stauffenberg had to survive the assassination attempt. He had to return to Berlin in one piece to direct Operation Valkyrie, the takeover of the Nazi government by Reserve Army units. It was this complication, the fact that Stauffenberg had to perform not one but two impossible jobs—kill Hitler and also direct the Reserve Army takeover of the country—that partly explains what would happen next.

As Stauffenberg, Haeften, Stieff, and Röll climbed aboard the plane, Stauffenberg and Haeften waved goodbye to their brothers, who remained behind.

It was only 350 miles northeast from Rangsdorf Airfield to the small military landing strip outside of Hitler's infamous Wolfsschanze, or Wolf's

The ruins of Hitler's secret headquarters in the forests of Prussia, now within the borders of Poland, can still be seen today. Hitler spent more than eight hundred days in this heavily guarded compound of bunkers and fortresses. *Shutterstock*

Lair, his secret military headquarters near Rastenberg, East Prussia (now part of Poland). The flight would take about two hours.

Stauffenberg was familiar with Hitler's military headquarters. In fact, he had been there only five days earlier, on July 15, when he aborted another bombing attempt because none of the other top Nazi leaders, such as Hermann Göring and Heinrich Himmler, were present. At that time, the other organizers of the plot to kill Hitler were convinced that they had to eliminate all of the top Nazi leadership in one fell swoop. But now Stauffenberg believed they were running out of time. Hitler had to be killed immediately; otherwise, they might not get another chance.

The Wolf's Lair was an elaborate compound of some sixteen hundred acres[7] located in the middle of a thick forest, divided into three concentric security zones. These zones were manned by some of Hitler's most loyal bodyguards, soldiers from the SS Reichssicherheitsdienst and the twenty-thousand-man-strong Führerbegleitbrigade. The outer zones were heavily guarded, protected by land mines, steel fencing and strictly monitored checkpoints. The innermost security zone, where Hitler stayed, contained a series of ten bomb-proof bunkers, including the Führerbunker, made out of steel-reinforced concrete six feet thick.

There were numerous wooden buildings inside the compound perimeter, including barracks, a radio and telex center, a cinema, a tearoom, mess halls, and so forth. Many top officials of the Reich, including Martin Borman, Hermann Göring, and Nazi Foreign Minister Joachim von Ribbentrop, also had quarters in this complex.

For all practical purposes, the Wolf's Lair was impenetrable to conventional attack, though Hitler feared that an airborne commando unit might succeed in landing inside the perimeter.

As the war turned against Nazi Germany in 1942, Hitler spent no fewer than 800 days in this security bubble—safe, he thought, from attempts by the Allies or disloyal Germans to kill him. He would freely walk about the grounds, often taking his beloved dog Trudi on long strolls.

The Allies knew the precise location of the Wolf's Lair, but both the Western Allies and Stalin had decided against an assassination attempt. Incredibly, they had concluded that Hitler was more valuable to them alive than dead. The military experts believed that it was Hitler's own blundering errors—such as the decision to invade Russia in 1941—that had brought the war effort so close to its inevitable conclusion. The Allies feared that, were Hitler killed, his far more capable generals might be able to regroup, perhaps in the natural fortress of the Bavarian Alps, and significantly prolong the war.

And once Hitler was holed up in his heavily guarded Wolf's Lair compound, the days of lone assassin attempts on his life by ordinary Germans were probably over. The only serious threat to Hitler came from within his own army. Yet, surprisingly, the guards at checkpoints throughout the Wolf's Lair complex—and at Hitler's personal residence, the Berghof, in the mountains of Bavaria—routinely checked credentials but never searched the belongings of top military officials entering. Had

The sheer scale of the Allied invasion at Normandy stunned Germany's high command and may have strengthened the resolve of Stauffenberg and other plotters that, for the good of Germany and what was left of Europe, Hitler had to be killed. *United States Coast Guard*

they done so, they would have discovered the secret bombs that Stauffenberg and others had brought into the inner sanctum of the Nazi regime on more than one occasion.

Hitler's security forces knew that there were civilian plots against the Führer's life. As a result, fewer and fewer officials were allowed to see him. What his security guards did not suspect was an attack from within the top echelons of the military itself.

By this time, most of the German General Staff knew that the war was lost. Just over a month earlier, on June 6, the long-dreaded Allied invasion of the European continent occurred, at the beaches of Normandy in France. Code-named Operation Overlord, it was the largest seaborne invasion in history: more than 156,000 soldiers aboard 6,500 ships from the United States, Britain, Canada, and Free France, and more

JUST THE FACTS

The D-Day invasion, Operation Overlord, involved:

> 156,115 U.S., British, and Canadian troops
>
> 6,939 ships and landing vessels
>
> 2,395 aircraft and 867 gliders

than 200,000 vehicles hit the beaches in successive waves along five locations on the Normandy coast. They were supported by 13,000 aircraft raining down death and supplies from the skies. After the beachhead was secured, it's estimated that up to 1.3 million men came ashore to push towards Germany.

After a month of fierce fighting in the bocage, the French name for the dense hedgerow country near the beaches, the Allies finally liberated the heavily fortified French port of Cherbourg. The invasion had succeeded.

Just a few days earlier, on June 22, the Soviet Red Army had launched a major offensive from the east (code-named Operation Bagration) with 120 divisions. More than 2.3 million Soviet soldiers advanced against a battered and retreating Germany army of only 800,000 men.

Stauffenberg's plane landed at the Wolf's Lair airstrip at a quarter past 10:00 on the morning of July 20. It was already sweltering when the men climbed out of the plane into the bright Prussian sunshine. Within fifteen minutes, Stauffenberg and Haeften were on their way through the thick woods to the Wolf's Lair compound, a drive of about four miles. On Haeften's lap were two identical briefcases, each holding one of the rectangular blocks of plastic explosives. The plan was for Stauffenberg to arm both and place them at strategic locations in the underground briefing room where he would present his report to Hitler. The combined blasts in such a small space would kill everyone in the room.

Within twenty minutes, the staff car had arrived at the first main checkpoint, through which they passed without incident. The next checkpoint was two miles away, through a minefield. They had to pass through yet another checkpoint—and then another—before they finally entered a large open area that was patrolled by heavily armed members of the SS. This was the most secure area in the entire Third Reich, requiring a special pass issued by Heinrich Himmer's personal Chief of Security. Incredibly, at none of these checkpoints were the possessions of Stauffenberg or his companions subjected to search.

Seemingly without a care in the world, Stauffenberg descended from the staff car in which he rode, casually handing his briefcase containing the plastic explosives to Haeften. He then announced that he was walking over to the mess hall for some breakfast.

Haeften took the briefcase containing the plastic explosives with him and went with General Stieff to a meeting in the main Army bunker.[8] Before Stauffenberg went into his meeting with Hitler, he and Haeften would exchange briefcases.

But for now, Stauffenberg sat at a large table outside the mess hall, under an oak tree, where he was joined by the operations officer at Wolf's Lair, Captain Heinz Pieper. Observers would later marvel at how relaxed Stauffenberg had seemed. He was waiting calmly to meet the most dangerous man in Europe—a man who, had he known what Stauffenberg was planning to do, could have ordered him shot on the spot or gruesomely tortured to death. Yet Stauffenberg sat contentedly in his seat, calmly eating his breakfast.

A Historical Enigma

It's difficult for modern readers to appreciate the historical enigma that is Adolf Hitler. By some accounts a polite, modest man in person, kind to dogs and children and a longtime vegetarian, he bewitched an entire nation with his magnetic speeches and appeals to restored German greatness.

Yet Hitler was more than just a populist. He instigated the greatest crimes against humanity the world has ever seen: the deliberate attempt to systematically annihilate eleven million Jews in Europe and, once that was accomplished, to kill untold millions more Gypsies, Poles, Russians, and others.

Hitler was obsessed with the Germans' supposed need for *Lebensraum*, living space. The "final solution" to this problem, in his view, was the literal extermination of entire populations. The Nazis set about this task by creating six industrialized death camps in Poland—Chelmno, Belzec, Sobibor, Treblinka, Auschwitz, and Majdanek—that were able to kill up to ten thousand prisoners per day.

When World War II was over, the battle-hardened Allied armies stood in horror at what they discovered: the mountains of human hair shaved off death-camp victims, the collected gold teeth, the enormous piles of emaciated human bodies.

In the end, the U.S. Holocaust Museum estimates the Nazis murdered in cold blood as many as 17 million people—6 million Jews, 5.3 million Soviet civilians, 3 million Soviet prisoners of war, 1.9 million Polish civilians, 250,000 people with disabilities, 300,000 Serbs, up to 220,000 Roma, and more.[9]

Eighty years later, historians still struggle to grasp the magnitude of the slaughter Hitler and his followers unleashed. The Germans alone lost between 4.4 and 5.5 million soldiers and another 400,000 civilians killed in Allied bombing attacks. The Russians lost 10 million soldiers and at least 16 million civilians, including deaths from famines. Altogether, historians estimate that World War II, the Holocaust, and war-related famines ended up killing between 50 and 75 million people over 15 years.[10] The killing only stopped when one man, Hitler, was dead.

Yet the mystery is how anyone from such a modest background could set in motion evil on such an apocalyptic scale. Hitler started out in life as an impoverished, somewhat dreamy artist and would-be architect, eking out a living selling cheap watercolor postcards on the streets of Vienna.

Adolf Hitler, fourth from the left in the top row, is seen here in a class picture taken in 1899, when he was just ten years old. *Wikimedia Commons*

He was born on August 20, 1889, in the small town of Braunau am Inn but raised in a suburb of Linz, Austria, in what was then the multiethnic Austro-Hungarian Empire. Hitler's father died in 1903 when he was just fourteen. His mother died four years later, leaving Hitler an orphan. As a result, the future dictator left the Realschule or secondary school in Linz, also attended by the famous Jewish philosopher Ludwig Wittgenstein, without graduating. He was technically a high school dropout.

Following his mother's death in 1908, Hitler received a small inheritance. Just eighteen, he moved to the bustling Austrian capital of Vienna with a childhood friend named August Kubizek. In his memoirs of his childhood friendship with Hitler, Kubizek claimed that, while Hitler at first saw himself as an artist and tried to earn a living through art, he ultimately came to believe that he was destined for a career in politics.

EYEWITNESS ACCOUNT

"Hitler's father would definitely have been anti-Jewish.... At [high school], Hitler must have known something of the political aspects of the Jewish question . . . for when I got to know him he was already openly anti-Jewish."

—*August Kubizek, Hitler's childhood friend*[11]

Either way, Hitler's money soon ran out. He was often homeless, forced to seek refuge in shelters and soup kitchens.[12]

Without his secondary school leaving certificate, or *Abitur,* Hitler could not gain admission to a university. The famed Vienna Academy of Fine Arts twice rejected his application. He was also turned down by the School of Architecture (most of Hitler's watercolors were of buildings, not of people).

Vienna at this time was a cosmopolitan melting pot of ideas, both good and bad. It was there that Hitler was exposed to a wide range of pan-Germanic and anti-Semitic currents, a fact he documented in detail in his autobiography, *Mein Kampf* (*My Struggle*). He described his time in Vienna as "five years of misery" and said that it was there that he became aware of two "menaces" to the German people—Marxism and Jews—which he soon decided were one and the same.[13] Yet strangely, while Kubizek claimed Hitler was overtly anti-Semitic even in his adolescence, the future dictator apparently had some Jewish acquaintances, or at least business partners, in Vienna.[14]

After five years in Vienna, and perhaps to escape the Austrian draft, in 1913 Hitler moved to Bavaria, to the boisterous southern German city of Munich, then, as now, a center of German art and culture. When World War I broke out in August 1914, the failed artist promptly

Adolf Hitler (seated, far right), shown here with comrades from the Bavarian Reserve Infantry Regiment 16, served as a courier during World War I. Like many Germans, he came to believe the false claim that the German military had been winning World War I but was betrayed by corrupt politicians who formed the Weimar Republic. *Deutsches Bundesarchiv*[15]

enlisted in the Bavarian Army—even though he was not a German citizen and thus technically ineligible.

Hitler served with distinction throughout the war. He held the dangerous but lowly position of dispatch courier, carrying messages from front-line positions to commanders in the rear. Hitler was thus present at many of the most famous battles of World War I, including the Battle of the Somme, where a shell fragment wounded him in the leg. A mustard gas attack also temporarily blinded Hitler at the end of the war, landing him in a hospital. For his injuries, he was twice awarded the Iron Cross for bravery.

Then, for Hitler, the real disaster occurred. The Armistice agreement that ended the bloody fighting at 11:11 a.m. on November 11, 1918 (still celebrated as "the eleventh minute of the eleventh hour of the eleventh day of the eleventh month") struck Hitler and many other battle-weary German soldiers as a hideous betrayal.

Many Germans would come to believe in the now-discredited "stab in the back" (*Dolchstosslegende*) theory of the war: that the German army was victorious on the battlefield but betrayed by cowardly politicians back home—particularly by the liberal republicans who, just as the war was ending, overthrew the constitutional German monarchy and instituted, largely peacefully, what became the Weimar Republic. The widely acknowledged vindictiveness of the Versailles Treaty imposed by the Allies—the terms of which made Germany's economic recovery difficult—contributed to the acceptance of this false theory. In truth, Germany was not winning but losing the war when it finally capitulated. However, that may not have been evident to the millions of German soldiers in the field.

Later, Nazi propaganda would take advantage of widespread resentment over Germany's defeat in World War I to build popular support. The Nazis would claim that the "architects" of Germany's defeat and the creation of the Weimar Republic were primarily Communists and Jews out to weaken Germany's national identity. This propaganda seemed plausible because of an attempt by German Communists, inspired by events in Russia in October 1917, to take advantage of the turmoil in Germany and seize power by force—just as the Bolsheviks had done.

The so-called Spartacist uprising broke out in January 1919 led by two openly Marxist intellectuals, Karl Liebknecht and Rosa Luxemburg. The new Social Democrat government crushed the revolt with the help of recently deactivated units of the German military, the so-called *Freikorps*. Both Liebknecht and Luxemburg were eventually beaten to death by soldiers and became martyrs to the communist cause. Luxemburg was Jewish—as were some other members of the German Communist Party. German anti-Semites made use of this fact to portray Jews in general as closet communists and enemies of the German people, plotting to defeat Germany from within.

American newspapers from 1919 onward show the alarm with which the world viewed the political chaos then raging in Germany. It was this chaos that helped the Nazis build support among large swaths of the German populace. *Wikimedia Commons*[16]

This was the swamp of anti-Semitism, paranoia, and fetid resentment that the young Hitler encountered in the 1920s. After the war ended and his eyesight returned, Hitler was released from the hospital. For a time, he remained in the Army. He had nowhere else to go and no real career prospects. In Munich, the World War I veteran encountered fellow soldiers who were similarly enraged at how the war had ended. And the Germany Army, then known as the Reichswehr (Reich Defense), gave him a new assignment: Hitler was to become an intelligence operative and infiltrate a new political party known as the

Deutsche Arbeiterpartei (DAP) or German Workers Party, then organizing in Munich. In other words, Hitler was ordered to spy on the very group he would one day lead. Hitler's own leap into politics thus came about almost by accident.

Hitler began attending meetings of the small group. When Hitler joined a few months later, he was only the fifty-fifth member.[17] The young soldier was quickly impressed by the political outlook of the people he was supposed to be spying on: founders Anton Drexler, a left-wing political organizer who combined socialist and anti-Semitic views with a strong German nationalism, and Dietrich Eckart, a successful journalist, playwright, and anti-Semitic theorist who became Hitler's mentor. Eckart introduced Hitler to more elite German social circles.

During a meeting of the DAP at the Sterneckerbräu brewery in Munich, Hitler got into a heated argument with a man who criticized the group's anti-capitalist outlook and who insisted that Bavaria should form a new country with Austria. The DAP opposed both the Marxists and the conservative German aristocracy, railing against capitalist profiteers while also strongly opposing Communism. Hitler's fiery, impassioned defense of the DAP's unusual views greatly impressed the members of the group. He soon became not only a member of the party but also its most celebrated speaker. Hitler gave his first formal political speech on October 16, 1919, at the Hofbräukeller restaurant on the Wiener Platz in Munich. He was a natural if unpolished speaker—and he worked hard practicing his delivery and even his hand gestures. Within months, the DAP was drawing crowds as large as two thousand to hear Hitler speak.

By early 1920, Hitler had resigned from the Army and joined the DAP full time, eventually convincing members to add the word "Socialist" to the party name, changing it to the Nationalsozialistische Deutsche Arbeiterpartei (National Socialist German Workers Party) or Nazi Party for short. An instinctive marketer and propagandist, Hitler wanted to emphasize both the *nationalist* aspect of the Party's program—he called for the unification of all German-speaking peoples into one state or Reich—and its anti-liberal or *socialist* outlook.

EYEWITNESS ACCOUNT

"I looked around the hall and could see no one I knew. 'Where is Hitler,' I asked a middle-aged journalist next to me. 'See those three over there? The short man is Max Amann, the one with the spectacles is Anton Drexler, and the other is Hitler.' In his heavy boots, dark suit and leather waistcoat, semi-stiff white collar and odd little mustache, he really did not look very impressive—like a waiter in a railway-station restaurant."

—*Ernst Hanfstaengl, German American and early Nazi supporter*

Yet Hitler wasn't a socialist in the normal understanding of the term. When the party founder, Drexler, proposed that the group merge with the German Socialist Party, another group that combined nationalism and socialism, Hitler rebelled and insisted that either he or Drexler had to go. In Hitler's view, big business was a necessary evil that the state should *control*, not eliminate or replace, as the true socialists wanted to do. Hitler portrayed himself as an advocate for the average working man against a corrupt financial elite, but he was also vehemently opposed to "Bolshevism." He was thus for *national* socialism as opposed to the *international* socialism advocated by the Communists. The party overwhelmingly elected Hitler as their new head.

It was during this period that the still small organization adopted the ancient Hindu good luck symbol of the right-facing swastika (which the Germans called the *Hakenkreuz* or hooked cross) as its symbol. It also began using the one-armed Roman salute adopted by the Italian fascists. Many future leaders of Nazi Germany joined the party around this time, including Rudolf Hess and Hermann Göring.

Hitler's rapid rise to power, and the enormous success of the new party in gaining recruits, quickly went to his head. Under his leadership, the Nazi Party soon had tens of thousands of members, some organized into a paramilitary militia known as the Sturmabteilung (SA), or Storm Troopers, who dressed in brown shirts and quasi-military uniforms. Inspired by the success of the Italian fascists' successful March on Rome and rapid seizure of power in 1922, Hitler decided that the time had come for his own group to take quick, decisive action. As a result, he organized the attempted coup d'état that would become known as the Beer Hall Putsch.

Over a period of two days, November 8 and 9, 1923, Hitler and thousands of his followers attempted to force their way into Bavarian military headquarters and take control of the Bavarian state government. They thought that if they could somehow gain control of the Bavarian military, they could then do the same with the main German Army in Berlin. The city of Munich was already in chaos at this time; demonstrations and

Early Nazi supporters, sporting swastika armbands, gathered in Munich's Marienplatz on November 9, 1923, during Hitler's failed attempt to stage a "putsch," or coup d'état. Sixteen of Hitler's followers were killed during clashes with police. *Deutsches Bundesarchiv*[18]

Hitler, far left, served only eight months in prison for his role in the failed coup attempt against the Munich government. He used his time in Landsberg Prison, during which he is shown here in 1924, to dictate his book, *My Struggle* (*Mein Kampf*), to his follower Rudolf Hess (second from right). *Wikimedia Commons*[19]

violent street clashes with police were common. Bavaria had been declared in a state of emergency. A top Bavarian official, Gustav von Kahr, was ruling by martial law.

On November 8, Hitler and six hundred of his heavily armed storm troopers burst into a large political meeting that Kahr was holding in the Bürgerbräukeller, a large beer hall in Munich. Unable to be heard above the din of the crowd, or simply to wake the dozing attendees up, Hitler dramatically fired a handgun into the ceiling of the beer hall. He then climbed up on a chair and announced to the crowd that the Revolution had begun! In effect, Hitler held the political leaders in attendance hostage and wouldn't allow them to leave, insisting that he was now taking control of the government of Bavaria. After making numerous speeches that appeared to win over the crowd of some three thousand, Hitler

EYEWITNESS ACCOUNT

"Late on the evening of the Putsch a knock came at the door and outside stood Hitler, Dr. Walter Schultze, a physician in one of the S.A. battalions, and two or three others. Hitler's dislocated shoulder was drooping and he was in considerable pain...Hitler asked if he could stay the night. My wife, in total ignorance of all that had occurred, let him in and the others went away. She gave him a little attic-bedroom I had fitted up with my books, while she slept downstairs..."[20]

—*Ernst Hanfstaengl, German American businessman in whose Munich home Hitler stayed after the failed Putsch*

finally released the officials he had taken prisoner. That was a mistake. Over the course of the night, Bavarian officials regrouped and instructed police and military officials to fight back.

The next day, Hitler and his top lieutenants, unsure of what to do, organized a march of some two thousand Nazi supporters to the military barracks in Munich. But the professional soldiers guarding the building were ready and waiting for them. They opened fire on Hitler and his supporters, killing sixteen Nazi Party members. Hitler managed to escape and go into hiding in the home of a gregarious German American businessman named Ernst Hanfstaengl. But two days later, Hitler and his fellow ringleaders were hunted down, arrested, and charged with treason.

Surprisingly, Hitler soon won the sympathy of the trial court judges, most of whom shared his vision of a revitalized Germany. After a widely publicized trial, Hitler was given a sentence of only five years imprisonment, in Landsberg Prison—and he ended up serving only eight months. Moreover, the trial itself brought him maximum publicity for his cause.

Hitler used his brief imprisonment—during which he was allowed to receive visitors daily—to dictate to his deputy, Rudolf Hess, his life story up to that point and his political manifesto: *Mein Kampf*. It was in *Mein Kampf* that Hitler announced to the world, at least in outline, his political goals and philosophy. Even before Hitler took over, careful readers of Hitler's writing—such as Nicholas Fairweather, writing in the March 1932 issue of the American magazine *The Atlantic*—could foresee that, were Hitler to put his ideas into practice, it would mean war on a global scale. The very extremism that attracted so many discouraged Germans to Hitler's cause virtually guaranteed that Hitler's "struggle" would result, as he put it, either in "total victory" or his own premature death. In effect, Hitler bet everything he had, and everything his nation had, in a game of Russian roulette.

Yet the game wouldn't end before an extraordinary chain of events had played out. First, there would be the incredible twists and turns of many plots against Hitler's life, brushes with death so close that the Nazi dictator credited Providence with miraculously keeping him alive to lead the Reich. As Allied soldiers closed in during the final days of the war, the mysteries multiplied with body doubles, cover-ups, mass suicides, conflicting (and burning) evidence, and deliberate government disinformation that made what happened to the Führer a puzzle still unsolved at the beginning of the twenty-first century—a puzzle that fueled conspiracy theories that have endured to this day.

This book will review the evidence and resolve, as much as possible, the few remaining mysteries. It will follow the valiant attempts of the now mostly forgotten Georg Elser to kill Hitler and the courageous German dissidents in the Wehrmacht—Claus von Stauffenberg, Ludwig Beck, Henning von Tresckow, Friedrich Olbricht, and Erwin von Witzleben— as they struggled to bring down the entire Nazi government in a brilliant but flawed coup d'état. Finally, it will examine piece by piece the latest revelations about Hitler's ultimate fate.

We begin in the middle of the story, with Stauffenberg's "July 20 plot" against Hitler's life, which itself involves more than one enigma.

2 SAVING GERMANY FROM THE NAZIS

itler got up earlier than usual on this hot Thursday morning in July 1944—at nine o'clock. In contrast to the luxury of the New Reich Chancellery in Berlin and his Berghof residence in the Bavarian Alps, Hitler's living quarters at the Wolf's Lair in East Prussia were genuinely Spartan: just a single bed, chairs, and a table.

Normally, Hitler's habit was to stay up until well past midnight talking to aides and to sleep late the next morning. This was, in fact, what the Führer had done the night before, staying up past 2:00 in the morning chatting with two of his secretaries, Christa Schroeder and Johanna Wolf, about earlier, happier days. He had taken his usual sleeping pill but left orders that he be awakened by 9:00.

July 20 would be a special day: Hitler was expecting a visit that afternoon from Benito Mussolini, the recently deposed strongman of Italy and a longtime ally. Hitler admired Mussolini. The Italian dictator's quick seizure of power in the early 1920s had inspired Hitler's attempt to do the same in Munich—with, as we have seen, far less successful results. What's more, there were many parallels between the ideology of Italian fascism and that of Nazism.

Yet Mussolini did not reciprocate Hitler's admiration. Secretly, he found Hitler boorish and his racial theories of Aryan superiority ludicrous. But the Italian leader needed Hitler and German support—now more than ever.

A year earlier, on July 10, 1943, Allied forces had landed in Sicily and encountered little resistance from the Italian military. Two weeks later, the Italian dictator was overthrown by members of his own Fascist Party. Mussolini was arrested and eventually held incommunicado at an isolated luxury resort high in the mountains of Abruzzo in central Italy. Then, on September 3, 1943, the Italians essentially switched sides in World War II, agreeing to an armistice with the Allies.

The Germans responded to what they perceived as treachery by sending reinforcements to the front in central Italy—and rescuing Mussolini in one of the most daring raids of the war. On September 12, ten German glider planes carrying nine commandos each landed silently on a high alpine meadow near the Hotel Campo Imperatore, where Mussolini was guarded by two hundred Italian Carabinieri. At around two in the afternoon, the German commandos stormed into the hotel and took control without firing a single shot. Ten minutes later, a small single-engine plane landed in the meadow and whisked Il Duce off to safety. He was flown first to Vienna, then to Munich, and finally to a meeting with Hitler at the Wolf's Lair.

Now, a year later, Hitler would meet Mussolini again. This time, the former dictator of Italy would arrive by train.

The Nazi Seizure of Power

Hitler's first attempt to take power by acting outside of the law—the failed Beer Hall Putsch of 1923—resulted in the deaths of sixteen of his followers and a five-year prison term for him (of which he served less than one year). In the late 1920s, therefore, the gang of thugs, anti-Semites, dreamers, and profiteers who made up the early Nazi Party took a new tack. They pretended to be a legitimate political movement and sought to gain power through the democratic process. Perceptive observers, such as the German novelist Thomas Mann, could see that the Nazis' willingness to act within the confines of the law was strictly tactical—and temporary. Like the Bolsheviks in Russia, the Nazis planned on achieving total power by force the moment they had an opportunity.

The Nazis built up their organization from just fifty-five members when Hitler joined the German Workers Party (DAP) in 1923 to a hundred and thirty thousand just five years later. Yet in the German parliamentary elections of 1928, they managed to win only twelve seats in the Reichstag. And then, luckily for the Nazis, disaster struck.

At this time, the Weimar Republic had dozens of political parties and, as in all parliamentary systems, required coalitions of disparate groups to form governing majorities. To many Germans, the various social democratic and liberal parties seemed ineffectual, out of touch. The only parties with vigorous platforms for change—and concrete proposals for confronting the growing economic crisis—were the German Communists (Kommunistische Partei Deutschlands or KPD) and the National Socialists. For the German middle classes, who had seen what the Communists had done in Russia—conducting summary executions of tens of thousands during the Red Terror and after—the Communists were not an attractive option.

The Nazis were the beneficiaries when, in October 1929, the U.S. stock market plunged 24 percent over a period of forty-eight hours, triggering a worldwide financial collapse and the start of what became the Great Depression. Thousands of workers in Germany suddenly lost their jobs, banks closed, and the already-fragile German economy ground to a screeching halt. To make matters worse, American bankers began calling in the loans that had been helping to prop up the Weimar Republic's economy since 1924. Virtually overnight, the apocalyptic warnings of the Nazis concerning international capitalism and predatory bankers suddenly seemed prophetic, vindicated by events. By the end of 1929, 1.5 million Germans had lost their jobs; by the end of 1933, unemployment hit 25 percent. The Nazis surged in popularity.

A Nazi campaign poster for the 1928 elections clearly shows the party's openly violent intentions towards Germany's Jewish population. "Choose List 10," the poster advises, referring to the party's number on the ballot. *Everett Historical / Shutterstock*

Moreover, Hitler and his fellow Nazis had their fingers on the pulse of the German people. They knew precisely which themes would resonate politically—the working underclass against the greedy war profiteers—even if they had little intention on following through on their promises. "Work, freedom and bread!" promised one Nazi poster in 1931. Recent research has shown that while the Nazis claimed they would "put Germany back to work"—and their propaganda always showed roads being built and factories humming—in fact, Nazi domestic work programs ended up doing little for the German economy. Similarly, while Hitler portrayed himself as a German nationalist intent on peacefully rebuilding the country, he was, in fact, an imperialist intent on conquering most of Europe, even if it risked destroying the country he claimed to love.

Yet the relentless propaganda was effective.

In the German federal elections of September 1930, the Nazis received 6 million votes (18 percent of the total), winning 107 seats in the Reichstag and becoming Germany's second-largest political party. It was at this time that the Nazis began to reveal their true intentions, engaging in violent street battles with Communist groups and attacking Jewish businesses and individuals. They were not yet, however, strong enough to seize power.

In March, 1932, the German presidential elections pitted Hitler against the popular conservative incumbent and war hero Paul von Hindenburg and the leader of the Communist Party, Ernst Thälmann. Hindenburg won decisively, securing 49.5 percent of the vote while Hitler won 30 percent and Thälmann only 13 percent. Yet because Hindenburg hadn't received an absolute majority of the vote, a second election was held in April. This time, Hindenburg received 53 percent of the vote and Hitler 36 percent. Hindenburg dismissed Heinrich Brüning as chancellor (prime minister) and appointed Franz von Papen, an aristocrat like himself.

However, Von Papen had virtually no support, and so, three days after his appointment, Hindenburg dissolved the Reichstag and called for new parliamentary elections. This gave the Nazis yet another chance to use the democratic process to further their own undemocratic ends.

During the Great Depression, when millions of Germans were hungry, the Nazis promised "work, freedom and bread," as this poster from 1931 shows. *Everett Historical / Shutterstock*

There were two more elections—one in July and another in November. In the July 1932 elections, the Nazis picked up 37 percent of the popular vote and won a total of 230 seats, becoming the largest party in Germany. The Social Democrats took 21.5 percent of the vote and 133 seats. And the Communist Party won 14.3 percent of the vote and 89 seats. The rest of the popular vote, about a third, was split between three smaller parties: the Catholic-dominated Center Party, the German National People's Party (a conservative nationalist party), and the Bavarian People's Party (BVP). But in the November election, the last free election in Germany before 1949, Nazi support actually slipped. Their share of the popular vote fell from 37 percent to just 33 percent, and they lost 34 seats in the Reichstag. At the same time, the Communists picked up 11 seats.

Hitler paying his respects to his political rival in the 1932 presidential elections, the German aristocrat and president Paul von Hindenburg, after Hindenburg appointed Hitler chancellor. Following Hindenburg's death in 1934, Hitler assumed dictatorial powers and abolished the office of president. *Deutsches Bundesarchiv*[1]

EYEWITNESS ACCOUNT

"By that fateful act [the Enabling Act] the Reichstag not only eliminated itself from the government, but also limited the powers of the president. Hindenburg could still sign decrees, but he could scarcely obstruct his chancellor any longer. On that day in Potsdam Hitler successfully made a snatch at absolute power."

—*Hans Gisevius, German diplomat and July 20 plot survivor*[2]

Yet with no party in the clear majority, Hitler began negotiations to form a coalition government. After months of squabbling, the Nazis agreed to form a coalition with the German National People's Party. Because of this successful coalition, on January 30, 1933, Hindenburg reluctantly appointed Adolf Hitler Chancellor of Germany. It was a fatal error. From that moment, the Nazis acted with lightning speed to seize total control of the government.

Just a month after Hitler took office, a fire broke out in the German legislature, or Reichstag building. It was allegedly set by a twenty-four-year-old Dutch Communist named Marinus van der Lubbe. The Nazis immediately blamed the incident on the entire Communist establishment. Because of the fire, Hitler was able to talk Hindenburg into issuing the Reichstag Fire Decree, an emergency order allowing the government to temporarily suspend most civil liberties, including freedom of the press, and to arrest anti-government conspirators. Given what had happened in Russia, the earlier Spartacist uprising, and the Reichstag fire, it was at least possible that Communists could be planning a coup.

A month later, the Nazi members of the Reichstag maneuvered to push through another major usurpation of power, an amendment to the Weimar Constitution known as the Enabling Act (Gesetz zur Behebung der Not von Volk und Reich or Law to Remedy the Distress of

People and Reich). This piece of legislation allowed the government to enact laws directly, without the consent or control of the Reichstag. It was an unprecedented and blatant attempt to seize dictatorial power—and it worked.

Because of various parliamentary maneuvers by Nazi leader Hermann Göring, the new president of the Reichstag—such as banning outright the votes of Communist deputies—the Enabling Act passed with 83 percent of the vote. Only the leader of the Social Democrats, Otto Wels, spoke out publicly against the legislation. These two legal maneuvers—the Reichstag Fire Degree and the Enabling Act—handed virtually limitless power to Hitler's new government within two months of the election. And if Hitler's critics and opponents had any doubts about how the Nazi leader would use his new dictatorial powers, those doubts were soon eliminated entirely. Just three months later, all political parties except for the Nazis were banned outright.

By the middle of the following year, the Nazis had amassed sufficient power to do away with even the appearance of due process. Between June 30 and July 2, 1934, in a series of extra-judicial executions that would be known as the Night of the Long Knives, Hitler and his top aides set about systematically eliminating their political opponents, many within their own ranks.

Units of the Nazis' new paramilitary force, the Schutzstaffel (SS), arrested and summarily executed dozens of opposition political leaders and rivals of Hitler within the Nazi Party. At least eighty-five and as many as two hundred people were killed in one forty-eight-hour period. Ironically, they included Ernst Röhm, the homosexual leader of the Sturmabteilung (SA) or "Storm Battalion," with some two million men in brown-shirt uniforms. The professional German military viewed the street-fighting thugs of the SA with disdain, so Hitler's elimination of Röhm had the unexpected effect of quieting things down in Germany.

In was also during this period that Hitler began taking action on one of his top priorities, a priority that baffled even many of his fascist allies: his obsession with eliminating the Jews of Europe.

After the Nazis took power, supporters organized boycotts of Jewish businesses and tried to intimidate ordinary Germans from buying from Jewish shops. These signs read, "Germans, defend yourselves. Do not buy from Jews." *Deutsches Bundesarchiv*[3]

In his memoir of his time with Hitler in Linz and Vienna, Hitler's roommate August Kubizek reported that the future German leader was "openly anti-Jewish" even in secondary school. Kubizek recalled that once when they were strolling about, Hitler had spotted a synagogue and blurted out, "That doesn't belong in Linz." When Kubizek invited the hungry young artist to eat with him at the university cafeteria to which he, Kubizek, had access, Hitler almost refused on account of the presence of Jewish students.[4] By the time he dictated the first volume of *Mein Kampf* in 1924, Hitler's hatred of Jews was all-consuming. As his biographer Ian Kershaw has pointed out,[5] Hitler argued in *Mein Kampf* that if during World War I, "twelve or fifteen thousand of these Hebrew corrupters of the people had been held under poison gas...the sacrifice of millions at the front would not have been in vain."[6] In another chilling passage, the future Führer wrote that the German masses "will succeed only when, aside from all the positive struggle for the soul of our people, their international poisoners are exterminated."[7] From the very beginning, Hitler and the Nazis portrayed Jews as a virus, a disease, that had to be eliminated from the German body politic.

Hitler pursued his war against the Jews with single-minded ferocity. As early as 1933, the year he took power, German law sharply restricted the number of Jewish students at German schools and universities and then limited the amount of "Jewish activity" in the medical and legal professions. In 1935, the Nuremberg laws codified in law Nazi racial doctrines, stripping all Jews of their citizenship and making it a crime for a Jew to marry or have sexual relations with a German. Over the next four years, the legal restrictions became increasingly onerous, with beatings, burnings, and legally sanctioned destruction of property. This campaign of terrorism culminated, in 1938, with the Kristallnacht, the night of broken glass, when Jewish shops and synagogues all across Germany were simultaneously ransacked and destroyed.

When World War II broke out, Hitler began mass deportation of Jews from Germany to ghettos and then concentration camps in Poland—largely on the pretext that they were "enemy aliens" and therefore potential spies. Strangely, there weren't actually that many Jews in Germany to begin with. Before the Holocaust began, there were only 565,000 German Jews, representing less than 1 percent of Germany's total population of about 67 million. In contrast, there were millions of Jews living in Poland and Eastern Europe—three million in Poland alone. Yet Hitler was determined to make Germany "*Judenrein*," or free of Jews.

Once Hitler began his suicidal attack on Russia in June 1941, he and top Nazi leaders decided to take their war against the Jews to its murderous conclusion: they opted for what they called "the Final Solution"—that is, to simply exterminate all the Jews in Europe on an industrial scale.

When shooting people and burying them in mass graves—the method used by the notorious SS death squads known as the Einsatzgruppen

The scale of the industrialized Nazi genocide against the Jews, Slavs, and other "inferior" people in the East only became clear after the war. This photo shows German officers "selecting" Hungarian Jews for death at the Auschwitz II–Birkenau death camp in German-occupied Poland, around May 1944. *Wikimedia Commons*[8]

in the early days on the Eastern Front—proved costly and inefficient, Hitler's war planners began building camps specifically designed for mass genocide by means of poison gas. It is now estimated that, by the end of the war, Nazi death camps and execution squads had managed to kill at least six million Jews (two thirds of all the Jews in Europe) and at least five million others, including Poles and Serbs, Soviet prisoners, Gypsies, disabled people, Jehovah's Witnesses, homosexuals, and others.

Early Plots

Despite what some would claim later, Hitler's rapid and undemocratic seizure of power appalled many ordinary Germans. This was particularly the case after Hitler dropped the pretense of merely restoring German dignity after World War I and began invading neighboring

EYEWITNESS ACCOUNT

"Every day that the Russian war lasted, the crimes that were committed behind the fronts grew more and more fearful. The atrocities committed by the SD police against Jews, captured commissars, and guerrillas had no parallel in the whole bloody history of the Gestapo tyranny. For a time it might be possible to cover up this terrible shame and guilt, but that could not be done forever. Too many people knew or suspected what was going on."

—*Hans Gisevius, German diplomat and July 20 plot survivor*[9]

countries one after the other—first Austria and Czechoslovakia (1938), then Poland (1939), then Denmark and Norway, Belgium, the Netherlands, and France (1940) followed by Yugoslavia and Greece (1941). As outlined in *Mein Kampf*, this had been Hitler's plan all along: to conquer living space in Eastern Europe and fill it with German colonists. Nevertheless, the invasions struck many top-ranked German military officials as potentially suicidal, especially if they roused Britain and America to declare war; but Hitler's fateful decision to open a second major front and awaken the slumbering Russian bear in June 1941 was widely seen as the last straw.

There were thousands of civilian, political, and ecclesiastical opponents to the regime, such as the famous Protestant theologian Dietrich Bonhoeffer and the outspoken Catholic archbishop of Münster, Clemens August Graf von Galen. Yet the real threat to Hitler came from within the Wehrmacht itself. As early as 1938, top military officials began openly questioning what the Nazis were doing and then plotting their overthrow.

One of the first plotters had been an early supporter of the Nazis: General Ludwig Beck, chief of staff of the Army High Command (OKH).

General Ludwig Beck (1880–1944), chief of staff of the German Army High Command (OKH), opposed Hitler's military adventurism in 1938 and was forced to resign. He became the early leader of a group of Wehrmacht officers determined to remove Hitler from power. He attempted suicide the night of the July 20 assassination attempt. *Deutsches Bundesarchiv*[10]

Out of pragmatic rather than moral concerns, Beck consistently opposed Hitler's military ambitions as premature and potentially disastrous for Germany. When he was forced to retire in 1938 because of his outspoken opposition to Hitler's invasion plans, Beck and his circle became the nucleus for the anti-Nazi resistance movement in Germany. He quickly contacted top government and military leaders and began plotting a putsch or coup d'état to remove Hitler from power.

Among those who became part of Beck's unofficial resistance movement were Admiral Wilhelm Franz Canaris, chief of German Military Intelligence; General Hans Paul Oster, also a top official of German Military Intelligence who used his position to aid Jews fleeing the regime; and General Erwin von Witzleben, commander of the Third Military District, which included Berlin.[11] Eventually, the group would number hundreds of top military officials and political leaders, including economist and former Reichsbank president Hjalmar Schacht (co-founder of the German Democratic Party), the diplomat Hans Bernd Gisevius, and the monarchist politician Carl Friedrich Goerdeler.

Goerdeler, an economist, former mayor of Lepzig, and, for a brief time, the Reich price commissioner, was an especially noteworthy member of the group. Although culturally anti-Semitic, Geordeler was a devout Protestant Christian and early on opposed all acts of violence and economic intimidation against Jews. After 1938, he joined the anti-Nazi resistance movement, traveling abroad to warn the Allies of the Nazi threat and to ask for assistance for Polish Jews.

Unfortunately for Germany and the world, the German resistance initially spent more time debating and arguing than actually plotting. The members disagreed amongst themselves about key issues. Some were sympathetic to the Nazi cause but thought Hitler himself mad. Others were socialists who wanted to plan for a post-Hitler Germany before they took action. Men such as Goerdeler spent months debating who should be the future king of Germany after the Nazis were overthrown. Still others had moral or religious scruples against assassination and preferred that Hitler be deposed and then put on trial, not killed outright.

For a long time, the plotters' fears about Hitler's military ambitions seemed not just unjustified but positively wrong. At first, Germany's armies went from victory to victory, seemingly unstoppable. General Beck's dire warnings about what would happen if Germany invaded Czechoslovakia were proven false. Despite their bluster, the Allies at first did nothing—just as Hitler had predicted. As a result, Hitler became not merely popular but adored, a living symbol of a newly rejuvenated Germany. In this environment, a direct attack against the regime appeared doomed to failure—especially given how thoroughly the Nazi party had taken over Germany's civic organizations.

Yet while political and military leaders dithered, others took matters into their own hands. By some estimates, there were no fewer than forty attempts to kill Adolf Hitler after his entry into politics in the early 1920s,[12] the vast majority of them perpetrated by lone-wolf assassins who acted without any support.

As early as 1921, at a beer hall in Munich, someone took a shot at Hitler; similar assassination attempts followed in Thuringia and Leipzig in 1923 and then again in 1929, when a member of the SS planted a bomb under a stage where Hitler was to speak. Hitler only survived the latter attempt when the would-be assassin accidentally locked himself in a bathroom and was unable to detonate the bomb.

Throughout the 1930s, there were additional ad hoc attempts to assassinate the Führer, many of them crackpot. A man named Ludwig Assner sent a poisoned letter to Hitler, but it was intercepted. In 1934, 160 men organized a conspiracy to infiltrate the SS to monitor Hitler's movements; they were soon discovered and quickly arrested.

In 1936, a German Jew named Helmut Hirsch—a member of the bizarre Nazi splinter group known as the Black Front, whose members believed that Hitler had betrayed the Nazis' original anti-capitalist principles—was involved in a plot to plant two suitcases of explosives at Nazi headquarters in Nuremburg. Hirsch was betrayed by a Gestapo agent and arrested. His case became an international cause célèbre after the intervention of the Red Cross and the U.S. Ambassador to Berlin. Despite the public outcry, Hirsch was executed by guillotine.

Maurice Bavaud's Suicidal Plan

Another bizarre lone-wolf attempt to kill Hitler involved a dreamy Swiss Catholic seminarian named Maurice Bavaud. Only twenty-five years old, Bavaud was a member of a secret society of anti-Communist seminarians known as the Compagnie du Mystère, founded by a deranged fellow seminarian named Marcel Gerbohay. Gerbohay, who fancied himself a descendant of the Romanoff dynasty that had ruled Russia for 350 years until it was overthrown by the Bolsheviks in 1917, believed that Hitler had been chosen by God to stop the Communist onslaught.

When it appeared, in 1938, that Hitler was not only not going to stop the Communist onslaught but was actually preparing to cooperate with it in dividing up eastern Europe, Gerhohay decided that Hitler must be stopped at all costs. He somehow talked Bavaud into leaving the peaceful confines of the Saint Ilan Seminary in Saint-Brieuc, Brittany, to travel to Germany on a quixotic quest to assassinate Hitler.

Bavaud made his way by train first to his native Switzerland, where he stayed for a few weeks with his family in Neuchâtal, helping out with the family grocery business and reading *Mein Kampf* in French translation.

Finally, on October 9, 1938, Bavaud decided the time to act had come. After visiting relatives in Germany, he took a train to Basel, where he was somehow able to get his hands on a pistol—a Schmeisser 6.35-mm semi-automatic.

From there, Bavaud went back to Germany and made a series of vain attempts to see Hitler in person. His plan, apparently, was to pose as an admiring tourist, walk up to the Führer, and then simply shoot him in the head—despite the fact that, as a Catholic seminarian, he had no experience whatsoever with firearms.

Between October 25 and 31, Bavaud traveled from Berlin to Berchtesgaden, Hitler's mountain retreat in the Bavarian Alps, and to Munich in a desperate effort to get close to Hitler. Wherever he showed up, he would discover that the Führer was no longer there. This phenomenon—Hitler's erratic and unpredictable schedule—would bedevil would-be assassins for years. On October 25, Bavaud arrived in Berchtesgaden but was told that Hitler had left the day before.

Although he was Swiss, Bavaud only knew a few words of German. But he met a friendly German policeman who spoke French. Bavaud explained to the policeman that he was a great admirer of Hitler and wanted to see him in person. The policeman replied that this was likely impossible unless he was a foreign dignitary or someone similarly important. The policeman added, however, that Bavaud's best chance to see the Führer would probably be in early November, in Munich, where Hitler came every year to commemorate the failed Beer Hall Putsch of 1923. The Führer always marched in a parade along the same route that he and his fellow plotters had taken when marching to the military headquarters during the putsch. If Bavaud watched the parade, the policeman explained, he might be able to see Hitler as he walked by.

Bavaud took the policeman's advice and, on October 31, boarded a train to Munich, where he rented a room. He spent the next week getting to know the city and the parade route that Hitler would likely take. Since taking power in 1933, the Nazis had gone out of their way to make a big deal out of November 9—the Der Neunte Elfte (the Ninth of the Eleventh)—the date of Hitler's failed attempt to take over the Bavarian government.

In addition to Hitler's annual speech in the Bürgerbräukeller, where he had announced the revolution, the Nazis reenacted the march that Hitler and his fellow Nazis had undertaken to the Feldherrnhalle, the war memorial on Munich's Odeonsplatz where the Bavarian military had exchanged fire with the Nazi plotters, killing sixteen. The so-called Blutfahne or blood flag, stained with the blood of the fallen Nazis, was ritually displayed. Hitler would lay a wreath at the Feldherrnhalle. Tens of thousands of Germans crowded into Munich for these ceremonies every year, a security nightmare.

On November 9, Bavaud was ready. Early in the morning, he walked over to Munich's Marienplatz—an enormous open plaza in the center of the Alt Stadt or old city. The parade route went right by this area, and there were large bandstands erected along the route. Bavaud was able to get a front row seat but then realized he wouldn't be able to see because of the rows of SA security personnel lining the street. He climbed higher into the bandstand, a poor location from which to fire a pistol, when suddenly the crowd erupted in a frenzy of excitement. The Führer was coming!

Bavaud got ready. Hitler was marching along the parade route in the old uniform of the SA—brown jodhpur pants tucked into knee-high black boots, a red swastika armband on his left arm—and without a hat. Nazi flags were everywhere. Suddenly, the crowd stood at attention, everyone raising their arms in the Roman salute. This completely blocked Bavaud's view.

Adding to his problems, Bavaud could see that Hitler was actually on the far side of the very wide boulevard, far beyond the range of his .22 caliber pistol, which he barely knew how to fire anyway. Surrounded by screaming Nazi supporters and facing rows of armed SA guards, the young dreamer instantly knew he had no chance to complete his mission on this day.

Distraught, Bavaud decided to make one last effort. Remembering what the German policeman had told him about foreign dignitaries, Bavaud bought some expensive stationery and forged a fake letter from the French foreign minister. It was a letter of introduction to Bavaud himself, stating that Bavaud had an important piece of correspondence from the minister that he was to deliver to Hitler personally.

Bavaud heard on the street that Hitler was returning to his residence in Berchtesgaden, so, once again, he took a train to the tiny Bavarian village. His plan was to present his fake letter to the Nazi security guards and thereby gain an audience with Hitler. But when he arrived, he discovered that Hitler wasn't there. He was still in Munich. As a result, Bavaud returned to Munich only to learn that Hitler had just left for Berchtesgaden.

Realizing he was clearly out of his depth, Bavaud gave up. Now out of money, he took a train to Paris where he planned to ask the Swiss Embassy for money to return to Switzerland. When a train conductor discovered that he was traveling without a ticket, Bavaud was arrested and then searched. The police found his pistol and the fake letter addressed to Hitler, so the Gestapo was alerted. Upon interrogation, Bavaud confessed that he was attempting to assassinate Hitler. After a brief trial, Maurice Bavaud was found guilty. Two and a half years later, on May 14, 1941, he was beheaded.

The Bomb Plot That Almost Prevented World War II

While Bavaud was doing his best to take a pot shot at Hitler in the bandstands of Munich, unbeknownst to him another plotter— with a far more ambitious and practical plan—was nearby. The night before, he had been busy scouting out the beer hall where Hitler spoke every year at this time.

His name was Johann Georg Elser, a thirty-five-year-old German cabinet maker and longtime opponent of Nazism with ties to leftwing political parties. He was known to have strong anti-Nazi views, refusing to say "Heil, Hitler," or to use the Nazi salute. And, despite recent conspiracy theories to the contrary, he almost certainly acted alone.

Like Bavaud, Elser knew that Hitler gave a speech every year at the famous Bürgerbräukeller beer hall in Munich on the anniversary of the 1923 putsch. He had come to Munich just the day before Bavaud's aborted assassination attempt, on November 8, with the germ of an idea in his head. After checking into a hotel, Elser headed straight for the Bürgerbräukeller. He had to wait until the thousands of Nazi supporters had heard Hitler's speech and left the building, after 10:00 or 11:00 p.m. Then he went inside.

It was an enormous rectangular structure, with a ceiling many stories high, that could hold up to three thousand patrons. At one end, there was a second-story balcony from which observers could look down at the main floor. On the ground floor, in front of a wooden pillar, a small stage had been erected with a podium on it. This was set up every year for Hitler and other Nazi dignitaries to use. It was on this stage, with an enormous Nazi flag behind it, that Hitler gave a speech each November commemorating the Beer Hall Putsch.

After inspecting the hall that night and over the course of the next few days, Elser began to formulate a plan—a daring, methodical, and patient plan that could have eliminated the entire Nazi leadership all at once and prevented the bloodiest war in history. As a result, he left and returned to his home in Königsbronn, a hundred miles northwest of Munich, and set to work.

Elser was originally a clock maker and cabinet maker, but he had recently been working in a munitions factory in nearby Heidenheim, where he was able to steal explosives. Over the course of many weeks, Elser slowly accumulated a stockpile of explosives and then, after he switched to a job in a rock quarry, of blasting caps and detonators. Although a self-taught amateur, he was determined to fashion a bomb

Johann Georg Elser (1903–1945), a German carpenter and ardent anti-Nazi, came very close to blowing Hitler up during annual ceremonies on November 8, 1939, at the Bürgerbräukeller beer hall in Munich. *Wikimedia Commons*[13]

that would accomplish his goals. Elser spent months designing and then testing various bombs, setting off the explosive devices in the woods near his parents' home.

Finally, in August 1939, when he felt his designs were good enough, Elser moved to Munich and rented rooms near the Bürgerbräukeller. He became a regular late diner at the popular restaurant and soon figured out how he could stay inside the building, undetected, after closing time. Over the next two months, Elser is estimated to have stayed inside the building at least thirty times. He systematically prepared a secret hiding place in the wooden pillar behind the speaker's platform where Hitler spoke every year and where he could place a large bomb.

Elser would work all night by flashlight, sneaking out in the early morning when workers came to start the day's routine. Finally, on the first two days of November 1939, the young carpenter began packing enormous amounts of explosives into the hollowed-out pillar, then installing the timing device and detonator that would ignite the explosives.

Unbeknownst to anyone, the most powerful men in Nazi Germany would soon be standing just a few feet away from a massive bomb.

Two days later, during a weekend dance festival, Elser returned to the beer hall. He bought tickets for the commemoration and then hid, once again, until past closing time. Now he would activate his

EYEWITNESS ACCOUNT

"The most amazing feature of [Elser's] bomb was the time fuse, which could be set ten days ahead of time. This was something that even experts had not yet accomplished. Otherwise, it was a rather primitive infernal machine. Nevertheless, its success indicated that even such old-fashioned objets d'art can produce, when well placed, tremendous explosive effects. After the explosion the hall was a shambles. . . . Elser found a place that was both effective and easy to work on unobserved—a column directly behind the speakers' desk."

—Hans Gisevius, German diplomat and July 20 plot survivor[14]

detonating timing device. Hitler usually began his annual speech at 8:30 p.m. and spoke for around two hours. Elser, therefore, set his bomb to explode one hour into Hitler's speech, around 9:20 p.m. on the night of November 8.

After leaving Munich on November 6 and visiting his sister overnight in Stuttgart, Elser returned to Munich the night before the Nazi rally. Leaving nothing to chance, he returned to the beer hall and made one final check on his bomb. Everything was ready. The next morning, November 8, he headed for the town of Konstanz on the border with Switzerland. He planned to be in Switzerland when the bomb went off.

Hitler arrived in Munch by private train. As usual, the Nazi faithful had packed the beer hall to bursting. And as Elser had hoped, virtually all of the top leaders of the Reich were there, including Joseph Goebbels, Reinhard Heydrich, Rudolf Hess, Alfred Rosenberg, Heinrich Himmler, and Julius Streicher.

But Hitler, preoccupied with the looming invasion of France, wanted to return to Berlin that night. As a result, his planned speech was moved up half an hour to 8:00 p.m. Even worse, Hitler decided to cut short his normally rambling oration so he could leave by 9:30 p.m. Hitler wrapped up his speech around nine to thunderous applause. At 9:07, the Führer left the building, followed into the street by hundreds of admirers.

Only a few hundred Nazis were left in the beer hall when, at precisely 9:20 p.m., just thirteen minutes after Hitler had left, Elser's bomb went off. The ear-shattering explosion blasted a hole in the ceiling, causing metal girders and glass to collapse in an enormous pile of debris. With Hitler and the other top Nazi officials having left the stage, sixty-three people were hurt, and eight were killed.

Forty-five minutes before the bomb exploded, Elser was stopped by German border guards just a hundred feet from the Swiss border. Like Bavaud, he was inexplicably carrying incriminating evidence with him. There were bomb-making diagrams and wire cutters in his pockets, which raised the border guards' suspicious. As the Gestapo was interrogating Elser, news arrived about the bombing in Munich. The next

German officials on November 9, 1939, surveying the destruction caused by Georg Elser's bomb. *Deutsches Bundesarchiv*[15]

day, his photo was on the front pages of newspapers in Germany and all over the world.

Before Stauffenberg, Elser came the closest to anyone to killing Hitler and ending the Nazi regime.

Unfortunately, his failed effort had a disastrous unintended effect. It would stymie attempts by the German anti-Nazi resistance to reach out to the Allies during the war. Top Nazi leaders could not accept that Elser had acted alone. Originally, they were convinced that he had to have had the assistance of British intelligence agents.

The Nazis brutally tortured Elser—as well as his mother, sister, brother-in-law, and former girlfriend. Gestapo agents forced Elser to watch as they tortured his family. As a result, Elser confessed to whatever the Nazis wanted. He cooperated fully. He demonstrated for Gestapo leaders precisely how he had made his bomb. He took them to the locations he had visited in pursuit of his plot. Yet it took months before Nazi intelligence officials reluctantly accepted that Elser had acted on his own initiative. As part of their investigations, Nazi intelligence officials pretended to be part of the resistance to Hitler and lured two British spies, based in the then-neutral Netherlands, to a meeting just across the German border. The Nazis kidnapped the British spies to learn the truth about Elser.

The captured British spies, Major Richard Henry Stevens and Captain Sigismund Payne Best, were held prisoners throughout the war but survived. Yet as a result of their capture, the British never again fully trusted any overtures from the German anti-Nazi resistance, always suspecting a possible trap. When no less an authority than Hitler's Deputy Führer Rudolf Hess piloted a private plane into Scotland in 1941, attempting to negotiate a separate peace agreement, the British simply arrested him, held him prisoner throughout the war, and turned him over to the Nuremberg War Crimes Tribunal after it was over. He would spend the rest of his life in Spandau Prison until his suicide in 1987 at the age of ninety-three.

Strangely, Elser was never tried for his crime and was not quickly executed, as other would-be assassins were. He spent most of the war in the Sachsenhausen concentration camp and then, in January 1945, was moved to the Dachau camp near Munich.

According to Best, who met Elser at Sachsenhausen, Elser claimed he had been recruited for the Munich bombing by top Nazi officials while he had been briefly detained at Dachau in the summer of 1939. It remains a mystery whether this is true—and, if true, whether the bombing was meant to really kill Hitler or to be a "false flag" operation, a deliberate near-miss designed to stir up public sentiment in support of Hitler's coming war against Britain. Most historians of World War II, including Hitler biographer Ian Kershaw, believe that Elser acted alone with no help from either British intelligence or high-ranking Nazis.[16]

Nazi officials played up Elser's assassination attempt, publicizing it in newspapers and holding ceremonies to honor those injured during the attempt. And in one of his final acts, on April 5, 1945, when the war was almost over, Hitler commanded the execution of all those conspirators against him still alive, including Elser and such famous political prisoners as Protestant pastor Dietrich Bonhoeffer. Four days later, on April 9, Elser was led to the crematorium at the Dachau concentration camp where he was met by the man in charge, SS-Oberscharführer Theodor Bongartz. Bongartz shot Elser dead at point blank range. His body was then quickly burned in the crematorium.

3 | SHOWING THE WORLD

espite his failure, Georg Elser showed the anti-Nazi resistance in Germany that the regime was vulnerable. The death of Hitler was an achievable goal. Hitler and other top Nazis had come very close to being blown to bits—as newspaper headlines all around the world loudly celebrated.

What Elser had failed to do, acting all by himself with homemade materials and with no training in explosives at all, perhaps an organized plot of professional soldiers might be able to pull off.

Yet over the next eighteen months, the anti-Nazi generals watched in dismay as Hitler swept from victory to victory. Betting that the timid leaders of the West would do nothing to stop him, Hitler abrogated the Versailles Treaty and spent the 1930s engaged in a massive program of rearmament. He grew the German military from a nominal force of 115,000 men in 1921 to an invulnerable war machine of up to 9.4 million at its height in 1943. One after the other, the nations of Europe fell to German armies—Belgium and the Netherlands, Luxembourg, and then France. Norway surrendered. Germany began bombing Britain. The Nazi juggernaut seemed unstoppable. What's more, German public opinion was clearly with the Führer.

Hitler's successful rearmament of Germany's military—exemplified in this photo of the Nazi Party Congress held in Nuremberg in 1938—allowed Nazi troops to conquer most of Europe in just three years. Hitler's opponents felt powerless to act against the regime in the face of his seemingly unstoppable success. *Shutterstock*

But then, in June 1941, Hitler made the key mistake of the war. He ordered his armies to attack his erstwhile ally, the Soviet Union, opening up a second front in what would become the Second World War.

Most of Hitler's generals were aghast. They knew very well what had happened to Napoleon when he attacked Mother Russia and faced the brutal Russian winters. They forthrightly questioned Hitler's plans. And a few began plotting Hitler's removal from power by any means necessary.

The leading figure in the evolving Wehrmacht assassination plot was Major General Henning von Tresckow, the forty-three-year-old chief of staff of the German Second Army. He succeeded the retired and now ailing General Beck as the primary leader of the military resistance to Hitler. Born into an aristocratic family in Magdeburg with three hundred

EYEWITNESS ACCOUNT

"Hitler's entourage certainly bore a measure of the blame for his growing belief in his superhuman abilities. Early in the game, Field Marshal Blomberg, Hitler's first and last Minister of War, had been overfond of praising Hitler's surpassing strategic genius. Even a more restrained and modest personality than Hitler ever was would have been in danger of losing all standards of self-criticism under such a constant torrent of applause."

—*Albert Speer, Hitler's architect and confidant*[1]

years of military heritage, Tresckow did not fit the stereotype of a Prussian officer. He was cosmopolitan and well-traveled, having visited both Britain and the United States in the early 1920s. Tresckow understood what Germany would face if America's industrial might were brought to bear against Germany.

Like many members of the resistance, Tresckow had been an early supporter of the Nazis but changed his mind after the Night of the Long Knives (when many military officials were murdered in cold blood) and after he learned about the mass executions of Jews and Russian soldiers in Eastern Europe.

By the time Georg Elser detonated his bomb in 1939, Tresckow was fully committed to overthrowing the Nazi regime and seeing Hitler dead. He recruited his cousin Fabian von Schlabrendorff, a German Army lawyer, to join the resistance, telling him that "both duty and honor demand from us that we should do our best to bring about the downfall of Hitler and National Socialism to save Germany and Europe from barbarism."[3]

What that barbarism entailed was evident to anyone who served on the Eastern Front. One of the most thoroughly documented acts of mass

Major General Hermann Henning Karl Robert von Tresckow (1901–1944), chief of staff of the German Second Army, was the driving force behind the plot in the German armed forces to kill Hitler. An early supporter of the Nazis, he became disillusioned by atrocities committed in the 1930s. *Deutsches Bundesarchiv*[2]

murder committed by the Nazis was the order, given during the invasion of the Soviet Union in June 1941, to summarily execute the Russian commissars, the political officers in Soviet military units. Earlier that year, in March, during a speech to senior officers, Hitler stated bluntly that the coming war against the Soviet Union was a "war of annihilation" that could not be conducted in a "knightly fashion."[4] For this reason, he explained, upcoming battles would require the "extermination of the Bolshevist commissars and of the Communist intelligentsia." Hitler dismissed the objection that German soldiers would be guilty of war crimes under the Geneva Convention, stating that the Soviet Union had never signed the Convention and, besides, this was a different kind of war. "In the East, harshness today means lenience in the future," he said.[5]

Hitler's instructions were then codified in a written order, the "Directives for the Treatment of Political Commissars" (Richtlinien für die Behandlung politischer Kommissare) or the Commissar Order for short. Issued on June 6, 1941, it explicitly stated that "in this battle mercy or considerations of international law is false." It decreed that commissars, recognizable by their special badge—a red star with a golden woven hammer and sickle on the sleeve—were not soldiers and therefore did not have "the protection due to prisoners of war under international law." What's more, the commissars were "originators of barbaric, Asiatic methods of warfare." The order was explicit: " ...if taken while fighting or offering resistance they must, on principle, be shot immediately."[6]

The German generals knew this order was illegal, a blatant violation of international law. Yet most carried it out anyway. They justified this war crime by saying the commissars were like spies, criminals who tyrannized the Russian population and should be treated differently than real soldiers.

It is estimated that thousands of Russian commissars were executed in the first months of Operation Barbarossa. It was a loss of innocence for many of those serving in the German Army, particu-

Major General Rudolph Christoph von Gersdorff (1905–1980) volunteered to become a suicide bomber and planned to kill Hitler (and himself) on March 21, 1943, but Hitler left the target location too quickly for Gersdorff to act. He was able to defuse the bomb he was carrying on his body. *Deutsches Bundesarchiv*[8]

larly for the professional officer corps. Yet only a few actively resisted the order. One of the few who did was Henning von Tresckow, whom we have already met. At that time, he was a major serving as chief operations officer of the German Army Group Center under Field Marshal Günther von Kluge, who told commanders under his direction to ignore the illegal order.[7]

Soon after the Commissar Order was issued, Tresckow approached his superior officer about participating in a coup against the regime. At first, Kluge was open to such a plot. But then Kluge received government-issued checks from Hitler worth half a million Reichsmarks ($3.6 million today).[9] Hitler was not above bribing his generals when he felt it necessary. Kluge backed out.

Over the coming months, Tresckow quietly began recruiting other top Army officers for some type of action against Hitler. In addition to his cousin Fabian von Schlabrendorff, Tresckow managed to convince key military personnel to join the conspiracy, such as Rudolph Christoph Freiherr von Gersdorff, a thirty-seven-year-old professional soldier who oversaw military intelligence as part of Army Group Center; Colonel Hans Oster, head of foreign intelligence in the Abwehr, German Military Intelligence; and General Friedrich Olbricht, head of the General Army Office and deputy to the commander of the Reserve Army, General Friedrich Fromm.

Beginning in 1941, all of these men would risk their lives, and the lives of their families, in repeated efforts to remove Hitler from power. Hitler's preeminent contemporary biographer, Ian Kershaw, credits Tresckow as being the guiding force behind the conspiracy within the German Army to overthrow the Nazi regime.

At first, Tresckow and many of his fellow conspirators thought it would be best if Hitler were simply arrested, removed from power, and then put on trial. As early as 1941, Tresckow, Schlabrendorff, and other officers planned to arrest Hitler when he visited Army Group Center's headquarters at Borisov, in the Soviet Union.

But when Hitler showed up, he arrived in a fleet of vehicles and was surrounded by a small army of SS bodyguards. Tresckow and his group never got anywhere near the Führer, let alone arrested him. They quickly realized that the only way Hitler could be stopped would be by killing him.

As a result, Tresckow and the other conspirators began planning in earnest to assassinate the Führer the next year. Shooting him was impractical and likely to fail since he was under constant guard and was known to wear a bullet-proof vest. Moreover, Elser's explosion had demonstrated just how effective a bombing might be were it done correctly.

As a result, in 1942, Tresckow directed Gersdorff to begin acquiring and testing different explosive devices.[10] As an intelligence officer, Gersdorff had access to many different types of explosives, including captured British bombs meant for the French Resistance.[11]

Taking Advantage of Operation Valkyrie

Yet the conspirators realized that killing Hitler would not be enough. The Nazi regime was a vast and well-oiled machine, staffed with thousands of true believers, which could continue to function even after Hitler's death.

Hitler's top aides, such as Heinrich Himmler, Joseph Goebbels, Hermann Göring, and Martin Bormann, were more than capable of maintaining the Nazi reign of terror even after Hitler's death. Hitler's own detached style of governance—delegating most tasks to subordinates—proved that.

Tresckow insisted that the assassination of Hitler would have to be part of an overall military coup that would also result in the removal of all top Nazi leaders from power. The question was: how?

Working with General Friedrich Olbricht, the deputy head of the Reserve Army, Tresckow learned about Operation Valkyrie (Unternehmen Walküre). As we have seen, it was a pre-existing plan, already approved by Hitler, to use the

General Friedrich Olbricht (1888–1944) helped work out how plotters could take advantage of an existing Nazi plan, Operation Valkyrie, to take over the government after Hitler was dead. *Deutsches Bundesarchiv*[12]

EYEWITNESS ACCOUNT

"As soon as the code word 'Walkuere' was given, the troops stationed around Berlin would start moving. For the first three hours, however, only the guards regiment would be at our disposal, because giving the alarm, issuing live munitions, and getting the troops going would be time-consuming. These three 'stagnant' hours represented the real danger to us. During that period the Gestapo could get set to strike back. Therefore, it was especially important for us...to paralyze the Berlin police."

—*Hans Gisevius, German diplomat and July 20 plot survivor*[13]

organizational structure and resources of the Reserve Army to allow the Nazis to survive any attempted coup against their regime. Tresckow and Olbricht realized that the plan could be turned on its head. Instead of protecting the regime from a coup, Operation Valkyrie could be used to initiate one.

The basic idea was to blame the assassination of Hitler on disloyal Nazi officials and then to use the Reserve Army to arrest all top Nazis, seize control of all command and communications centers, and announce to the nation that the Army had taken control of the government in the face of an attempted coup.

Tresckow and Olbricht even drafted the precise words to be used in making the announcement to the German people: "The Führer Adolf Hitler is dead! An unscrupulous clique of party leaders without frontline service has exploited this situation to stab the fighting front in the back and to seize power for their own selfish ends. In order to maintain law and order in this situation of acute danger the Reich Government has declared a state of martial law and has transferred the executive power to [the head of the Reserve Army] together with the supreme command of the Wehrmacht."[14]

It was an ambitious plan that could very well have worked. But Tresckow realized there were weak points.

First, for Operation Valkyrie to succeed, it would require the cooperation of the top officials in the Reserve Army—particularly of Olbricht's commander, the devious, self-serving, and untrustworthy head of the Reserve Army, General Fromm.

Also, getting *access* to Hitler to plant a bomb would be very difficult. Since the 1939 assassination attempt, the Führer's scheduled public appearances had been all but eliminated. When Hitler did appear in public, it was often not for a prearranged event but on the spur of the moment.

Additionally, as the war turned against Germany after 1942, Hitler spent most of his time in virtual hiding at his tightly guarded Wolf's Lair bunker in East Prussia, surrounded by twenty thousand elite bodyguards. Also, his schedule was notoriously erratic. Hitler often changed his mind at the last minute. It would be very difficult for any plan to assassinate the Führer to succeed.

Yet Tresckow was determined to try.

The Generals Fail to Kill Hitler

On March 13, 1943, Hitler made a visit to Army Group Headquarters in Smolensk, then under the command of Tresckow's old boss Field Marshal Kluge. A group of sharpshooters with sufficient security clearances to enter the army perimeter were in on the conspiracy, and they had volunteered to set up a sniper position and shoot Hitler as he was returning to his car.

The conspirators were ready to put Operation Valkyrie into action. Their comrades in the top echelons of the Reserve Army were prepared. The plan was for the conspirators to activate Valkyrie and take control

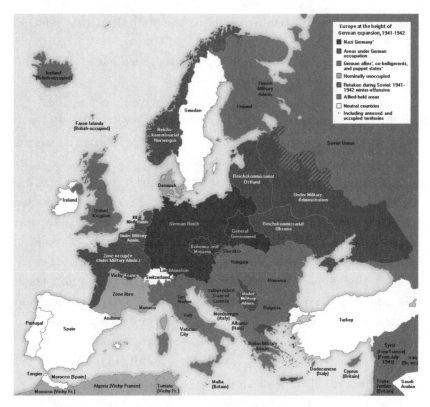

By 1942, Nazi Germany had attacked or invaded eleven countries and, through its Axis allies, had control over much of Europe. *Wikimedia Commons*[15]

of the central government the moment the assassins killed Hitler. The code word for success was "flash," and so the conspirators called their plot Operation Flash. Yet at the last minute, for unknown reasons, the snipers didn't fire.

Tresckow was furious. He decided that explosives were, as he had originally thought, the only realistic option. Before Hitler boarded his private plane for the return flight back to Berlin from Smolensk, Tresckow took one of the explosive devices sourced by Gersdorff—a British-made sabotage mine—and placed it in a package. He then asked a top Hitler aide if he would take the package back with him on the plane and give it to another general. It was, he said, two bottles of Cointreau, the orange-flavored liqueur much loved by many German officers.

The aide said he would be glad to do so. Right before Hitler's plane took off, Tresckow's cousin, the Army lawyer Fabian von Schlabrendorff, broke the fuse capsule on the detonator, sealed up the package, and handed it to the aide. This type of detonator would ignite in thirty minutes. When it did, it would blow Hitler's plane out of the sky.

But nothing happened. Hitler's plane landed without incident. The detonator failed to ignite the bomb. It was likely a dud.

The conspirators quickly realized that they were in mortal danger and that, were the bomb to be discovered, any hope of killing Hitler would be gone for the foreseeable future. They had to get the bomb back!

Tresckow telephoned the aide who had taken the package on the plane and asked him to hold on to it for a day. There had been some mix-up, Tresckow said, concerning who was to get the package. You know how those officers like their Cointreau! He then dispatched his loyal cousin to the Army High Command at Rastenburg carrying two real bottles of Cognac. Incredibly, Schlabrendorff was able to recover the package containing the bomb without incident and, once he was alone, somehow defused the detonator. Upon inspection, he discovered that it had been activated but the bomb had simply not exploded.

The whole incident was a disheartening fiasco. Yet the conspirators refused to give up. Frustrated, the idealistic Army intelligence officer Rudolf von Gersdorff volunteered to become, in effect, one of the world's first suicide bombers.

In a week, Hitler would make a rare public appearance at a ceremony honoring Germany's war dead. It was to be held in Berlin's Zeughaus, an enormous Baroque building that had once been used as a military armory. Constructed in the early 1700s, it stands in the center of the city near Berlin's Spree River on the beautiful tree-lined boulevard known as the Unter den Lindon.

The plan called for Gersdorff to take two medium-sized bombs and place one each in a pocket of his overcoat. He would attend the Memorial

Day ceremonies in the Zeughaus, activate the bomb detonators, and then stay close to Hitler until the bombs exploded, killing himself, Hitler and anyone in the immediate vicinity.

As usual, the problem was the detonators. In 1942, the typical delayed-action military detonator was maddeningly imprecise. The detonator was activated not by a clock-like timing device but by a kind of fuse. A spring-loaded firing mechanism was held back by a wire that, when released, would ignite a bomb. The detonator would be activated by someone breaking a capsule of acid in the firing cylinder, typically with pliers. When the acid ate away at the wire holding the spring back, it would release and ignite the bomb.

The fuses that the conspirators were able to acquire typically took approximately ten minutes to go off, give or take two or three minutes either way. They could go off early or late. Yet even trusted officers not in Hitler's inner circle rarely had a chance to be near the Führer for more than a minute or two.

The Memorial Day event in the Zeughaus called for a brief ceremony inside the Zeughaus main mall and then for Hitler to inspect an exhibition of captured Soviet military hardware on display there. Once that was done, Hitler would go to the cenotaph nearby for a wreath-laying ceremony.

The plot was put into operation. Gersdorff stood at the entrance to the Zeughaus as Hitler walked in. He raised his right arm in the Nazi salute and then squeezed the acid-release button in his left pocket to activate the two detonators. Everyone in his immediate vicinity should be dead within seven to ten minutes.

Gersdorff did his best to stay close to the Führer. Yet once again Hitler did what no one expected. He virtually raced through the exhibition hall, leaving the building in just two minutes, accompanied by his bodyguards. Foiled again, Gersdorff ran into a nearby lavatory and deactivated the bombs.[16] Even someone willing to blow himself up couldn't get close enough to Hitler for long enough for a bomb to kill him.

As if Hitler's uncanny luck were not enough, further disasters struck the resistance movement. The Gestapo arrested a number of resistance leaders accused of plotting against the Führer. These included the famous Lutheran pastor Dietrich Bonhoeffer, the members of the Catholic White Rose student movement in Munich, and even key figures in German military intelligence, such as Hans Oster. Finally, in October of 1943, Tresckow himself was transferred to the Eastern Front, now under the command of a fervent Nazi.

For this reason, he and his military colleagues in the resistance movement decided the key for success would be the Reserve Army, staffed as it was at the highest levels with anti-Hitler conspirators.

A break came in August, before Tresckow had to report for duty in the East. The conspirators had made a crucial new recruit: Stauffenberg. The young officer was still recovering from the wounds he had received in North Africa in April. But he had made up his mind that Hitler simply had to be removed before he brought Germany to utter destruction. Stauffenberg made a famous youthful boast about the German resistance: "Since the generals have failed to do anything, it's now up to the colonels."[17]

Surviving members of the resistance in the Germany Army reported that Stauffenberg reenergized the demoralized conspirators with his no-nonsense, take-charge style. He swept away all of the religious, political, moral, and logistical arguments against killing Hitler with the simple argument that something had to be done, immediately, to save Germany from destruction.

Stauffenberg met with Tresckow and other top conspirators, including the energetic anti-Nazi politician Carl Goerdeler, to discuss the crucial matter of how a successful coup d'état could be accomplished after Hitler was assassinated. Goerdeler and Stauffenberg cordially detested one another on sight. Goerdeler thought he could reason with Hitler, calmly explain that the best thing for Germany would be for the Führer to resign and name him, Goerdeler, as his successor. The military men, on the other hand, all agreed that Operation Valkyrie, which would

Major Axel von dem Bussche (1919–1993) volunteered in November 1943 to become a suicide bomber and kill Hitler during an inspection of new army winter uniforms. The attempt was canceled when the shipment of the uniforms was destroyed in a bombing raid. *Deutsches Bundesarchiv*[19]

give the plotters the use of the Reserve Army's parallel communications and operational systems, represented the best chance to take over the government.

At this point, Stauffenberg and Tresckow came up with an ingenious refinement to the original plan: they would blame Hitler's death not on anti-Nazi conspirators but rather on an ambitious cabal of traitors *within the Nazi Party itself.* This would allow the Reserve Army's soldiers to justify mass arrests of top Nazi officials. As the historian Joachim Fest puts it, the plotters would blame top Nazi leaders for the very coup which they, the plotters, would be carrying out against them.[18]

The tentative plan was to declare retired general Ludwig Beck, the widely respected former Wehrmacht Chief of Staff, head of state and chancellor. Field Marshal Erwin von Witzleben would be commander-in-chief of the Wehrmacht.

Tresckow explained to Stauffenberg the difficulty that the plotters had experienced in getting a bomb close enough to Hitler for a sufficient length of time for a delayed detonator to work. They needed someone who had regular access to Hitler and could either plant a bomb somewhere Hitler would remain for a fixed period or, as Gersdorff had attempted to do, remain in Hitler's presence until a bomb on the plotter's person was exploded.

EYEWITNESS ACCOUNT

"The successful struggle against National Socialism and its fanatical theories and aims, thus the way to the preservation of the people, goes only through the removal of Hitler's person and of what surrounds him."

—*Claus von Stauffenberg, February 3, 1943*[20]

Stauffenberg approached a number of fellow officers who had tentatively agreed to take on the assignment, including Major General Hellmuth Stieff, but all declined or stalled. Only one accepted immediately: a young Army captain named Axel von dem Bussche, twenty-four, who had witnessed the mass execution of Jews in the Ukraine and turned irrevocably against the regime.

The plan was to be a repeat of Gersdorff's effort and thus a suicide mission. The conspirators planned to lure Hitler out of his impregnable redoubt at the Wolf's Lair to view an exhibition of new uniforms and military equipment that was already planned. Bussche would show the uniforms to Hitler, activate a short-fuse grenade in his pocket, and then tackle Hitler and hold him down for the few seconds it would take for the explosives to detonate.

But as with the previous plots to kill Hitler, nothing came of this one.

The grenade was delivered to Bussche, but the presentation of military uniforms was postponed time and again. In November, Bussche was stationed close to the Wolf's Lair, but still no announcement of the event was made. Then the new uniforms were destroyed in an air raid. Finally, in January 1944, Bussche was wounded in battle and lost a leg.

As he was moved from hospital to hospital, Bussche had to somehow keep his stash of explosives hidden from prying eyes. The plotters tried to find a substitute assassin—Stauffenberg's own adjutant, Werner von Haeften, was asked—but possible candidates demurred for a variety of reasons, certain death not the least of them. As 1944 dawned, two men volunteered to sacrifice their lives—Lieutenant Ewald Heinrich von Kleist and Rittmeister Eberhard von Breitenbuch—but the limited public access to Hitler foiled their various attempts as well.[21]

Stauffenberg Takes Charge

Finally, in July 1944, the conspirators got a break: Stauffenberg was promoted to full colonel and appointed Chief of Staff of the Reserve Army, the very heart of the Wehrmacht plot to kill Hitler.

He soon realized that assassinating the Führer would inevitably be up to him. For one thing, as Chief of Staff of the Reserve Army, Stauffenberg now had rare and regular access to Hitler in person. Yet that opportunity presented a related difficulty. If Stauffenberg were to be killed in the assassination of Hitler, the likelihood that Operation Valkyrie would be put into motion was greatly reduced.

General Friedrich Fromm, Stauffenberg's new boss, was the only man in Germany besides Hitler who had the authority to order the Reserve Army into action, yet he would only take that step if he were certain that Hitler was dead and the coup would succeed. Stauffenberg knew that he had to be with the general every step of the way, helping him organize and rally the Reserve Army forces for a bloody takeover from the Nazis. This was Stauffenberg's dilemma. Yet once he was appointed Chief of Staff of the Reserve Army, he was determined to kill Hitler.

Over a series of three personal meetings with the Nazi dictator over the next two weeks, Stauffenberg carried enough plastic explosives with him to obliterate a small building. To each meeting he took, undetected, the two kilos of British plastic explosives that Gersdorff had acquired and two ten-minute acid-release detonators. Yet each time, Stauffenberg decided not to arm the bombs. He could have killed Hitler, but it would have been difficult not to kill himself at the same time—decapitating the conspiracy and putting Operation Valkyrie in jeopardy.

EYEWITNESS ACCOUNT

"I don't know whether Stauffenberg had always showed his ruder side. But now, consciously or unconsciously, he was trying to over-compensate for the inferiority feelings engendered by his mutilation. As he sat there with his arms dangling limply and his legs in their heavy top-boots sprawled out in front of him, I marveled at the vast difference between this Stauffenberg and the disciple of Stefan George whom I had imagined. I tried to see the connection between this unquestionably forceful but rather boorish person and the verses of the aristocratic poet."[22]

—*Hans Gisevius, German diplomat and July 20 plot survivor*

Stauffenberg's first opportunity to kill Hitler had occurred on July 6, when he was invited to a two-hour meeting at the Berghof, Hitler's personal residence in the Obersaltzberg region of the Alps. He brought the explosives with him in his briefcase. Yet he did nothing on this day.

His next chance came five days later, on July 11, at another meeting at the Berghof. On this occasion, Heinrich Himmler was not present, and the other key members of the conspiracy did not want Stauffenberg to act in Himmler's absence. Many of them believed that it was almost as important to kill Himmler—the Nazi fanatic at the head of Hitler's personal army, the SS—as it was to kill Hitler himself. Once again, Stauffenberg did nothing.[23]

Then, four days later, there was yet another meeting—this time at the Wolf's Lair in East Prussia. Stauffenberg was determined that this was to be the day, but then Hitler suddenly left the conference.

Because of a mix-up in communications, the Valkyrie Order was released—prematurely triggering the active coup. When the conspirators

Stauffenberg (on the far left) stands at attention during a meeting with Hitler at the Wolf's Lair on July 15, 1944. *Deutsches Bundesarchiv*[24]

realized that the bombing attempt had been called off, the order had to be quickly canceled. They made the excuse that it had been just a drill, but now the conspirators knew that they could only activate Valkyrie when they were certain Hitler was dead. Another slipup would spell the end of the plot to stop Nazi rule.

By this point, Stauffenberg was desperate. His next meeting with Hitler would again be in four days, on July 20 at the Wolf's Lair. This had to be the day, the young colonel told his fellow conspirators. They no longer had any choice. Whether or not Himmler and other top Nazis were present, on July 20 Adolf Hitler had to be killed and the elaborate plan to take over the German government put into operation. They had to make the attempt—or die trying.

The Wolf's Lair, 11:30 a.m.

It was now nearly four years since Elser had almost succeeded in blowing Hitler and many top Nazis to kingdom come. No one else had come as close. Stauffenberg was determined that failure was not an option this time. He would do everything in his power to place a deadly bomb as close to Hitler as humanly possible.

Stauffenberg astonished his adjutant Haeften with his steely nerves. Casually chatting and laughing with some of Hitler's most trusted associates at breakfast just after they arrived at the Wolf's Lair on July 20, he didn't appear to have a care in the world.

EYEWITNESS ACCOUNT

"When on the 11th of July Stauffenberg received orders to go to the Obersaltzberg to attend the military conference, he resolved to make the attempt on that day. He flew there in a special plane, taking with him in his briefcase the English delayed-action bomb. He intended to start its mechanism after he finished his report, and to leave his briefcase in the conference room with the remaining participants.... When the conference began, Himmler, the most dangerous Nazi next to Hitler, was absent. Stauffenberg considered this so serious a drawback that he didn't make the attempt.

"Shortly afterwards Hitler left for East Prussia. Stauffenberg went to the next conference there, on the 15th of July, and again took the delayed-action bomb with him. This time both Hitler and Himmler were present. Stauffenberg was about to start the time bomb's mechanism when Hitler unexpectedly left the conference room and did not return. Again the attempt had to be abandoned."

—*Fabian von Schlabrendorff, July 20 plot survivor*[25]

After a few minutes at the outdoor breakfast table, Stauffenberg spotted a longtime member of the anti-Hitler resistance, General Fritz Erich Fellgiebel, the fifty-seven-year-old head of Army communications. He hurried over to have a private word with him. It was Fellgiebel's task to cut off all communications from the Wolf's Lair once Stauffenberg's bomb was detonated and Hitler killed. Fellgiebel assured Stauffenberg that he was ready and able to accomplish his mission.

At twelve o'clock, Stauffenberg met with General Walter Buhle to go over the report that Stauffenberg was to deliver to Hitler on troop reinforcements from the Reserve Army. The two men then walked over to the office of another officer, Field Marshal Wilhelm Keitel, one of Hitler's most loyal generals. It was here that Stauffenberg received disconcerting news.

Because of Hitler's surprise meeting later that day with the Italian dictator Benito Mussolini, Stauffenberg's briefing had been moved up to half past noon, in just thirty minutes! In addition, Stauffenberg learned, the meeting was not to be held in the normal basement briefing room—a small windowless room made out of reinforced concrete, the perfect place for a bombing—but instead, on account of the oppressive heat, in a nearby wooden hut with large open windows.

Time was quickly running out.

Stauffenberg met his aide, Haeften, in the hallway outside of Keitel's office. He asked Keitel's assistant, Major Ernst John von Freyend, if there was a room available where he could change his shirt. With the blistering heat, it was a reasonable request. Freyend showed Stauffenberg to a small lounge in the same building where Keitel's offices were located.

Stauffenberg and Haeften went inside, shut the door, and quickly set about arming the two bombs. It was a delicate operation under the best of circumstances. Haeften had the briefcase carrying the two bricks of plastic explosives, each weighing 975 grams, just slightly more than two pounds.[26] Carefully, the two men pulled one of the bricks out of Haeften's briefcase.

The detonators were long metal cylinders of British manufacture, designed to be inserted into the thick clay-like plastic explosives. To arm the detonators, the men had to remove the fuses from the primer charges and break a glass capsule to release acid into the cylinder. Once released, the acid would seep into cotton balls surrounding a wire. When the acid ate through the wire, it would release a spring-loaded firing mechanism that would ignite the primer charge and set off the plastic explosives.[27]

Out of a sense of personal responsibility, Stauffenberg insisted on breaking the capsule himself, with a special set of pliers modified for his disabled left hand. Yet if he squeezed too much, he risked breaking the wire suddenly, releasing the firing pin and blowing up himself and Haeften.

The detonators were designed to go off in thirty minutes, but this was merely an approximation. As soon as the acid ate through the wire, the bomb would explode. Satisfied that it was armed, Stauffenberg and Haeften eased the first, now-live bomb into Stauffenberg's own briefcase.

Then disaster struck! Suddenly and unexpectedly, the door to the lounge abruptly opened inwards, striking Stauffenberg in the back.[28] A young sergeant, Werner Vogel, burst into the room just in time to see Stauffenberg stuff something into his briefcase.

Vogel breathlessly announced that there was an urgent telephone call for Stauffenberg from General Fellgiebel. Meanwhile Keitel's assistant, Major Freyend, was standing outside the room, yelling for Stauffenberg to "please come along!"

Startled, but with as much calm as he could muster, Stauffenberg hurriedly closed the latches of his briefcase. Haeften did the same with his briefcase, still containing the unarmed second brick of plastic explosives.

Some historians speculate that Fellgiebel's ill-timed telephone call changed the course of history. That call made it impossible for Stauffenberg to arm the second bomb, or even to place the second bomb from Haeften's briefcase into his own, alongside the previously armed bomb. Had he been able to do so, the first bomb would likely have ignited the second, even without a detonator. The explosive force of the two bricks of plastic explosives could have made the mission a success.[29]

But the unnerved Stauffenberg did not dare try anything with the second block of explosives. He didn't know whether the sergeant had seen what he had placed in his briefcase. And the Führer was now waiting impatiently for him!

Walking briskly with Major Freyend, Stauffenberg left the building where Keitel's office was located. The two men strolled quickly across a large open yard to the small wooden building being used as an impromptu briefing room.

Twice Stauffenberg declined Freyend's offer to carry his heavy brief-case for him. Instead, he asked Freyend for a special favor: Stauffenberg wanted to stand as close to the Führer as possible, he explained, so he could catch up and be ready to give his report.

Entering the wooden building via a side door, Stauffenberg turned right down a hallway past the telephone center and into the briefing room itself: a rectangular room with open windows all around.

In the center of the room was a long, narrow, and very heavy oak table upon which were laid large military maps. At the middle of the table, closest to the entrance and with his back to it, sat Adolf Hitler, poring over his maps.

As Stauffenberg entered the room, Hitler looked up at him. Stauffenberg stood at attention, meeting the Führer's eyes. Stauffenberg could see instantly that neither Himmler nor Göring was present.

There were twenty-four men in the room including Hitler. On Hitler's left stood Keitel, technically Commander-in-Chief of the German Armed Forces but in reality Hitler's most reliable yes man. On his right and next to the big table were Lieutenant General Adolf Heusinger, Deputy Chief of the General Staff, and Colonel Heinz Brandt, Heusinger's aide.

Gathered around both the left and right ends of the table were an assortment of top generals and their aides, including General Alfred Jodl, a war criminal who had carried out the executions of Russian commis-sars and who would succeed Keitel as the Chief of the General Staff of the Wehrmacht's High Command; General Walter Warlimont; the dip-lomat Franz von Sonnleithner, Foreign Minister Joachim von Ribben-trop's aide; and Nicolaus von Below, a Luftwaffe colonel who was one of Hitler's most trusted adjutants.

Keitel formally announced Stauffenberg's arrival. Hitler silently shook Stauffenberg's hand. Major Freyend gently requested that Stauffenberg be allowed to stand next to General Heusinger, on Hit-ler's immediate right, so he could hear what was being said.

As a result of his injuries, Stauffenberg's hearing was indeed poor, and it was a plausible excuse. But with Heusinger and Brandt crowding the table, Stauffenberg was only able to stand near the right-hand end of the table. Freyend then took Stauffenberg's briefcase from him and placed it on the floor, under the table.

General Heusinger continued with his part of the briefing on the battle situation on the Eastern Front. While he did so, Stauffenberg—at least according to some accounts—used his left foot to push the briefcase from directly in front of him, where Freyend had placed it, to as close to Hitler as possible, about six feet from the Nazi dictator.[30]

Satisfied that the bomb was as close to Hitler as it could possibly be, Stauffenberg signaled to Freyend with his raised left hand that he had to make a quick phone call, muttering as if he had forgotten something important.

The two men left the briefing room together and walked a few steps down the hallway to the telephone center in the same building. Freyend told the operator to call General Fellgiebel for Stauffenberg, and then, satisfied that this would be accomplished, returned to the briefing room. The moment he did so, Stauffenberg put down the receiver and quickly left the building.

According to some accounts, it was at this moment that General Heusinger's adjutant, Colonel Brandt, moved back into position on Heusinger's right and his foot struck Stauffenberg's briefcase beneath the table. Brandt, thinking the briefcase was in the way, may have moved it to the other (that is, the right) side of the thick oak table leg, effectively shielding Hitler.[31] Other accounts, including that of Stauffenberg's biographer, insist that Freyend had originally placed the briefcase to the right of the table leg, and that Stauffenberg had been unable to push it any closer to Hitler without drawing attention to himself.[32]

After leaving the building, Stauffenberg walked as fast as he could back towards where he had met with Keitel and then on to the adjutants' building, where Haeften and Fellgiebel were waiting for him. Haeften had spent the last few minutes locating the vehicle that was to drive them back to the air strip. Stauffenberg had left his belt and hat behind him in the conference room when he left, supposedly to make a phone call, to keep up the pretense that he was coming back.

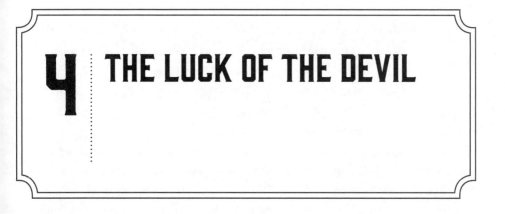

4 THE LUCK OF THE DEVIL

tauffenberg and Haeften were standing outside the Signal Office building, nervously chatting with General Erich Fellgiebel. Suddenly, the three men heard an explosion: a deafening blast of cracking wood and shattered glass that sounded like lightning, only much closer.

The low wooden building blew apart, flames shooting into the air. The blast slammed all twenty-four men inside the conference room to the ground, beams and plasterboard crashing all around them. Smoke filled the room. It was around 12:45 p.m.

"What's happening?" Fellgiebel asked, feigning ignorance.[1]

Both he and Stauffenberg knew what the explosion meant: Hitler was dead.

It was now Fellgiebel's crucial task to alert the core group of conspirators back at the Reserve Army headquarters in Berlin—that the actual coup itself, the overthrow of the Nazi government, should commence at once.

In addition, Fellgiebel was to cut off all communications from the Wolf's Lair to the outside world, at least to the degree that this was possible.

Startled by the size of the explosion, Stauffenberg and Haeften were convinced everyone inside the wooden barracks must have been killed. They quickly climbed into the car waiting for them and headed towards the gate leading out of Security Zone One. As they did so, both men could see a body being taken out from the rubble on a stretcher, covered by what they thought was Hitler's cloak.

In fact, three officers nearest the bomb were badly wounded and eventually died from their injuries: General Günther Korten, General Rudolf Schmundt, and Colonel Heinz Brandt. The stenographer for the meeting, Heinz Berger, had both of his legs blown off of his body and died later that same day. Three more generals in the room were badly injured and seventeen slightly injured.

Yet somehow Hitler survived.

He had been thrown violently to the floor of conference room, his face covered with black soot and his trousers shredded into ribbons. But once again, Hitler's amazing luck—what more than one observer called the luck of the devil—saved him. The open windows and wooden structure of the building diffused the force of the blast, as did the fact that Hitler had been sitting directly in front of the conference room doorway. In addition, the placement of Stauffenberg's briefcase on the right side of the table's heavy wooden leg shielded the dictator from much of the blast.

Coughing from the acrid smoke and badly dazed, Hitler managed to clamber to his feet. Not only was he alive; he had only minor injuries— a burst eardrum, it turned out, and some small burns, abrasions, and cuts. Helped by an equally shaken but unhurt General Keitel, Hitler staggered down the corridor that led from the conference room past the telephone center and outside. The two men, joined by two other Hitler aides, then limped uneasily towards Hitler's bunker, passing right by an astonished Fellgiebel.

Within two minutes of the explosion, Stauffenberg's car reached the first security checkpoint, which had been closed when soldiers heard the explosion. But in an area filled with land mines, explosions were not uncommon. Stauffenberg, with his aristocratic bearing, calmly insisted

EYEWITNESS ACCOUNT

"When I got to [the bunker] Hitler looked at me questioningly with great eyes and noticed my concerned expression. With a calm smile he said: 'Linge, somebody tried to kill me.'

"His uniform was in ribbons. His hair was singed and hung down in strands. My knees were trembling, but he acted as though nothing had happened. He was sitting on the round table. From his bared legs Dr. Hasselbach removed 200 wood splinters and dressed his wounds. Hitler's right arm hung down limply. His face and legs were still bleeding, but nothing else suggested the violence of the event."

—*Heinz Linge, Hitler's valet*[2]

that the guard open the gate immediately. The guard complied. As Stauffenberg and Haeften sped towards the second checkpoint, the dirt road took them back past the destroyed wooden barracks where the conference room had been.

But now a warning siren sounded—and the guards at the second security checkpoint refused to let them through. Stauffenberg got out of the car and demanded to use the guardhouse telephone, ordering the guards to call the Wolf's Lair military commander. They reached the commander's deputy, who had no idea why the alarm was sounding and so ordered the guards to let Stauffenberg pass. As the conspirators raced through the woods towards the landing strip, Haeften took the opportunity to toss the unused brick of plastic explosives out of the car—leaving a vital piece of evidence that investigators would later discover.[3]

At the airstrip, the driver maneuvered the staff car as close to the plane as he could. Stauffenberg and Haeften got out and marched about

Hitler's top aides, Martin Borman and Hermann Göring (center), inspect the conference room after the bombing attack on the Nazi dictator on July 20, 1944. *Deutsches Bundesarchiv*[4]

a hundred yards to the waiting Heinkel 111 aircraft, a twin-engine medium bomber that could make the flight back to Berlin in about three hours.

It was now about 1:15 p.m. Stauffenberg was sure that Fellgiebel had informed the main group of conspirators, back at Reserve Army headquarters, that Hitler had been killed. He was certain that Operation Valkyrie was already in operation. By now, the announcement of the Führer's death must have gone out by telex to key centers of the Reserve Army. Troops would soon surround the government district in Berlin, seize control of all telecommunications and radio centers, and release the statement about the supposed coup of disloyal Nazi Party leaders. All this would be coordinated with top-ranking conspirators at other locations around the Reich, including in Paris. By nightfall, the conspirators would have control of the German government. The two titular leaders

"Stauffenberg got in his car and drove through the camp, past the ruined hut. He saw the wounded officers lying in the grass, no sign of Hitler, just the smoking, shattered wooden remains and bleeding men. He must have thought his mission had succeeded, and he drove to the airfield convinced that Hitler was dead. But by the time Stauffenberg drove past the hut, the Führer was already back in his bunker, uninjured and fit and well."

—*Traudl Junge, Hitler's last secretary*[5]

of the coup—retired General Beck and Field Marshal von Witzleben—would broadcast an announcement to the German people.

Unfortunately, the flight back to Berlin meant a communications blackout for Stauffenberg. He wouldn't be able to contact Reserve Army headquarters until he landed and could use a telephone. That should be around 4:00 p.m.

He and Haeften had three long hours to think about all the steps they would have to take once they landed. By then, they thought, Operation Valkyrie would be in full swing, and most of the top Nazis already arrested. It was going to be a long day, Stauffenberg knew, but a glorious one! Hitler was dead—and there was a good chance that the new government could put an end to the war.

By the time Stauffenberg's Heinkel 111 took off, communications expert Fellgiebel faced a wrenching dilemma: he had seen with his own eyes that Hitler had survived the assassination attempt and was still very much alive. Yet he was supposed to alert the plotters in Berlin to initiate the coup.

What should he do?

An unknown German soldier holds up Hitler's tattered trousers after the July 20, 1944, blast. Later that day, Hitler would proudly show deposed Italian dictator Benito Mussolini the same shredded clothes. *Deutsches Bundesarchiv*[6]

Fellgiebel quickly took steps to cut off the Wolf's Lair's communications—something that the Nazi leadership also wanted him to do until they figured out what had happened.

But before he did so, Fellgiebel managed to get a telephone call through to the Reserve Army headquarters in Berlin.

His message was brief and cryptic. "*Etwas Furchtbares ist passiert!*" he shouted into the receiver. "*Der Führer lebt!*" *Something terrible has happened! The Führer lives!*

Back in Berlin, the leaders of the conspiracy didn't know what this meant. Did it mean that the bomb had never gone off? That Stauffenberg had been arrested before he could set it off?

Or did it mean the bomb had been detonated but Hitler hadn't been killed?

As a result, the conspirators, led by General Olbricht, decided to wait for more information. There had been too many false alarms, too many instances when Stauffenberg was going to ignite the bomb but didn't. The false alarm just five days earlier, on July 15—when an order to activate Operation Valkyrie had gone out and had to be canceled—made everyone in on the plot wary of taking action without knowing for sure that Hitler was dead. So they did nothing. During the three long hours that Stauffenberg was in the air, expecting the entire coup to be in operation, no orders were given. No one was arrested. Nothing happened at all.

And by 2:00 p.m., within an hour of the bombing, Hitler and the other top Nazis at the Wolf's Lair had identified Stauffenberg as the likely would-be assassin. At first, they suspected the foreign construction workers doing repairs at the compound. But then reports began to come in about Stauffenberg's hurried departure—and the fact that he had been seen leaving the conference room without his briefcase.

Hitler was in a state of posttraumatic euphoria, giddy with his own survival and more convinced than ever that he was invincible. "Well, ladies," Hitler told his young secretaries when they rushed to his side to reassure themselves that he was still alive, "once again everything turned out well for me. More proof that Fate has selected me for my mission."[7]

Hitler proceeded with his day as if nothing unusual had happened. At a delayed lunch, he proudly showed off his shredded trousers. After he was driven down to the Wolf's Lair railroad platform for his scheduled meeting with Mussolini, he brought the deposed Italian dictator back to the scene of the bombing and showed him the ruins.

Stauffenberg Arrives at the Bendlerblock

Stauffenberg's plane flew over Berlin, a large, modern city through which the River Spree flows from east to west. Looking out the window to the north, he could see the Tiergarten, a large central park, just south of the river. And he may also have been able to spot the Bendlerblock, the large complex of neoclassical buildings that then stood and today still stands just south of the Tiergarten, facing the Landwehr Canal.

At that time, the Bendlerblock housed the offices of many key military organizations, including the Reserve Army. And by the late afternoon of July 20, dozens of conspirators working in the Reserve Army and the Abwehr, German military intelligence, were anxiously awaiting word in their offices there.

Stauffenberg's plane landed earlier than expected, at 3:45 p.m.—not at Rangsdorf Airport, from which he had departed earlier that morning,

The Bendlerblock is an office building just south of Berlin's central park, the Tiergarten, that was the headquarters for the Reserve Army and the group of plotters who tried to assassinate Adolf Hitler on July 20, 1944. It now houses a museum of the German Resistance. *Wikimedia Commons*[8]

but likely at Tempelhof Airport, just three miles south of the Bendlerblock and the city center. As Stauffenberg climbed awkwardly out of the plane's hatch onto the portable stepladder, he half-expected to see the Gestapo waiting for him. Instead, no one was there at all except for his brother, Berthold. All was quiet, too quiet.

Apprehensive, Stauffenberg, Berthold, and Haeften hurried inside the airport hangar and quickly called the Reserve Army office. Haeften managed to get Olbricht on the phone. Speaking in code, he hurriedly told the general that the assassination effort had been a success. There was no time to waste.

But Stauffenberg sensed immediately that something was wrong. It was quickly apparent that Olbricht had so far done nothing about the coup itself. It was only after Stauffenberg himself got on the phone that Olbricht finally gave the orders to activate the Valkyrie plot—shortly before 4:00 p.m. and three hours after Hitler had survived the attack. Precious hours, and the element of surprise, had been lost.

Olbricht marched into the offices of General Fromm, the head of the Reserve Army. He announced that Hitler was dead and that it was time to activate Operation Valkyrie. The conspirators had long known that Fromm, who prided himself on always picking the winning horse politically, would join the plotters only if he were utterly convinced that Hitler was dead and the coup would succeed.

Olbricht told Fromm that he had the sheaf of special orders from the safe. He demanded that Fromm use his legal authority to finish the job, notifying all military units that the Army was stepping in to prevent a coup and that the military was now to answer to him. General Beck was arriving and would take control as head of state.

Fromm was skeptical. He feigned outrage. The activation of Operation Valkyrie five days earlier, on July 15, had earned him a stern dressing down from Field Marshal Keitel. He was not about to make the same mistake twice. Fromm immediately picked up a phone and dialed Keitel at the Wolf's Lair. Communications links had been restored, and Keitel came to the phone at once.

Keitel assured Fromm that Hitler was very much alive. Then he added, "And where, by the way, is your chief of staff, Colonel von Stauffenberg?"

A few minutes later, around 4:30 p.m., Stauffenberg's car was speeding into the central courtyard of the Bendlerblock complex. Despite his disability, Stauffenberg bounded up the stairways of the central office building, along with Berthold and Haeften, and the men burst into Olbricht's office, where most of the top conspirators were waiting.

"*Hitler ist tot!*" Stauffenberg announced with a flourish, out of breath. "Hitler is dead." He was met by complete silence. Stauffenberg had no idea of the quiet drama that had been unfolding over the past two hours.

General Friedrich Fromm (1888–1945), commander of the Reserve Army, ordered Stauffenberg's immediate execution to cover up the fact that he had advance knowledge of the assassination plot and would have supported it had it succeeded. He was implicated anyway and executed two months before the war ended. *Deutsches Bundesarchiv*[9]

As his staff quickly told him, General Keitel was claiming that Hitler was not dead but had survived the assassination attempt.

Stauffenberg insisted that this was nonsense. "Keitel is lying as usual," he replied. "I myself saw Hitler being carried out dead." And, he added, even if Hitler were still alive, the coup had to proceed as planned. The honor of Germany was at stake.

Stauffenberg's calm, determined manner stiffened the conspirators' backbones, and they sprang into action. The warren of Reserve Army offices became an instant swarm of activity as the conspirators issued military orders, fired off telex communications, and spoke on the telephone with wavering commanders in the field.

Remarkably, the plan worked better than might have been expected under the circumstances. In Paris, for example, more than a thousand SS soldiers were rounded up and arrested that night. The government district in Berlin was quickly surrounded by Reserve Army troops, just as had been planned. Even the offices of Joseph Goebbels, the Nazi minister of propaganda and one of Hitler's most trusted aides, were surrounded. Goebbels was sufficiently alarmed by these events that he took the precaution of putting a small box of cyanide capsules in his pocket, just in case.

Yet Fromm, the commander of the Reserve Army, was having none of it. He refused to sign any of the orders, confronted his deputy, and

EYEWITNESS ACCOUNT

"Olbricht and Stauffenberg returned to the office in which Beck and I were pacing back and forth. Both were exhausted as they informed us of the 'skirmish' they had just been through. Stauffenberg had no time to go into lengthy reflections on Fromm's behavior. Activity halted whenever he did not stand behind it with his organizational talent and impulsiveness."

—*Hans B. Gisevius, German diplomat and July 20 plot survivor*[11]

angrily demanded an explanation. If someone had ignited a bomb, Fromm said, then it must have been someone in Hitler's inner circle.

Stauffenberg shook his head and looked his superior in the eye. "I did it," he said. "I detonated the bomb during the conference in Hitler's headquarters."

The general was visibly astonished at this admission of guilt. He coolly asked if the colonel had a pistol and knew what to do with it at a time like this. "Count Stauffenberg, the assassination failed. You must shoot yourself at once."

"I shall do nothing of the kind."

Now Olbricht spoke up. "General Fromm, the moment for action has come. If we do not strike now, our country will be ruined forever."

"Does that mean that you, too, are taking part in this coup d'etat?"

"Yes, sir."

Fromm's face turned bright red with rage—and he promptly announced that Olbricht and Stauffenberg were under arrest. For a moment it looked as though the men would come to blows.

Finally, Olbricht spoke. "You cannot arrest us," he told Fromm calmly. "You do not realize who holds the power. We are arresting you."[10]

Major Otto Remer (1912–1997) was ordered by Hitler on the phone to stop the coup in Berlin. After the war, Remer became a Holocaust denier and neo-Nazi leader. *Deutsches Bundesarchiv*[12]

Fromm was placed in his office under guard while the conspirators returned to their telephones and telex machines. Rumors and conflicting reports were now ricocheting around the entire Reich, from Paris to Vienna.

Stauffenberg amazed his comrades with his calm determination as he cajoled commanders in the field, assuring them that Hitler really was dead. The truth was, even if Hitler was alive, the conspirators were still determined to overthrow the Nazi government.

The Empire Strikes Back

It almost worked. The Reserve Army troops at first were able to take control of key installations, even in Berlin.

But at 6:00 p.m., the conspirators faced a devastating setback in the person of an ardent young Nazi by the name of Major Otto Ernst Remer. Remer, who survived the war and became a leader of the neo-Nazi underground, commanded a unit of the Berlin Guard Battalion that had effectively sealed off the government district off Wilhelmstrasse and Goebbels' offices.

But Remer had his doubts about the Führer being dead. He was also smart enough to realize that if he aided a coup against Hitler, his own neck would be on the line. So Remer marched into Goebbels's home on the pretext of arresting him but in reality to see for himself whether Hitler was really dead. He arrived just as a member of the coup, Major Martin Korff, was himself attempting to arrest Goebbels.[13]

"Is the Führer dead?" Major Remer demanded.

Goebbels just smiled. "Would you like to speak with him yourself?"

The minister of propaganda promptly dialed the telephone number of the Wolf's Lair and managed to get the Nazi dictator on the line. "Remer, do you recognize my voice?" Hitler bellowed.

"Jawohl, mein Führer," the major said into the receiver.

Hitler replied that he was putting the young major personally in charge of the defense of Berlin. He was to stop this illegal coup at all costs.

The ardent young Nazi replied that the Führer could count on him.

Remer left Goebbels's residence and immediately began countermanding all of the orders coming from Stauffenberg's office that he could. Remer's most effective move was to order the removal of the military cordon that had been set up around the government quarter—the most visible sign that a new government was taking over.

By this time, the radio was broadcasting reports that Hitler had survived an assassination attempt. It quickly became apparent that, whatever coup had been planned, it was about to fall apart.

On the streets of Berlin, all was chaos. Military units were receiving contradictory orders. There were conflicting reports that Hitler had been killed and that he had survived the assassination. Under the circumstances, no one wanted to stick their necks out and take decisive action.

Only a small group of dedicated conspirators, led by Stauffenberg, refused to give up. They knew that their only chance was to bluff their way through the situation, to act as though Hitler was dead and hope that enough military units joined their cause to make their fiction a reality.

Stauffenberg continued to work the phones like a madman, telling field commanders that the Nazis were lying and that Hitler really was dead. He had seen it himself.

Around eight o'clock, a top member of the Army general staff, the sixty-two-year-old Field Marshal Erwin von Witzleben, himself a

Field Marshal Erwin von Witzleben (1881–1944), a leading conspirator in the plot to assassinate Hitler, would have become head of the Wehrmacht had it succeeded. He knew early on the plot had failed and angrily returned to his home, awaiting his certain arrest. *Deutsches Bundesarchiv*[14]

member of the conspiracy, arrived at the Bendlerblock office complex. Just as retired General Beck was supposed to be named chancellor of the new government, the plan had been for Witzleben, a veteran of World War I, to be named acting head of the Wehrmacht.

But Witzleben had just come from a meeting with other Army personnel. He knew that Hitler was very much alive. The entire coup had been bungled—and Witzleben knew what that meant for all involved. He was enraged.

Witzleben confronted Stauffenberg, Beck, and the other conspirators in Stauffenberg's office. Nothing that they had promised had come to pass, he said. Hitler was not dead but very much alive. The government quarter was open. Top Nazi leaders were not under arrest. Even the government radio station was operating normally, broadcasting regular reports about the Führer's miraculous escape from a vicious assassination attempt. After berating the dwindling group of conspirators for their incompetence, the field marshal stormed out of the building.

Meanwhile, General Fromm, inexplicably left unguarded, had been able to telephone key commanders of the Reserve Army and countermand Stauffenberg's orders. As he was Stauffenberg's superior, his orders were, of course, immediately obeyed.

By nine o'clock, the conspirators began to arm themselves. A group of Bendlerblock soldiers, Nazi loyalists who had not been part of the conspiracy, also acquired some small arms and headed towards Stauffenberg's office.

Suddenly, shots rang out in the hallway. Stauffenberg somehow managed to load his pistol with one hand and get off a round, but he was immediately shot in his upper left arm. He staggered back into his office and collapsed on the floor, blood everywhere. The colonel removed his eye patch with his one hand, despite his wounded arm.

Downstairs, troops stormed into the building, challenging the men inside with the question, "Are you for or against the Führer?"

Events were moving quickly. A group of soldiers headed to the private apartment where Fromm was being held and released him. With a group of soldiers behind him, the general marched down the hallway and burst

Stauffenberg's office in the Bendlerblock complex, where he desperately tried to convince military units to join the coup against Hitler, is now part of a museum dedicated to the German resistance. *Wikimedia Commons*[15]

into Stauffenberg's office. The small group of remaining conspirators stood defiantly before Fromm.

"So, gentlemen," the general announced, "now it's my turn to do to you what you did to me this afternoon."

Now armed with a pistol, Fromm declared that he was placing the conspirators under arrest and demanded their weapons.

Beck, the old retired head of the Wehrmacht, asked if he could keep his pistol "for private reasons." Fromm agreed but insisted that the old general "be quick about it." Beck tried to shoot himself in the head but bungled the attempt. He fired twice, grazing his skull once and merely wounding himself the second time, and collapsed onto the floor.

General Fromm told the conspirators that he would give them a few moments to write goodbye letters to their loved ones. Only Olbricht tried to write a few lines.

Fromm had already decided that, to save his own neck, he had to eliminate all the members of the conspiracy who knew of his own tacit involvement. He didn't have much time. Top Nazis were already on their way to the Bendlerblock.

"In the name of the Führer, I have convened a court-martial that has pronounced the following sentence," Fromm announced. "General Staff Colonel Mertz, General Olbricht, the colonel whose name I will not speak, and First Lieutenant Haeften are condemned to death."[16]

Stauffenberg announced that the coup was entirely his responsibility, that everyone else had been acting on his orders.

As he spoke, General Beck was moaning in agony on the floor. On Fromm's orders a staff sergeant dragged Beck into an adjoining room. A loud shot rang out.

Stauffenberg's brother Berthold watched in horror as the four condemned men were then led into the hallway, down a stairway, and outside into the inner courtyard of the Bendlerblock complex.

It was around midnight. The air was cool. A number of vehicles had parked in the courtyard, their headlights blaring. In front of one, a large pile of sand had been dumped. As they stepped into the courtyard, the four conspirators could see a line of ten soldiers, rifles at the ready, already lined up in front of the sand.

A soldier unceremoniously led Olbricht to stand in front of the sand. Within seconds, a barrage of shots rang out. Olbricht collapsed in a heap.

Next, it was Stauffenberg's turn.

Yet just as the members of the execution squad raised their rifles to shoot, Stauffenberg's loyal aide, Haeften, rushed in front of his commander. He was killed instantly.

The soldiers calmly chambered another round and then took aim at Stauffenberg again. In a gesture of defiance, the young count yelled out, "Long live sacred Germany," just as he, too, died in a hail of gunfire. The soldiers then lined up Mertz von Quirnheim and shot him as well.

A group of soldiers carried the body of General Beck down the stairwell and threw it on top of the others. The bodies would shortly be transported by truck to St. Matthew's Church in Berlin's large central

The site in the Bendlerblock courtyard where Stauffenberg and his fellow conspirators were executed by firing squad on July 20, 1944. *Wikimedia Commons*[17]

park, the Tiergarten, and quickly buried. The next day, Himmler ordered the bodies dug up, burned, and their ashes scattered.

After sending a telex message that the conspirators had all been shot, General Fromm stepped into the courtyard, giving a speech praising Hitler.

At that moment, Albert Speer, the civilian architect and now Hitler's Minister of Armaments and Munitions, came careening to a stop in the Bendlerblock courtyard in his white sports car. Next to him was none other than Colonel Remer. Speer told Fromm to get in. He was to drive him to Goebbels's headquarters immediately.

As he was leaving, another unit of soldiers arrived, under the command of the Viennese commando Colonel Otto Skorzeny, to take control of the Bendlerblock complex. Skorzeny, who had been involved in the recent successful operation to free Mussolini from captivity, set out to countermand all of the recent Valkyrie orders and arrest all the conspirators still in the Bendlerblock offices, including Stauffenberg's brother Berthold. Skorzeny also ordered that no more executions be carried out. Hitler and Himmler were determined to get to the truth of what had happened, and they wanted to interrogate all prisoners.

When Fromm arrived at Goebbels' office in the Propaganda Ministry, he was surprised to see Heinrich Himmler there. Himmler and Goebbels were fierce rivals, widely known to detest one another. Yet despite his position as head of the SS and chief of the German police, Himmler allowed Goebbels to take control of the situation—a role that the civilian propaganda minister relished.

Historians would marvel at how Goebbels behaved as though he had crushed the rebellion himself.[18]

"They had an enormous chance," Goebbels would say to Himmler. "When I think how I would have handled such a thing. Why didn't they seize the radio station and spread the wildest lies?"[19]

Fromm, too, did his best to take credit for crushing the rebellion. For the next two hours, over wine and cigars, Himmler and Goebbels had Fromm and some other generals rehearse the events of the day step by step. The Nazi higher-ups interrupted their accounts now and then with questions.

Some of the generals were allowed to leave once they had established their innocence. But Fromm was not. Goebbels was not the least bit fooled; he suspected, correctly, that Fromm had ordered Stauffenberg's quick execution to cover up his own complicity in the plot. The old general was placed under arrest; later he would face trial.

Back at the Wolf's Lair, as Hitler waited in the wood-paneled tea house for radio equipment to be set up, he practiced his address in front of a small group of subordinates and his personal secretaries. Around one in the morning, he addressed the entire German nation and most of Europe in a radio broadcast.

"Yet another of the countless attempts on my life has been planned and carried out," Hitler intoned quietly into the microphone, speaking in a normal tone, not in his half-shouting speechifying voice. "A very small clique of ambitious, wicked, and stupidly criminal officers forged a plot to eliminate me, and, along with me, virtually the entire leadership of the German High Command. The bomb which was planted by Colonel von Stauffenberg exploded two meters to my right. It seriously injured a number of my colleagues who are very dear to me; one has died. I myself am completely unhurt apart from a few minor skin abrasions, bruises, and burns. I interpret this as confirmation that Providence wishes me to continue my life's mission as I have in the past."

Hitler referred to the conspiracy a number of times as "very small" and called it a "small clique of despicable creatures." At this point, this is what Hitler actually believed to be true. He insisted that those responsible would be hunted down and brought to justice, adding ominously, "we will settle accounts as we National Socialists are accustomed to."[20]

Despite the decisive action against the conspiracy's leaders, the Nazis still had a lot of work to do. They quickly realized that the "small clique" had somehow succeeded in sparking local rebellions throughout the Reich, from Paris to Prague and Vienna.

General Carl-Heinrich von Stülpnagel (1886–1944), military commander of occupied France and a member of the July 20 plot, successfully arrested Gestapo leaders in Paris during the coup attempt. When it failed, he was arrested and executed. *Deutsches Bundesarchiv*[21]

In Paris, rebellious Wehrmacht leaders acted with particular decisiveness. They knew about the planned assassination, and they also knew just how dire the Reich's prospects actually were. The Allies' massive invasion at the beaches of Normandy had made them see that Hitler's days were numbered no matter what happened with the assassination attempt.

As a result, the German military commander in Paris, General Carl-Heinrich von Stülpnagel, a member of the conspiracy, issued pre-arranged orders to his officers to act at specific times. In this, the Paris uprising was better organized than the one in Berlin.

Stülpnagel succeeded in having more than a thousand Gestapo and SS soldiers in Paris arrested in one fell swoop—just as Stauffenberg and his comrades were being arrested.

Like many of the anti-Hitler conspirators, Stülpnagel was no hero. In fact, he was himself a war criminal, having ordered the deportation of French Jews to death camps and supervised the SS death squads, the Einsatzgruppen, in mass executions of Jewish prisoners in eastern Europe. But he knew that Hitler was leading Germany to utter destruction.

From the beginning, the fatal flaw in the Valkyrie plot was that too many of the conspirators had a wait-and-see attitude toward the entire effort—including the head of the Reserve Army, General Fromm. In

Paris, this attitude was exemplified by Stülpnagel's nominal superior, Field Marshal Günther von Kluge. Like many top German officers, Kluge knew about the conspiracy to kill Hitler and would have supported the coup had it succeeded. But he wasn't about to risk his own neck to ensure its success. Yet this wait-and-see attitude ultimately did little to save the lukewarm conspirators from Nazi vengeance.

Late in the evening, Stülpnagel visited Kluge at his headquarters near Paris. Over dinner, Stülpnagel told the general about the mass arrests of the Gestapo that would shortly take place. Kluge, horrified, informed him that Hitler had in fact survived the assassination. Kluge ordered the general to release his prisoners at once—something Stülpnagel would reluctantly do the following day. Kluge then relieved Stülpnagel of command and gave him a piece of advice: "Put on some civilian clothes and disappear."[22]

Stülpnagel returned to his residence in Paris at the Hotel Majestic around midnight. The bar and restaurant were full of German officers celebrating the arrests. Just as Stülpnagel entered the officer's mess, the voice of Hitler came on the radio, speaking about his miraculous deliverance and the small group of despicable criminals who had acted against him.

Stülpnagel soon learned that loyal Nazi units were preparing to attack the military barracks where the SS and Gestapo prisoners were held and free them. With typical ruthlessness, Stülpnagel considered briefly whether he should order the mass executions of the prisoners, burning his bridges and forcing others to join him, but quickly dismissed the idea.[23] Instead, he ordered the prisoners' release.

The released soldiers all came to the officers' mess where Stülpnagel was and sat down together to a late-night dinner with champagne. "So, Herr General," one of the released SS officers said to Stülpnagel, "you seem to have bet on the wrong horse."

The next day, Stülpnagel got the call: he was to return to Berlin at once. On the trip back to Germany, the disgraced general had his driver stop outside of Verdun, near the Meuse Canal, where Stülpnagel had fought in World War I. The driver heard a shot ring out. When he investigated, he discovered that Stülpnagel, like Beck, had failed in his effort to kill himself. Instead, he was now blind. He was put in the car and brought back to Berlin, where he would stand trial for treason.

The situation in Paris was played out all across the Reich. Small pockets of resistance succeeded at first but were quickly overcome once the news of Hitler's survival reached the provinces.

The truth was that the plot was almost certainly doomed from the start by a lack of adequate preparation. There were too many loose ends, too many key personnel who were not fully committed to the coup and who waited to see which way to jump.

Yet Operation Valkyrie actually worked better than anyone could have expected under the circumstances.

And for Stauffenberg, success had never been the point.

He was determined that, come what may, someone should make a stand . . . to show the world that not everyone in Germany had gone along with Hitler. The attempt was what was important—even though he knew that in the process he was sacrificing not merely his own life but the lives of hundreds, possibly thousands of others, perhaps including those of his own family.

5 THE AFTERMATH

By the time Hitler addressed the German people by radio early on the morning of July 21, 1944, Heinrich Himmler had already begun organizing an extensive investigation. He appointed SS Obersturmbannführer Georg Kiessel to head up a special commission, made up of more than four hundred investigators in eleven agencies, designed to root out every last member of the assassination plot.

The Nazis would also use the excuse of the assassination investigation to eliminate the last vestiges of domestic resistance to the regime, arresting old political enemies and dissidents as well as those directly involved in the plot. Eventually, the Gestapo investigators would arrest more than five thousand people, most of whom were ultimately executed. Those rounded up included peaceful critics of Nazi Germany, such as the members of the so-called Kreisau Circle, a group of two dozen aristocratic dissidents who met in Kreisau, Silesia. Among its members were three Jesuit priests—one of whom, Alfred Delp, SJ, was later executed.[1]

At first, Hitler planned on staging a massive show trial along the lines of the ones Stalin had arranged in the 1930s in Moscow, parading the supposed criminals before the eyes of the German people. "This time I'll fix them," Hitler roared to his top aides. "There will be no honorable bullet for...these criminals, they'll hang like common traitors!...The sentences will be carried out within two hours! They must hang at once, without any show of mercy."

Yet the investigators very quickly discovered, to their astonishment and horror, that the plot to kill Hitler was far larger than just the "tiny handful of criminals" that Hitler had spoken of during his radio address. In fact, it involved hundreds—even thousands—of top Nazi officials, politicians, generals, intellectuals, newspaper men, and even members of Hitler's inner circle. The opposition to the Nazi regime was far more substantial than even Hitler's most paranoid and suspicious security chiefs had suspected.

The first wave of arrests, which began on July 21, numbered about five hundred people.

First arrested were the staff members who had assisted Stauffenberg and Olbricht at the Bendlerblock complex—such as Oberstleutnant Robert Bernardis, who had issued the Valkyrie orders under Olbricht's command, and Major Hans-Jürgen von Blumenthal. Also arrested at the Bendlerblock was the aristocrat Ulrich Wilhelm Graf Schwerin von Schwanenfeld. Others directly involved, who were arrested the next day, included General Hans Oster, the head of the Abwehr, German military intelligence, and General Helmut Stieff.

Stieff had flown to the Wolf's Lair with Stauffenberg. He endured brutal torture for days without revealing the names of his fellow conspirators. Erich Fellgiebel, the communications chief at the Wolf's Lair, was also arrested. He was tortured for more than three weeks and never revealed what he knew about the plot.

Some of the conspirators, after hearing Hitler's voice on the radio and knowing their ultimate fate, committed suicide rather than surrender and betray their comrades under torture. For example, key conspiracy leader General Henning von Tresckow, then stationed on the Eastern Front in northeastern Poland, pretended he was fighting

EYEWITNESS ACCOUNT

"How skeptically Hitler viewed every report is shown by the following example: I was standing beside him when he was told that Generaloberst Fromm had had Stauffenberg and Olbricht shot in Berlin. Outwardly calm, but very wound up, he listened to the report. 'Fromm had Stauffenberg executed?' he murmured. Then he ordered: 'Dig him up, dig up Stauffenberg immediately.' After the exhumation had confirmed that Stauffenberg had indeed been the victim, Hitler did not react as Bormann had expected, but concluded spontaneously, 'Fromm is the leader. This is how he got rid of his accomplices and those who could put him in the frame.'. . . Hitler's rage caught up with him on 19 March 1945 when [Fromm] was executed on the Führer's personal orders."

—*Heinz Linge, Hitler's valet*[2]

off an attack of partisans, put a hand grenade next to his head, and detonated it. Just hours earlier, he had explained to his aide and cousin Fabian von Schlabrendorff—another conspirator who endured agonizing torture without betraying his friends—why what they did was right.

"Hitler is the archenemy not only of Germany but of the whole world," Tresckow told him. "When, in a few hours' time, I go before God to account for what I have done and left undone, I know I will be able to justify in good conscience what I did in the struggle against Hitler. God promised Abraham that He would not destroy Sodom if just ten righteous men could be found in the city, and so I hope that for our sake God will not destroy Germany." Miraculously, Schlabrendorff survived the war.

Many other conspirators killed themselves. General Edourd Wagner, who had arranged for Stauffenberg's return flight from the Wolf's Lair to Berlin, shot himself in the head on July 23.

But as the historian Joachim Fest illustrates, dozens of other conspirators did not attempt to escape, either through fleeing the country or by committing suicide. Instead, they felt it was their moral duty to speak out against the regime, to have their say in court.

Some of these clung to cherished German ideals of personal honor, truth-telling, and the refusal to retreat, to "stand your ground." As a result, hunting down the perpetrators was relatively easy for the Gestapo. Many conspirators simply waited calmly for the inevitable knock on the door. A few even turned themselves in, the agony of not knowing their fate being too much for them.

Fest cites the strange case of Tresckow's brother, Gerd, then serving in Italy. Gerd tried repeatedly to turn himself in even though he had not actually been involved in the plot. His superiors rebuffed him at first, but finally arrested him. He would commit suicide in a concentration camp.[3]

As the arrests continued, the Gestapo began accumulating substantial evidence of how widespread the conspiracy actually was.

When they raided the hotel room of the anti-Nazi politician Carl Goerdeler—one of the possible chancellors in a post-Nazi government—they discovered a treasure trove of documents, including the manuscript of an address to the German nation that Goerdeler had hoped to give as chancellor. There had already been a warrant out for Goerdeler's arrest before, for various other offenses, and he had been in hiding in Berlin waiting for the bomb to be detonated. He eluded capture until mid-August.

But unlike the military prisoners—many of whom endured nightmarish torture without talking—the politician Goerdeler was never tortured and yet freely cooperated, naming names and betraying hundreds of people the Nazis hadn't known about. He was finally executed by hanging in February 1945, along with Father Delp.

The Gestapo had a major break on July 23 when they searched a house that had been bombed in an Allied raid. Inside it, they found documents that implicated high-ranking members of the Nazi government in the plot—including Admiral Wilhelm Canaris, former chief of the Abwehr; his successor, Colonel Georg Hansen; and former economics minister Hjalmar Schacht.

Canaris's involvement in the plot stunned the Nazis. A decorated war hero, member of the Nazi Party, and German nationalist, Canaris had joined the anti-Nazi underground early in the war. As chief of military intelligence, he was in a position to do a lot of damage to the Nazi cause and to undermine their goals—particularly their determination to annihilate the Jewish people. Indeed, Canaris used his position to save hundreds of Dutch Jews by issuing phony Abwehr identity papers, and he intervened personally to save the life of the Lubavitcher Rebbe in Warsaw, Rabbi Yosef Yitzchok Schneersohn. The Rebbe's followers would later petition the Israeli government to have Canaris named a Righteous Gentile at the Yad Vashem Holocaust Memorial in Jerusalem—a petition that was ultimately rejected.[4] Yet Canaris was merely the tip of the proverbial iceberg. The more the Gestapo dug, the more evidence they found of a vast conspiracy.

What Happened to Stauffenberg's Family

Around seven in the evening of July 20, Stauffenberg's thirty-one-year-old wife Nina was called to the telephone at the family's lavish estate in Lautlingen, set among the rolling green Swabian hills in south-west Germany.

Visibly pregnant with their fifth child, daughter Konstanze, Nina was hearing the news that all military wives dread.

Yet in her case, the situation was even worse: Nina was informed that there had just been news reports on the radio that her husband had tried to blow up Adolf Hitler—and failed! Her hands visibly shaking,

Nina almost dropped the receiver of the phone as she collapsed onto a nearby armchair.

Their four children were upstairs playing: Berthold, then age ten; Heimeran, eight; Franz-Ludwig, six; and Valerie, just four. Nina did not know what to tell her children. At this point, her husband was still alive, desperately trying to bluff his way through a coup d'état. Within hours, he would be dead.

Nina decided to wait for more information, but the news was even worse the next day. She learned that her beloved husband of eleven years had been summarily executed the night before as a traitor. Nina gathered the two oldest boys around her and broke the news to them. They couldn't believe what they were hearing. "Papa made a mistake and that is why they shot him," Nina told her two boys. She told them this because she knew the Gestapo would certainly interrogate the children.[5]

Stauffenberg's eldest son, Berthold, had desperately wanted to join the Hitler Youth. Now he was being told that his father had tried to murder the Führer. "Our world broke apart in an instant," Berthold would recall. "I was a conformist and my dearest wish, which my mother fortunately prevented, was to march through our home town carrying a flag at the head of the junior branch of the Hitler Youth."[6]

With Nina at the Lautlingen estate was Stauffenberg's mother, the Countess Caroline, and Caroline's brother Count Üxküll (Uncle Nux), along with the wife of Stauffenberg's brother Berthold, Maria (Mika) Classen. They all knew that it was only a matter of time before the Gestapo arrived. Later that evening, July 22, detectives and soldiers marched into the grand house, searched it top to bottom, and arrested Nina and Uncle Nux, taking them to a prison camp near Rottweil, in southern Germany. Nina was soon transferred to the Gestapo prison off Alexanderplatz in Berlin. In January of 1945, she would give birth to Stauffenberg's daughter Konstanze, and then she and her daughter would be transferred to St. Joseph Hospital in Potsdam.

The secret police returned the next day to Lautlingen and took away the Countess Caroline and Uncle Nux's wife, Alexandrine, who had worked as the head of the local Red Cross. They were held in solitary confinement at the Balingen district court prison. The Stauffenberg children were allowed to stay in Lautlingen until August 17, when they, too, were taken away—to a Nazi-controlled orphanage in Bad Sachsa, in Lower Saxony, where they were held under the name Meister. Eventually, all of the Stauffenberg property was confiscated, and eight Gestapo officers moved into the lavish estate along with their families. The old Countess Caroline was released in November and allowed to stay in the family estate.

Stauffenberg's brother Berthold, who had seen him off on the morning of July 20 from Rangsdorf Airport, had watched as his brother was led out into the courtyard and shot. He was arrested that night at the Bendlerblock complex and then interrogated with ferocious cruelty for the next three weeks.

Stauffenberg's other brother Alexander was in Athens, Greece, serving as an artillery lieutenant, when he heard the news of the assassination plot. He had known nothing about it because of his marriage. In 1937, Alexander had married a famous German aviator, engineer, and Luftwaffe test pilot, Melitta Schiller, who was part Jewish. Alexander's brothers suspected that Melitta might be under Gestapo surveillance, so they decided not to tell Alexander about their plans.

Alexander had a chance to escape to Egypt but feared for his wife's safety were he to do so. He decided to return to Berlin by train on July 22 and was able to warn his wife before he left. A few hours later, she was arrested by the Gestapo and brought to the same prison in Berlin where Nina was. Melitta was held until September 2 but then released on account of her importance to the German war effort. An expert in night-landing instrumentation and dive bombers, she was able to use her position to help her husband and the entire Stauffenberg family over the coming months.

When Alexander arrived in Berlin on July 26, he, too, was promptly arrested. He was transferred to various concentration camps, including Buchenwald.

One of the first things that Hitler and his deputy Heinrich Himmler agreed upon was the necessity of eliminating all the family members and associates of the conspirators. It wasn't enough to arrest those directly responsible for the conspiracy, probably around two hundred people in all. For the cancer to be utterly eradicated, the Nazis had to ensure that it had not spread to other parts of the body politic. This policy, known as *Sippenhaft,* or "blood guilt," was introduced in 1943 as a means of threatening disobedient soldiers. The wives and children of Wehrmacht deserters, for example, were sometimes executed in retaliation. After the July 20 plot, Nazi leaders used the *Sippenhaft* policy to arrest hundreds of family members and associates of the conspirators.

Hitler had made it clear that he wanted the entire Stauffenberg family wiped out. "The Stauffenberg family will be exterminated, root and branch," Himmler declared in an August 3 address to the Gauleiters, the Nazi Party leaders in charge of local governments. "That will be a warning example, once and for all."[7]

Many Stauffenberg family members were arrested, including Stauffenberg's eighty-five-year-old uncle Berthold, the brother of his late father and the living patriarch of the family, as well as numerous cousins. Yet the Stauffenbergs had powerful friends among the members of the German aristocracy, and considerable pressure was brought to bear on Himmler and other top Nazi leaders not to harm Nina, the old countess, and especially Stauffenberg's young children.

Luckily for the family, Hitler and his henchmen had bigger problems to worry about in the coming months than the fate of the Stauffenbergs. The Soviet Red Army was rapidly approaching Berlin from the east while the Western Allies were now trying to cross the Rhine and enter Germany proper.

Alexander Stauffenberg's wife Melitta, the aviatrix, provided considerable help to the family in the months after their arrest. At considerable risk, given her Jewish heritage, she visited her husband twice in the Buchenwald concentration camp. Melitta was also able to discover the orphanage where the Stauffenberg children were being held and visited them there at Christmas, bringing presents. A few days later, in January

1945, Melitta also visited Nina at St. Joseph's Hospital in Postsdam, bringing her news of her children's well-being.

Four months later, on April 9, as the Soviet Red Army was approaching Berlin and the war in Europe was coming to a close, Melitta's unarmed Bücker 181 trainer was shot down by an American fighter near Stasskirchen.[8] She somehow landed the plane but died from her wounds two hours later. Alexander survived the war but was devastated by his wife's death. He would go on to become a famous ancient historian at the Ludwig-Maximilian University in Munich.

In April 1945, as French troops occupied Lautlingen, a French military commander gave Countess Caroline's sister-in-law Alexandrine, the wife of Uncle Nux, a military vehicle so she could go in search of the Stauffenberg children. Despite the advancing Soviet army, Alexandrine was able to reach Bad Sachsa, where all the children—Stauffenberg's four and his brother Berthold's two—were still living in the Nazi-controlled orphanage. The children were brought back to Lautlingen just hours before the Red Army arrived at Bad Sachsa.

Nina and her newborn daughter had been transferred to German-occupied territory in the South Tyrol and held as hostages there. Guards had orders to kill Nina, but she was eventually liberated by advancing Allied troops, released, and reunited with all of her children at the family estate at Lautlingen. Berthold's wife Mika was also reunited with her children there.

Conspirators on Trial

The arrest of the Stauffenberg family members was merely the beginning of a purge that would occupy Germany for eight months and shape the rest of the war effort.

The machinery of Nazi vengeance worked quickly. Within days, most of the main conspirators, those who had participated directly in the plot, were arrested. And within two weeks or so, the trials began.

The Volksgerichtshof, or People's Court, led by Nazi fanatic Roland Freisler (1893–1945), tried the participants in the July 20 assassination plot against Hitler, including top generals and a field marshal. All were condemned and executed by hanging in Plötzensee Prison in Berlin. *Deutsches Bundesarchiv*[9]

They were held in the so-called People's Court (Volksgerichtshof), a special Nazi-controlled judicial venue that operated outside the normal structure of the German legal system.

Headed by a screaming Nazi fanatic named Roland Freisler, the People's Court dealt with primarily "political" crimes, such as treason and black marketeering. The court normally met in an ornate four-story building off Potzdammer Platz in Berlin, but for the trials of the July 20 conspirators it was moved to the far more imposing Great Hall of the Berlin Chamber Court (Kammergericht) on Elssholzstrasse.

It was a kangaroo court. The defense lawyers, primarily ardent Nazis, often offered no defense at all. Many times, the presiding judge simply passed sentence without even hearing any evidence. That was how Sophie and Hans Scholl, the founders of the anti-Nazi student group the

White Rose, had been condemned to death the previous year for passing out leaflets critical of the regime.

The first eight members of the conspiracy to appear before Freisler were Field Marshal Erwin von Witzleben, General Helmuth Stieff, Erich Hoepner, Paul von Hase, Peter Yorck von Wartenburg, Robert Bernardis, Friedrich Klausing, and Albrecht von Hagen.

Freisler presided in a long red robe beneath a bronze bust of Hitler and surrounded by swastika flags. More than three hundred carefully selected spectators, including journalists, sat in the galleries. The entire spectacle was filmed for newsreel releases and for Hitler. The videos of the proceedings still exist and can be seen on YouTube.

The prisoners were brought before the court one by one, dressed in shabby civilian clothes that were so oversized that the men had to hold their pants up with one hand as they addressed the court. Most bore obvious signs of torture and walked with difficulty.

The idealists among the accused, those who had failed to flee the country or had even turned themselves in out of a desire to testify about their motives in court, would be sorely disappointed.

When Hitler faced his own treason trial after the failed Beer Hall Putsch in 1923, he had used the twenty-four-day proceedings to make lengthy political speeches that ended up being a major public relations triumph, one that paved the way to his election a decade later. The Führer had no intention of allowing the conspirators a similar opportunity to speak out against the government. Freisler made sure that the accused were only allowed to say a sentence or two before they were cut off. Most of the proceedings were simply Freisler screaming insults and accusations from the bench.

At Hitler's instructions, the military officers accused had already been court martialed and now stood trial as civilians.

Everyone present knew that the men's fates were sealed. The proceedings were merely a formality. Freisler bellowed at the defendants in a mad rage—so loudly that the sound technicians recording the events had to ask him to lower the volume for their equipment.

The first of the accused conspirators to stand trial was Field Marshal Witzleben—the man who was to take over command of the Wehrmacht after the assassination and who had appeared at the Bendlerblock briefly on July 20 to berate Stauffenberg for his incompetence.

Witzleben clutched at his pants to keep them up as Freisler screamed at him that he was a traitor. The general even had his false teeth taken from him as an extra humiliation. Yet the old soldier, then sixty-two, was defiant. "You can hand us over to the hangman," Witzleben yelled back. "In three months, the enraged and tormented people will call you to account, and will drag you alive through the muck of the street."

In fact, however, the people did no such thing. As we will see shortly, the people instead rose up in defense of Hitler, enraged by the idea that traitorous military officers such as Witzleben and Stauffenberg had been undermining the German war effort, possibly for years.

Freisler was eventually killed, but not by the German people. Six months later, in February 1945, bombs from an Allied air raid struck the courthouse, and a heavy beam crushed the judge. Facing the court that day was one of the few July 20 plotters to survive the war, Fabian von Schlabrendorff, who had smuggled a bomb onto a plane Hitler flew in but which, for unknown reasons, had failed to detonate. Despite a week of torture at the Gestapo's hands, Schlabrendorff escaped execution. On the day of his trial, an Allied bomb scored a direct hit on the courtroom, knocking down a heavy steel beam that collapsed and struck Freisler dead. In his hands were found the court documents for his next case, that of Schlabrendorff. The courageous anti-Nazi fighter went on to serve on Germany's highest court, the Bundesverfassungsgericht or Federal Constitutional Court, after the war.

One by one, the others of the first eight accused July 20 conspirators had their handful of minutes in court. All were condemned to death, with the sentences to be carried out immediately. They were taken from the Berlin Chamber Court to Plötzensee Prison, about fifteen minutes north. This prison, which is still a functioning prison today, was where many enemies of the Nazi state were executed. In

EYEWITNESS ACCOUNT

"On the 3rd of February [1945], when my case had just been called before the 'People's Court,' the air-raid sirens sounded. . . . A terrible bombardment began. It was easily the heaviest daylight [raid] ever launched by American bombers on Berlin. It felt as if the world's end had come. In the middle of this howling tornado there was a deafening crash. The 'People's Court' had received a direct hit, and burst into flames. It shook to its foundations and split open. Part of the ceiling collapsed into the cellar: a heavy beam crashed with its full weight on the head of president of the 'People's Court,' Feisler, who was still holding the files of my case in his hand."

—*Fabian von Schlabrendorff, July 20 plot survivor*[10]

1937, a one-story brick work shed was designated the execution site for the prison. Between May 1937 and August 1939, 124 people were beheaded there by means of a guillotine brought from Bruchsal Prison in Baden. With the advent of the war in 1939, the number of executions increased markedly—from 192 in 1940 to 1,158 by 1943. People were executed for desertion but also for being conscientious objectors and for "subversion of the war effort," for example by passing out anti-Nazi flyers. By the end of the war, more than 30,000 death sentences had been handed out.

The condemned were brought one by one into a small room with a low ceiling and meat hooks hung from a steel girder. The room, usually dark, was now brightly lit by photography lights. Film cameras were set up to record the condemned men's agonies. Observers noted the bottle of cognac sitting on a bare table. It was not for the prisoners but for the executioners.

The execution chamber in Plötzensee Prison where the July 20 plotters were stran-
gled, now a memorial, still contains the meat hooks from which the condemned
men were hanged to writhe in agony. *Wikimedia Commons*[11]

The condemned men had been forbidden any religious rites or last
words. They were brought in one at a time, handcuffed, through a black
curtain covering the side door. The full-time executioner, a sadist named
Wilhelm Röttger, simply looped a thin hemp cord—not, as is reported,
piano wire—around their necks and unceremoniously hoisted them up
to the ceiling. The men's necks were not snapped, as in a normal hanging.
Instead, they writhed in agony from choking. A few died quickly but
some took as long as twenty minutes to expire.

Both film and still pictures were taken. Historians have established
that films were indeed made of the executions, although the actual footage has never been found; it is presumed destroyed. It was widely
reported[12] that Hitler watched the films for entertainment. In his memoirs, Albert Speer reported seeing still photos of the executions on
Hitler's desk.[13]

All of the condemned conspirators met the same fate. Three days later, on August 10, Stauffenberg's brother Berthold was executed in the same way, along with General Erich Fellgiebel, Alfred Kranzfelder, Fritz-Dietlof von der Schulenburg, and Georg Hansen. Röttger ordered some of the men, including Berthold Stauffenberg, raised and lowered a number of times to prolong their agony.

General Fellgiebel, who had withstood the most barbaric torture the Gestapo could deliver without betraying any secrets, had also refused to cower before Freisler. He told the Nazi judge that he had better hang him quick because otherwise "you will hang earlier than we."[14]

Through the rest of August, the biggest-name conspirators were brought before Freisler, condemned to death, and quickly executed. Yet very soon Hitler, Goebbels, and other top Nazis decided that the trials were having mixed results—although they continued with less publicity up until Freisler's death in February 1945. On the one hand, the trials certainly demonstrated that, just as Hitler claimed, the German war effort had been undermined by traitors within the German military establishment. Yet at the same time, the number and rank of the conspirators also showed that the opposition to the Nazi regime was far more extensive than the public had been led to believe.

As a result, while the Gestapo continued to arrest hundreds and then thousands of opponents of the regime in the months after the trials began, many of these arrests were done quietly, and those arrested were either killed outright or held as prisoners. Although the Plötzensee Prison itself lists only eighty-nine members of the July 20 plot executed, it's estimated that altogether as many as seven thousand people were arrested in the months after the plot, and nearly five thousand of those were executed.

Incredibly, the British government speculated over radio broadcasts about the names of possible anti-Nazi conspirators—who were then promptly hunted down by the Gestapo and arrested. The historian Joachim Fest emphasized the courage of the conspirators who endured weeks of Gestapo torture in an effort to save their comrades only to have

Dietrich Bonhoeffer (1906–1945), the influential Protestant theologian, was an outspoken opponent of the Nazi regime and active member of the resistance but did not take a direct part in the July 20 bombing. Nevertheless, he was executed just two weeks before the end of the war. *Deutsches Bundesarchiv*[16]

their efforts undermined by the Allies. "As if to do Hitler one last favor," Fest wrote, "British radio began regularly broadcasting the names of people alleged to have had a hand in the coup."[15]

As the trials dragged on, the Gestapo also continued to discover documents that implicated prominent people in Germany.

For example, in September 1944, the discovery of some military intelligence documents showed that the famous Protestant theologian and author Dietrich Bonhoeffer had connections to some of the conspirators, in particular the head of military intelligence, Admiral Wilhelm Canaris.

Bonhoeffer was arrested while preaching at his church and held at different locations, including the Buchenwald concentration camp. In February 1945, Canaris's secret diaries were discovered, further implicating Bonhoeffer and others. Hitler read the diaries and, in a rage, ordered that those named in them be exterminated.

At dawn on April 9, 1945, just two weeks before the U.S. Army liberated the Flossenbürg concentration camp in Bavaria, where Bonhoeffer and other political prisoners were last held, Bonhoeffer was brought outside, stripped naked, and hanged. Executed at the same time were Canaris, Canaris's deputy and fellow July 20 conspirator General Hans Oster, and other German resistance fighters.

The Forced Suicide of Field Marshal Erwin Rommel

After the first wave of executions of those directly involved with the July 20 assassination plot, the Nazi secret police soon turned its attention to the wider conspiracy—the apparently quite large group of German politicians, intellectuals, and military officers who knew about the plot but did not report it.

The documents the Gestapo discovered in the homes and offices of the conspirators showed that the opposition to Hitler within the upper echelons of the military was far more widespread than Hitler and his closest aides had ever suspected.

Perhaps the biggest personal blow to Hitler involved the field marshals. Field marshal was the highest rank in the German military, the equivalent of a five-star general in the United States. (The British general Bernard Montgomery also held the rank of field marshal.) Unusually, the Nazis had created twenty-six field marshals. They wore a special uniform, and as a symbol of their rank they carried ornate ceremonial batons manufactured by jewelers at great expense.

The field marshals were expected to be the most loyal of Nazis. Yet as they were generally professional military men, that was, in reality, not the case. Among those officers eventually executed for their roles in the July 20 plot were twenty-six colonels, nineteen generals—and three field marshals.

The first field marshal proven to be involved was Erwin von Witzleben. He was in the very first group of conspirators to be executed on August 7.

Next was Field Marshal Günther von Kluge, a career Prussian military officer who thought Hitler's military recklessness could destroy Germany. He was among the circle of officers who secretly planned on overthrowing Hitler after the invasion of Poland in 1938.

Like many top generals, Kluge knew about the conspiracy to kill Hitler and tacitly supported it if it succeeded but would not risk his neck by overtly helping it. Kluge was the commanding officer of Henning von Tresckow, the most important figure in the conspiracy after Stauffenberg.

At one point in 1941, Kluge had promised Tresckow he would help arrest Hitler—but that was before the Nazi Führer had sent Kluge a check for five hundred thousand Reichsmarks.

By the time the bomb went off in the Wolf's Lair, Kluge was the commander of the German forces in the West, meaning France. At that point, Germany was desperately trying to prevent the Allies from capturing a seaport along the Atlantic coastline from which they could quickly flood Europe with troops and supplies. Kluge quickly realized that the German military had little chance of success.

Hitler already suspected that Kluge had known about the assassination attempt, and in fact he had. On August 15, Kluge's military vehicle was damaged in an Allied bombing raid, and his communications were cut off for hours. Hitler became convinced that Kluge was then secretly negotiating with the Allies for a surrender. He therefore relieved Kluge of command, sent Field Marshal Walter Model to replace him, and ordered Kluge to report to Berlin in person immediately.

Kluge assumed he was implicated in the July 20 plot. On his way back to Berlin, he wrote Hitler a fawning goodbye letter in which he swore his personal loyalty to the Führer and then, on August 19, he swallowed a cyanide capsule.

But the biggest blow of all was the discovery, or at least the emergence of credible evidence, that Field Marshal Erwin Rommel had known about the assassination plot—and done nothing to prevent it. The evidence for his involvement is ambiguous.

Early accounts after the war, such as that of journalist William Shirer, claimed that Rommel knew about the plot and supported it. But while he certainly knew some of the active plotters, such as Stülpnagel, historians today doubt that Rommel had any specific knowledge of the Stauffenberg plot. Rommel's wife would say after the war that the field marshal was opposed to assassinating Hitler because he feared it would lead to civil war. He did believe the military situation for Germany was grim, and he was open to negotiating a surrender with the Allies, but it's not proven that he supported the assassination effort.

Yet there was enough evidence, not least the suicide of Kluge, to at least suspect Rommel of prior knowledge. Just five days before the bomb exploded next to Hitler, Rommel had written a forceful letter to the Führer in which he boldly insisted that "the unequal struggle is heading for its end," meaning, of course, that the war was lost.

Two days later, Rommel's car was strafed by Allied aircraft, and he was wounded. As the field marshal recovered from his injuries, the military situation in France continued to worsen for the Third Reich. British and American forces, including those led by General George Patton, were now pushing towards Germany itself.

What ultimately led Hitler to turn against his favorite general

Field Marshal Erwin Rommel (1891–1945), known as the Desert Fox for his exploits in North Africa and widely considered Nazi Germany's most capable general, was indirectly implicated in the July 20 assassination plot against Hitler. He agreed to commit suicide by poison in exchange for his family's being let alone by the Nazis. *Deutsches Bundesarchiv*[17]

was the testimony under torture of Lieutenant-Colonel Cäsar von Hofacker, a cousin of Stauffenberg's who had worked with the conspirator Stülpnagel in Paris. Hofacker had tried to draw Rommel into the conspiracy, but the field marshal was noncommittal. According to the American war correspondent William Shirer, Rommel was opposed to killing Hitler, as his widow would later say. Yet after days of nightmarish torture by the Gestapo, Hofacker claimed that Rommel had pledged his support in general terms. At the very least, the field marshal had known about the assassination plot in advance.

This was the final blow for Hitler, the ultimate betrayal.

Known as the Desert Fox for his brilliant tactical maneuvers in North Africa, Rommel was a legend in Nazi Germany and beyond. U.S. general George Patton famously studied Rommel's classic text on tank tactics before battling him in North Africa and the Ardennes. Moreover, Rommel had served early on as the commander of Hitler's personal army, the Führerbegleitbatallion, whose job it was to protect the Führer from assassination attempts.

On October 7, Rommel was summoned to Berlin. He had been resting at his home on the outskirts of Ulm, a quiet town near Munich where Albert Einstein was born and the two anti-Nazi martyrs, Sophie and Hans Scholl, grew up.

Rommel sent word back to Berlin that he was too ill to travel.

As a result, Hitler wrote the field marshal a letter, in Field Marshal Keitel's name, insisting that he report immediately or face trial for treason.

On October 14, two generals, Wilhelm Burgdorf and Ernst Maisel, drove to Rommel's estate with a small detachment of soldiers, arriving around noon. The soldiers quietly surrounded the perimeter of Rommel's property while the two generals climbed out of their green car and went through the garden gate. Inside the impressive, three-story house was Rommel's fifteen-year-old son Manfred; his personal aide, Captain Hermann Aldinger; and Rommel's wife of twenty-eight years, Lucie-Marie.

The generals asked courteously if they might speak with the field marshal alone. Rommel's family knew that he was under suspicion.

Manfred, who had been drafted into the Luftwaffe the year before at age fourteen,[18] would say later that the generals' courtesy led him to believe that they were not going to arrest his father. Relieved, Manfred went upstairs to look for a book.

Burgdorf and Maisel handed Rommel the letter signed by Keitel as well as the written transcript of Hofacker's statements under torture.

The generals then explained to Rommel that he had two choices. He could return with them to Berlin, stand trial for treason before the People's Court, and face almost certain execution. His property would then be confiscated by the state and the members of his family possibly subject to arrest as well. Or Rommel could swallow poison and be given a state funeral, with his family left alone.

Shaken, Rommel asked for a few moments to think about it. He went upstairs to speak with his wife, Lucie. He told her bluntly, "I'll be dead in fifteen minutes."

The truth was that Hitler didn't want Rommel to be tried or to shoot himself. The scandal of yet another war hero—Germany's most celebrated soldier, in fact—turning against Hitler would further undermine the public's faith in their leader.

Rommel faced his young son on the landing outside his bedroom, pale with grief. "'I have just had to tell your mother that I shall be dead in a quarter of an hour," he said to Manfred. "I am to have the chance of dying by poison. The two generals have brought it with them. It's fatal

Nazi generals visited the home of Erwin Rommel in Herrlingen, near Ulm in southern Germany, on October 14, 1944, to offer him the choice of committing suicide to save his wife and son. The home is now a museum. *Wikimedia Commons*[19]

At the Yalta Conference, the Western Allies agreed that the Soviet Red Army would be in charge of liberating Berlin and that Hitler and other top Nazi leaders would be executed. There was little chance that Hitler would be captured alive. *U.S. National Archives*

in three seconds. If I accept, none of the usual steps will be taken against my family, that is against you. They will also leave my staff alone."

"Do you believe it?" Manfred asked, tears welling up in his eyes.

"Yes," the old general replied. "It is very much in their interest to see that the affair does not come out into the open. By the way, I have been charged to put you under a promise of the strictest silence. If a single word of this comes out, they will no longer feel themselves bound by the agreement."

Manfred wanted to fight. He asked his father why they couldn't shoot their way out. "There's no point," Rommel replied, knowing that the Gestapo had the grounds surrounded. "It's better for one to die than for all of us to be killed in a shooting affray. Anyway, we've practically no ammunition."

Rommel's aide Aldinger now joined them. He, too, wanted to fight. But Rommel explained the situation to his young assistant. "It's all been prepared to the last detail," he said. "I'm to be given a state funeral. I have asked that it should take place in Ulm. In a quarter of an hour, you, Aldinger, will receive a telephone call from the Wagnerschule reserve hospital in Ulm to say that I've had a brain seizure on the way to a conference."[20]

The general glanced at his watch. His time was up.

Manfred helped Rommel put on his long leather field coat. The two soldiers and Manfred walked down the driveway toward the garden gate where the Nazi generals were waiting. Manfred remembered the crunch of the gravel driveway under his father's boots.

Rommel carried his field marshal's baton with him. As they approached the gate, the two waiting generals stood and raised their hands in the Nazi Roman salute. "Herr Field Marshal," General Burgdorf said, standing to the side. An SS soldier opened the door of the car for Rommel to get in. Rommel then turned to his young son. He looked him in the eye, shook his hand one last time and turned quickly and stepped toward the car. He climbed inside along with the two generals and the doors were slammed shut. As they drove away, Rommel did not look back.

The car drove less than half a mile up the road and pulled over near a clearing before the forest. The driver and Maisel got out, leaving Bergdorf and Rommel in the back seat alone. Rommel swallowed the poison capsule that Bergdorf handed to him. Just as he had said, he was dead within minutes. Twenty minutes later, Manfred heard the phone ring in the study and Aldinger answering it. The voice on the other end told the captain that Rommel was dead—the field marshal had suffered an unexpected brain seizure.

Rommel was given a lavish state funeral, as promised. His young son and wife were left in peace. The public was told that the general, who was fifty-one when he died, had succumbed to the wounds he had suffered when his vehicle had been attacked by Allied planes. "With him,

EYEWITNESS ACCOUNT

"It was not then entirely clear what had happened to [my father] after he left us. Later we learned that the car had halted a few hundred yards up the hill from our house in an open space at the edge of the wood. Gestapo men, who had appeared in force from Berlin that morning, were watching the area with instructions to shoot my father down and storm the house if he offered resistance. [General Ernst] Maisel and the driver got out of the car, leaving my father and [General Wilhelm] Burgdorf inside. When the driver was permitted to return ten minutes or so later, he saw my father sunk forward with his cap off and the marshal's baton fallen from his hand."

—*Manfred Rommel, Rommel's son*[21]

one of our best army leaders has passed away," Hitler announced. "His name has entered the history of the German people."

The forced suicide of Rommel symbolically marked the end of the German resistance against Hitler. The numerous plots against the Nazi dictator had all failed, although not for lack of courage on the part of the plotters. It was now clear that the only way Hitler would be stopped would be through victory on the battlefield. In four months, the Western Allies would meet with the Soviets at a conference in Yalta in the Crimea to discuss the final phase of the war in Europe and to negotiate the new map of postwar Europe. The participants—U.S. president Franklin Roosevelt, British prime minister Winston Churchill, and Soviet premier Joseph Stalin—agreed that Germany had to surrender unconditionally and that Hitler and other top Nazi leaders would be executed. As a result, few observers believed that Hitler would ever be captured alive. The failure of the Stauffenberg plot had reinforced Hitler's decision that Germany would fight to the death, setting the stage for the final apocalyptic drama—Hitler's own Götterdämmerung—in Berlin. "In this war there can be no compromise, there can be only victory or destruction," Hitler declared after the Stauffenberg bombing. "And if the German people cannot wrest victory from the enemy, then they shall be destroyed. Yes, then they deserve to perish."[22]

6 THE BEGINNING OF THE END

fter Stauffenberg's failed assassination attempt, the war went from bad to worse for Germany on both Western and Eastern fronts. But in the late summer and fall of 1944, the German people rallied in defense of their country and their leader.

The regional Nazi political chieftains known as Gauleiters organized huge outdoor rallies across the country to celebrate Hitler's "miraculous" survival—which was, according to the government, proof that Hitler was destined to lead Germany in the fulfillment of its historic mission to save Europe from the Slavic hordes and Communism.

In reality, Hitler's popularity had been steadily falling in the months before the assassination attempt as the stunning military victories early in the war turned into defeats—and the costs of the war became evident to everyone.

But the attack against Hitler's life changed everything.

First, it meant a savage crackdown on dissidents unlike anything Germany had seen before—and Germany had seen a lot.

Despite their proclaimed Germanophilia, Hitler and his top lieutenants never trusted most of the central institutions of German life: the professional military, the aristocracy, the court system, the churches, and

EYEWITNESS ACCOUNT

"The assassination attempt of 20 July was the greatest possible misfortune for Germany and Europe. Not because it was made but because it failed. Hitler saw all the unfortunate coincidences that foiled the plot as his personal success. His confidence, his certainty of victory and his sense of security, his consciousness of power and his megalomania now really passed beyond all bounds of reason. If recent military defeats might perhaps have made him ready to compromise . . . now he thought that Fate had confirmed his own worth, his ideals, his power and all that he did."

—*Traudl Junge, Hitler's last secretary*[1]

the big German companies. They now decided to trust only the most loyal Nazi Party officials.

In the past, the Nazis' schemes had sometimes been stymied or at least moderated by these older German institutions. For example, the Nazis often sought legal sanction for their outrages, as flimsy as they were, and they were occasionally blocked. After July 20, these German institutions were simply ignored. The Nazi Party itself took over Germany in toto.

Hitler promoted Goebbels, his minister of propaganda—who was possibly an even more murderous fanatic than Hitler himself—to the new post of Reich Plenipotentiary for the Total War Effort, allowing him to rule by unilateral decrees and directives. The net result was that any hope of a regime change, or of replacing Hitler with someone who could end the war peacefully and quickly, was now gone. The German people realized that they were now stuck with Hitler and the Nazis until the bitter end. There would be no other assassination attempts, no coups, no separate peace with the Americans over against the hated Russians.

Just as the plotters had foreseen, the German people were by and large genuinely outraged at the assassination attempt against Hitler. The idea that German military officers would attempt to murder their leader in the midst of a world war—a war in which Germany was fighting for its very life—struck even non-Nazis as reprehensible and treacherous. As one of Hitler's biographers notes, fully a third of the German population believed the attack on Hitler to be unjustified, even immoral, as late as the 1950s.[2]

Stauffenberg had predicted this. If the assassination attempt failed, he said, the plotters would go down in history as traitors. After the war, the German populace and government leaders largely ignored the actions of the German resistance because they reflected badly on the millions of people who did nothing to resist the regime. Only in recent years have the heroism and dedication of Tresckow, Beck, Olbricht, and Stauffenberg and their many fellow conspirators been recognized and celebrated.

The July 20 bombing strengthened the regime in the short term, but it ultimately undermined its legitimacy in the eyes of the German population. The fact that top-ranked German military officers—including many colonels, generals, and at least two field marshals—had taken part in the plot at first provided a plausible explanation for why Germany's military situation had so inexplicably deteriorated. It was clear that traitors within the German Army had been secretly undermining Hitler all along. But eventually, the German people came to an even more troubling conclusion: Hitler and the Nazis had failed the German people.

Hundreds of thousands of German soldiers—cherished sons, husbands, and fathers—had been killed in what looked increasingly like a doomed war effort, particularly against Russia. Hitler had admitted as much in his July 20 radio address. "It is intolerable that at the front hundreds of thousands and millions of brave men are willing to make the ultimate sacrifice," he said, "while here at home a small clique of ambitious, despicable creatures constantly tries to undermine" the nation.

It turned out that the Führer wasn't the unqualified genius the Nazis had said he was; instead, he was an ordinary man, one who had been duped by his own most trusted associates. In the final months of 1944, the Gestapo noted that Germans on the street were saying *Guten Tag* again, not *Heil, Hitler*. The cult of the Führer was losing adherents.

At this point, Hitler and his most loyal aides also began to sour on the German people. Following the bombing, Hitler issued statements implying that perhaps the German people themselves were to blame for the faltering war effort. More ominously, the Führer hinted that it would be better for Germany to be utterly destroyed than to capitulate to the Allies and the Communist hordes now on their doorsteps.

In short, the July 20 bombing marked the beginning of the end for Germany. Over the next nine months, from July 1944 to May 1945, more Germans would be killed than in the previous six years of the war. The country would be utterly destroyed by nonstop bombing raids and the combined armies of the United States, Russia, Britain, and other Allies. Few major cities were spared. Some of Germany's most historic towns were severely damaged, including Stuttgart, Hamburg, Düsseldorf, Münster, Cologne, Munich, Leipzig, Jena, and even Martin Luther's Erfurt. Berlin would be reduced to a pile of burning rubble. Following Stauffenberg's last failed attempt to kill Hitler, an average of 13,536 German civilians were killed every month in massive bombardments that leveled entire districts. In one notorious attack on the historic city of Dresden, more than 20,000 civilians died in a single day.[3]

Of course, the Nazis had also bombed British cities, but the number of German casualties ended up being much higher. It is estimated that up to 43,000 British civilians died from Nazi air raids, primarily during the Battle of Britain, while about 410,000 German civilians died in the final months of the war. The Royal Air Force and the U.S. Army Air Forces dropped thousands of tons of ordnance on cities such as Hamburg, Kassel, Darmstadt, Pforzheim, and Würzburg. Allied commanders believed that the surest way to spare civilian casualties, in both Germany and Japan, was to end the war as quickly as possible.

Escalating the Final Solution

It is also true that as the war moved to its inexorable conclusion, Hitler and the Nazis diverted badly needed resources from the war effort in order to complete the greatest act of genocide in history—the systematic annihilation of the Jews of Europe. As we saw earlier, there were relatively few Jews living in Germany proper even at the beginning of the war—only about 565,000 out of a total German population of 67 million. The original Nazi plan appears to have been to force Jews, Gypsies, and other despised groups to emigrate to lands far from Europe, such as Palestine. For this reason, the Nazis launched a campaign of brutal harassment against the Jewish population to force them to leave the Reich, making it illegal for Jews to work in many professions, for example. Before the start of World War II, about half of all German Jews emigrated, most of them to the United States or Palestine.

But with the invasion of Poland in 1939, suddenly more than 3.5 million Polish Jews came under direct German occupation. And the attack on Russia (Operation Barbarossa) in June 1941 brought millions more Jews within the reach of Nazi authorities. In addition, Jews also lived in countries occupied by or allied with the Germans, such as France and Italy. The Nazis estimated that there were eleven million Jews total in all of Europe. And it appears that sometime in 1940 or 1941, Hitler decided that forced emigration was not a realistic policy. He decided, instead, on mass murder—though some historians believe that genocide had been Hitler's plan all along, since the 1920s.

The speed with which the Nazis carried out the genocide continues to astonish historians. On January 20, 1942, fifteen top Nazi leaders gathered in the Berlin suburb of Wannsee, where Stauffenberg and his brother had a home, to discuss what Hermann Göring had described as the "final solution to the Jewish question."

In January 1942, top Nazi leaders gathered at this palatial villa in the Berlin suburb of Wannsee, where the "final solution to the Jewish question," the systematic annihilation of Europe's entire Jewish population, was revealed. *Wikimedia Commons*[4]

Heinrich Himmler's deputy, Reinhard Heydrich, head of the SS's own secret police known as the SD, met with the officials at a lakeside villa. The two-story neoclassical villa, which is now a museum dedicated to the Holocaust, had been purchased by the SS to use as a guest house for visiting Nazi officials. At the conference Heydrich revealed for the first time the regime's plan to systematically murder all eleven million Jews living in Europe. The Holocaust was not decided upon at this conference, as is sometimes claimed. The purpose of the meeting was merely to *inform* key government personnel of what was already happening— the creation of large camps where Jews and other people the Nazis deemed subhuman could be systematically killed and then cremated.

Much of the detail was only revealed orally. After the war, Allied soldiers discovered by accident a single copy of written minutes—or "protocols"—from the conference, in which the plans were hidden under a myriad of bureaucratic euphemisms and obfuscations. The protocols spoke of mass "evacuations" and deportations. Among those present at the conference, however, was Adolf Eichmann, one of the chief organizers of the deportations to death camps and the one

OFFICIAL DOCUMENTS

"In the course of this final solution of the European Jewish Problem, approximately 11 million Jews are involved. . . .

"Under proper direction the Jews should now in the course of the Final Solution be brought to the East in a suitable way for use as labor. In big labor gangs, with separation of the sexes, the Jews capable of work are brought to these areas and employed in road building, in which task undoubtedly a great part will fall out through natural [means].

"The remnant that finally is able to survive all this—since this is undoubtedly the part with the strongest resistance—must be treated accordingly since these people, representing a natural selection, are to be regarded as the germ cell of a new Jewish development. (See the experience of history.)"

—*Official Minutes of Wannsee Conference, written by Adolf Eichmann*[6]

responsible for drafting the protocols. In his testimony at his trial in Jerusalem in 1961, following his capture by Israeli agents in Argentina, Eichmann explained that the details of mass killing were spoken about openly. "[I]n very blunt words they referred to the matter, without putting it down in writing," Eichmann testified. "There was talk of killing and eliminating and exterminating."[5]

While Hitler himself did not attend the Wannsee Conference, there is no question that the directive to annihilate the Jews of Europe came from Hitler himself. In early 1942, Hitler ordered the head of the SS, Heinrich Himmler, to eliminate all of the Jews living in Poland by the end of the year. As a result, Himmler launched Operation Reinhard, in which Jews were transported by train to three death camps in Poland—Belzec, Sobibor, and Treblinka. An Israeli historian studying the raw data on 480 train deportations from 393 Polish towns discovered that an astonishing 1.3 million people were gassed in just three months, September through November 1942.[7]

Cornered

Yet while Hitler was preoccupied with murdering Jews, the war was not going according to plan. In the West, the Allies were moving slowly up the Italian peninsula, having reached Rome in June 1944. American and British troops liberated Paris in August.

British and American forces then began a slow, inexorable march towards Germany. On the Eastern Front, the situation was even worse for the Germans. In July and August 1944, the Soviet Red Army initiated a major offensive that forced German troops to retreat from Eastern Poland and the Ukraine.

It was then that Hitler made another strategic error that would cost his people, and all the enslaved people of Eastern Europe, dearly. Rather than reinforce his armies battling the hated Russians, at the end of 1944, Hitler decided to launch a major counterattack against the Western Allies in the Ardennes forest of Belgium—a maneuver that came to be known as the Battle of the Bulge. It was a last desperate roll of the dice, and it would end in disaster.

The Battle of the Bulge was the second deadliest battle in American history, but it ended up costing the Germans what remained of their reserve armor. Yet because of the high Allied casualties and a number of tactical misadventures, the Western Allies became cautious. Despite the vehement protests of some commanders, such as General George Patton, the British and Americans let the Russians take the lead in attacking Germany from the East.

OFFICIAL DOCUMENTS

"During his retreat, the enemy will leave behind only scorched earth and will abandon all concern for the population.

"I therefore command—

1. All military traffic, communications, industrial and supply installations as well as objects within Reich territory that might be used by the enemy in the continuation of his fight, either now or later, are to be destroyed.

2. It is the responsibility of the military command posts to execute this order to destroy all military objects, including traffic and communications installations.

The Gauleiters and Commissioners for Reich Defense are responsible for destroying the industrial and supply installations, as well as of other objects of valuable [sic]; the troops must give the Gauleiters and Commissioners for Reich Defense the assistance they need to carry out this task.

3. This command is to be transmitted to all troop commanders as promptly as possible; orders to the contrary are null and void."

—*Adolf Hitler*[8]

In January 1945, the Soviets launched a major offensive that would eventually take them all the way to Berlin. At this point, Hitler was forced to abandon his Wolf's Lair fortress in east Prussia and return to Berlin.

On January 16, he took up residence in the recently completed Führerbunker below Albert Speer's New Reich Chancellery building, already badly damaged by Allied bombing attacks. At first, Hitler would work upstairs in his large study in the Reich Chancellery, only returning to the Führerbunker to sleep at night. But with Allied air raids increasing in both frequency and intensity, Hitler soon moved down into the underground complex permanently, coming up only to walk his beloved dog Blondi in the Reich Chancellery garden.

By February, no fewer than eighty-five American and British divisions were pushing their way towards the Rhine and preparing to enter Germany itself. In early March, troops led by the British commander Montgomery and by the American George Patton managed to cross the formidable river, and the entire world knew it was now only a matter of time before Germany was defeated and the Nazi regime ended.

The German military fought heroically, as everyone predicted it would. The combat in the last months of the war was ferocious. In the East, German women committed suicide in large numbers to avoid the Soviet rape gangs—and there were isolated incidents of rape by the Western soldiers as well.[9]

On March 19, Hitler issued what became known as his scorched earth order: He ordered Albert Speer, the armaments minister, to destroy all German industrial and military facilities so that they would not fall into enemy hands. "If the war is lost, the people will be lost also," Hitler told Speer. "In any case only those who are inferior will remain after this struggle for the good have already been killed."[10] Speer, mindful of what this would do to the German civilian population after the war, deliberately ignored the order. He did everything he could to make sure it was never implemented.

On April 16, the Soviets began the final assault on Berlin, attacking from the east and the south. By this point, the Germans had about forty-five thousand troops left defending the city and another forty thousand boys and old men in the so-called Volkssturm or citizen militia. Around the Reich Chancellery area, there were only about two thousand German soldiers. They faced a Soviet force of some 1.5 million soldiers and a seemingly limitless supply of artillery that rained down death and destruction on an hourly basis.

By Hitler's fifty-sixth birthday, on April 20, 1945, the city was surrounded, with the few German tank units still functioning pinned down by Allied fire. A week later, Soviet troops captured Templehof Airport, and Soviet tanks were proceeding cautiously down the main Berlin streets, encountering fierce resistance but unstoppable. By the end of April, the few German troops left standing had almost run out of ammunition.

At this stage of the war, everyone, both in and outside of Germany, wondered what Hitler's end game might be. Would he attempt to flee the country? Commit suicide? Or regroup in the Alps and try to prolong the war? The Allies had no intention of providing Hitler with another opportunity for a show trial. Documents declassified in 2005 revealed that Churchill especially opposed Allied plans for war crimes trials and wanted to summarily execute leading Nazis, including Hitler.

The Allies weren't taking any chances. There had been rumors that Hitler might attempt to leave Berlin for his mountain hideaway in Berchtesgaden—as indeed many of his top aides had been recommending for weeks. As a result, a few days after Hitler's fifty-sixth birthday, 359 Avro Lancaster heavy bombers took off from British airfields and flew to Hitler's Bavarian residence. The planes dropped an estimated 1,400 tons of bombs on the complex, destroying the homes of some top Nazis but leaving Hitler's residence, the Berghof, only partially damaged. Most of the 3,000 employees of the facility were safe in bunkers deep underground. After the raid, the German military, on Hitler's orders, finished the job begun by the British bombers and destroyed the Berghof.

Yet the raid only heightened the mystery around what would happen with Hitler. Even at this stage, many were speculating that Hitler would attempt to escape justice. The Nazis still had substantial resources at their disposal—submarines and long-range aircraft that could transport the Führer and his soon-to-be bride anywhere in the world. Hitler's precise whereabouts were still a mystery and, as we shall see, would remain so for decades to come. Western intelligence agencies would not know what really happened to Hitler for at least twenty-five years after the war ended. Although there were reports of his suicide, no trace of his remains was found by Western investigators.

The military forces that arrived at Hitler's bunker, Soviet intelligence officers, at first claimed that Hitler's body had been burned—but then quickly reversed themselves and insisted that the evidence showed Hitler had actually escaped. When American forces finally arrived in Berlin two months after the ceasefire, all they found were empty bomb craters—and no sign of Hitler's body. These are the facts underlying a mystery that endured for more than seventy years.

7 | RUMORS OF HITLER'S ESCAPE

O ver the decades, both professional historians and amateur conspiracy theorists have raised questions about many details of the
official account of Hitler's death. In the next chapter, we will take
a closer look at the findings of the investigation that, as we have already
seen, Hugh Trevor-Roper, Army major and Oxford historian, undertook
for British intelligence in September of 1945.

Around the same time, the U.S. Federal Bureau of Investigation (FBI)
opened an official investigation to determine whether there was any truth
to rumors that Hitler had escaped Europe and was living in Argentina
under an assumed name. The details of this investigation—and a similar
inquiry conducted by the CIA a decade later, in 1955—were only declassified in 2014 by presidential executive order, although some of the
material in them had been made public as early as the 1950s.

The more than seven hundred pages of declassified FBI documents
formed the basis of a number of recent books—and a three-year History
Channel reality series called *Hunting Hitler*—examining whether Hitler
managed to escape.

Seven hundred pages of confidential reports sounds like a lot of
information. But as anyone who reads through the documents will

> ⌐ 105-410
>
> was one of four men who met HITLER and his party when they landed from two submarines in Argentina approximately two and one-half weeks after the fall of Berlin. ████████continued that the first sub came close to shore about 11:00 p.m. after it had been signaled that it was safe to land and a doctor and several men disembarked. Approximately two hours later the second sub came ashore and HITLER, two women, another doctor, and several more men, making the whole party arriving by submarines approximately 50, were aboard. By pre-arranged plan with six top Argentine officials, pack horses were waiting for the group and by daylight all supplies were loaded on the horses and an all-day trip inland toward the foothills of the southern Andes was started. At dusk the party arrived at the ranch where HITLER and his party, according to ████████, are now in hiding. ████████most specifically explained that the subs landed along the tip of the Valdez Peninsula along the southern tip of Argentina in the gulf of San Matias. ████████told ████████that there are several tiny villages in this area where members of HITLER's party would eventually stay with German families. He named the towns as San Antonio, Videma, Neuquen, Muster, Carmena, and Rason.
>
> ████████maintains that he can name the six Argentine officials and also the names of the three other men who helped HITLER inland to his hiding place. ████████explained that he was given $15,000 for helping in the deal. ████████explained to████████that he was hiding out in the United States now so that he could later tell how he got out of Argentina. He stated to████████that he would tell his story to the United States officials after HITLER's capture so that they might keep him from having to return to Argentina. He further explained to████████that the matter was weighing on his mind and that he did not wish to be mixed up in the business any further.

A screen capture of the redacted document in FBI files about a story that a *Los Angeles Examiner* reporter heard from an anonymous source in an L.A. bar on July 29, 1945. The source claimed that he was among a group of Argentine officials who met Adolf Hitler when he came ashore from a German submarine two and a half weeks after the fall of Berlin. *Federal Bureau of Investigation*

discover, a disconcerting amount of the material consists of letters from ordinary citizens to the FBI claiming they had seen Adolf Hitler in some unlikely location—such as working at a downtown New York lunch counter—or offering their personal theories about what happened to the German dictator.

In many cases, the correspondents simply passed on articles they had read in the popular press about the possibility that Hitler had escaped. One informant wrote in July 1946 to say that "while spending a short time between trains" in Charlottesville, Virginia, he had been "so sure of seeing Hitler that I can't get the experience out of my mind."[1] The FBI dutifully noted each report and forwarded them to different offices in the agency. In many cases, FBI Director J. Edgar Hoover responded to the informant by letter, thanking him or her for the valuable information.

Yet despite the many seemingly crackpot observations and theories in the FBI documents, there are a few reports that the FBI appears to have taken more seriously—and that formed the basis for most of the theories of Hitler's escape that would arise in later decades. An FBI document dated September 21, 1945, for example, describes a meeting on July 29 of that year between a reporter for the *Los Angeles Examiner* newspaper and an unnamed man who claimed to have been an official in the Argentine government. According to the reporter, the man told him that he was one of four men who had met Adolf Hitler about two and a half weeks after the fall of Berlin, when the dictator came ashore from a German submarine at the tip of the Valdez Peninsula in the Gulf of San Matias, along Argentina's southern coast.

The informant claimed it was about 11:00 p.m. when a large group came ashore from two submarines, including Hitler, two women, two doctors, and about forty more men. The Germans were met, the informant said, by Argentine officials, including himself, who brought with them pack horses and supplies. The large party proceeded to hike into the southern Andes, traveling all day until it reached a ranch where, the informant continued, Hitler was still hiding among German families in the area. He named some Argentine villages where a large number of Nazi fugitives were staying, including San Antonio, Videma, Neuquen, Muster, Carmena and Rason, closest to the coast. The official claimed he had been paid $15,000 to help Hitler and the others reach their destination.

The FBI dismissed this account as being unworthy of follow-up investigation, but reports from and about Argentina continued to pour into the agency's various field offices. One account, dated November 3, 1945, was a letter claiming to contain information from an anonymous source to the effect that Hitler was living in a "great underground establishment beneath a vast hacienda" located 675 miles west of Florianopolis and 430 miles northwest of Buenos Aires. According to

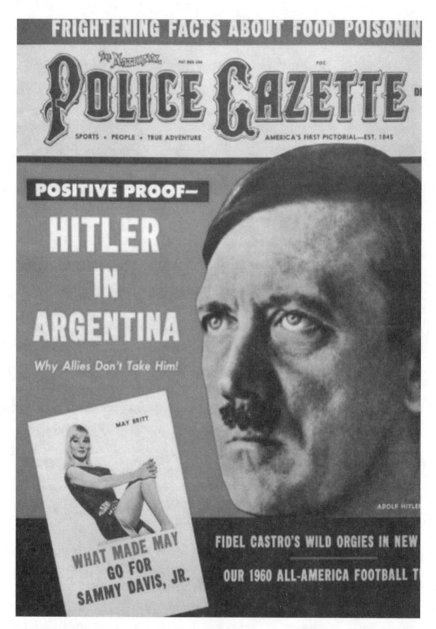

Throughout the 1940s and '50s, popular tabloids featured stories claiming Hitler had faked his suicide and escaped with Eva Braun to a hideaway in South America. *National Police Gazette*[2]

the letter, the underground hideout, which led to special elevators, was reached via a secret entrance in a wall operated by photoelectric cells. This account was featured at the beginning of the History Channel's three-year series *Hunting Hitler* as the jumping-off point for the cable channel's investigations.

FBI Director J. Edgar Hoover himself forwarded another report, dated November 13, 1945, about a possible "Hitler Hideout" in Argentina, to investigators in the U.S. Embassy in Argentina. It claimed that a wealthy German woman and ardent Nazi, a Mrs. Eichhorn, ran a spa hotel in the village of Falda where she had invited the former Führer to seek refuge if he ever needed an escape. Later documents would identify the woman as Ida Bonfert Eichhorn. Along with her husband Walter, she was an early supporter of the Nazis going back to the days of the Beer Hall Putsch in 1923, and she ran the once-luxurious Eden Hotel in Falda. The hotel, which still exists, is said to have been a favorite of local German expats and Nazi supporters throughout the 1930s.

While apparently skeptical, the FBI seems to have followed up on the more credible accounts. The agency eventually dispatched investigators to Argentina in 1946 and 1947. Based in the U.S. Embassy in Buenos Aires, they attempted to track what leads they had, even visiting the Eden Hotel. But they were unable to produce any credible proof that Hitler had escaped or was living in Argentina.

Yet reports continued to trickle in to the FBI, the CIA, and British intelligence.

An October 3, 1955 CIA memo contains a brief report that Hitler survived the war and lived in Colombia for several months in 1954. An editor of a local newspaper, Phillip Citroen, a former German SS agent, is said to have claimed he met Hitler at Residencies Coloniales in Tunja, Boyaca, Colombia, an area heavily populated with escaped Nazis. The CIA memo contained a grainy photograph of a man bearing a remarkable resemblance to the German dictator. The informant claimed that the Germans in Tunja followed the mysterious figure "with an idolatry of the Nazi past, addressing him as 'der Führer' and affording him the

OFFICIAL DOCUMENTS

"SECRET
"DATE: 17 October 1955
"TO: Chief, WH
"FROM: Chief of base, Maracaibo
"SUBJECT: Adolf Hitler

1. With reference to the intimation submitted by Station Caracas concerning the alleged report that Adolf HITLER is still alive, the files of the Base contain similar information received from the same source, who resides in Maracaibo . . .

2. An undated memorandum, believed to have been written in about mid February 1954, reflects that Phillip CITROEN, who was co-owner of the former *Maracaibo Times*, told a former member of this Base that while he was working for a railroad company in Columbia, he had met an individual who strongly resembled and claimed to be Adolf HITLER. CITROEN claimed to have met this individual at a place called "Residencies Coloniales" in Tunja (Boyaca), Colombia, which is, according to the source, overly populated with former German Nazis. According to CITROEN, the Germans residing in Tunja follow this alleged Adolf HITLER with an 'idolatry of the Nazi past, addressing him as Der Fuhrer and affording him the Nazi Salute and storm-trooper adulation.'

3. CITROEN also showed the member of this Office a photograph which was taken in Colombia of himself standing next to the alleged HITLER. This photograph was borrowed for few hours to be reproduced, but unfortunately the negatives were too poor to make copies from. The original was returned to its owner and could not be easily obtained again. Because of this and the apparent fantasy of the report, the information was not submitted at the time it was received."

—*George M. Warbis*[3]

Nazi salute and storm-trooper adulation."[4] When the CIA memo was declassified in 2017, it triggered headlines across the world.[5]

Not surprisingly, tales such as these have spawned a small industry of Hitler conspiracy theories. Books elaborating on the theory that Hitler escaped to Argentina have appeared regularly every few years beginning at the turn of the millennium.

The revival of this theory seems to have been sparked by the publication, in the year 2000, of the Spanish-language book *El Escape de Hitler: Su Vida Invisible en la Argentina, las Conexiones Con Evita y Perón* (*Hitler's Escape: His Invisible Life in Argentina and the Connections with Evita and Peron*) by an Italian journalist with the American-sounding name of Patrick Burnside. Burnside's book was followed by a series of three books by the Argentine journalist Abel Basti, all published in Spanish and never translated. First, in 2004, Basti wrote *Bariloche Nazi: Sitios Relacionados Al Nacionalsocialismo* (*Barliloche Nazi: Historical Sites Related to National Socialism*). This was followed two years later, in 2006, by *Hitler en Argentina* (*Hitler in Argentina*) and then, in 2010, Basti published *El exilio de Hitler: Las pruebas de la fuga del fuhre a a la Argentina* (*Hitler's Exile: The Proof of Hitler's Escape to Argentina*).

These Spanish-language titles were soon followed by similar books in English, including Gerrard Williams and Simon Dunstan's *Grey Wolf: The Escape of Adolf Hitler* (2011), Peter Levenda's *Ratline: Soviet Spies, Nazi Priests, and the Disappearance of Adolf Hitler* (2012), and Jerome R. Corsi's *Hunting Hitler: New Scientific Evidence That Hitler Escaped Nazi Germany* (2014). Also popular are three self-published books by a man named Harry Cooper. Cooper's books have a novel twist. They are based on the claims by a Spanish-German "double agent," Don Angel Alcazar de Velasco, who Cooper says was personally involved in the operation to smuggle Hitler and Martin Bormann out of Berlin and into Argentina. Both Corsi and Cooper have been criticized by activist groups, such as the Southern Poverty Law Center, for alleged ties to extremist organizations. In Cooper's case, the groups cited by the SPLC include Willis Carto's Holocaust-denial organization, the Institute for Historical Review.[6]

The Hitler conspiracy books point to the lack of definitive proof in the consensus account of Hitler's death (the dearth of physical evidence and conflicting reports from surviving witnesses on minor details) and establish the existence of a colony of Nazi refugees in South America. What they don't do, however, is provide any convincing documentary or physical evidence that Hitler actually lived there among them.

Most of the books make the following points:

1. The bodies of Hitler and Eva Braun were never found by American or British officials. *True.*

2. Soviet troops, who reached Hitler's bunker first, gave conflicting accounts of what they found there, eventually insisting that Hitler likely escaped after the war after leaving behind a body double who had been shot in the head. *True.*

3. German soldiers and aides living in Hitler's underground bunker also gave conflicting accounts of what happened in the final days of April 1945—and had a strong motive to cover their Führer's tracks if he had managed to escape. *Mostly true.*

4. Tunnels from Hitler's bunker to the Berlin subway system may have existed, and there is proof that daring aviators were able to fly in and out of Berlin during this period. This means that Hitler and Braun likely could have escaped from Berlin as late as April 29 or even 30. *True.*

5. The Nazis had plenty of looted money, gold, and other valuables stashed in hidden accounts that could have financed an escape attempt and a life of exile. *True.*

6. Nazi submarines capable of reaching Latin America continued to operate throughout May 1945, and records show that at least two visited the Argentine coast in July and August 1945. *True.*

7. Hundreds if not thousands of Nazis were able to escape from Europe and make their way to German colonies in Latin America, including such war criminals as Adolf Eichmann and Joseph Mengele. *True.*

8. Recently declassified FBI, CIA, and British intelligence files contain hundreds of reported sightings of Hitler after his alleged suicide—a few from reputable sources. The FBI and intelligence services continued to investigate these reports as late as the 1950s. *True.*

An ambitious author can dedicate a chapter or two to each of these points, and most of the "Hitler escaped" books do just that. They fill up page after page with background material—little-known details about the exact type of Nazi submarines remaining in the Atlantic, say, or what is known about the Berlin subway system. They also spend a lot of time and space on the German colonies in Latin America.

Historians have long known that some Nazis were able to escape Europe at the end of the war. The most notorious examples are the war criminals Adolf Eichmann and Dr. Josef Mengele. In 1960, Israeli commandos were able to kidnap Eichmann, who was living quietly at a house he built in Buenos Aires, and fly him to Israel to stand trial for war crimes. But Mengele, the sadistic Auschwitz death camp physician who performed horrific medical experiments on Jewish prisoners, was able to live relatively undisturbed for decades in Argentina, Paraguay, and Brazil, only dying in 1979 from a stroke while swimming off the Brazilian coast. By some estimates, there were as many as 60,000 Nazi refugees living in Argentina by the end of the war. Today, it is estimated that 3 million out of Argentina's total population of 45 million are of German descent.

The problem is that none of the major themes enumerated above is disputed by mainstream historians. In fact, almost every mainstream historian and researcher who believes Hitler committed suicide in the bunker acknowledges all of these points. They are so well documented as to be virtually unimpeachable. Yet none of these points, either alone or together, adds up to any sort of proof that Hitler got away.

That's why most of the "Hitler escaped" books spend, say, two hundred out of two hundred fifty pages on background material—interesting chapters on Nazi gold, reported sightings in the FBI files, the inconsistencies in the early Soviet accounts of what they found in the bunker—and give very little, if any, space to Hitler's supposed life in Argentina. In other words, what these books don't have is anything resembling proof that Hitler actually did escape.

The Hitler conspiracy books raise interesting questions. They propose fascinating theories. They put forth various hypotheses. But at the end of the day, when you examine the evidence they put forth to make the case that Hitler escaped alive, you find that they have virtually none. Almost all of the purported evidence is hearsay—one person, who is now dead, telling someone else that he or she knew someone who once saw Hitler. For example, the account in FBI files that launched the History Channel's *Hunting Hitler* series is a report from a journalist that he met an anonymous source one night in a club in Los Angeles who told him he had met Hitler in Argentina. The reporter didn't know his source's name, he only met him once, and, despite weeks of searching, he never saw him again. In the end, the entire claim that Argentine officials met Hitler on a beach came from a journalist hearing one guy brag in an L.A. bar. Many of the Hitler sightings in these books are like this, as we will see.

Grey Wolf

Of the recent "Hitler escaped" books, Gerrard Williams and Simon Dunstan's *Grey Wolf: The Escape of Adolf Hitler* is undoubtedly the most substantive and certainly the most influential. Williams is a veteran journalist who worked at the BBC, Reuters, and SkyTV, while Dunstan is a military historian, the author of more than a dozen books. *Grey Wolf* caused a sensation when it was first published in 2011, and it was made

IN THEIR OWN WORDS

"We never wanted this story to be true. It was originally intended to be a quixotic but thought-provoking 'conspiracy theory' television documentary. However, extensive research...backed up by the testimonies of many eyewitnesses...told a completely different [story] from the accepted 'history' of World War II. In the words of Winston S. Churchill, 'History is written by the victors.' Never has this been more true than the untold account of Hitler's escape from the ruins of the Third Reich in April 1945.

"The horrifying reality, we believe, is that at the end of World War II, the most evil man in the world, Adolf Hitler, escaped from Germany and lived out his life in Argentina—and that his deputy, Reichsleiter Martin Bormann, and Heinrich 'Gestapo' Müller, a key figure in the planning of the Final Solution, also escaped justice and joined him there. . . .

"There is no concrete forensic evidence that it was Adolf Hitler and Eva Braun who died in the Führerbunker—no eyewitness to the moment of death. The famous 'Hitler Skull' fragment held in Moscow for decades has finally been DNA-tested. It is that of a woman under the age of forty and it is not Eva Braun."

—*From the Preface, Simon Dunstan and Gerrard Williams,* Grey Wolf: The Escape of Adolf Hitler[7]

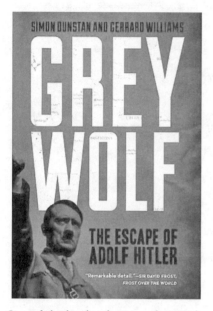

One of the books claiming that Hitler did not die in Berlin but escaped to Argentina is *Grey Wolf: The Escape of Adolf Hitler* by Gerrard Williams and Simon Dunstan.

into a documentary in 2014. Moreover, one of its authors, Williams, served as a consultant to and appeared on the History Channel reality series *Hunting Hitler*, which began in 2015.

Despite this, *Grey Wolf* was dismissed out of hand by some professional historians as unsubstantiated lunacy. The book is "2,000% rubbish," declared historian Guy Walters when it first appeared. "It's an absolute disgrace. There's no substance to it at all. It appeals to the deluded fantasies of conspiracy theorists and has no place whatsoever in historical research."[8]

The book's central thesis is a detailed elaboration of the old claim, first announced publicly by Joseph Stalin, that Hitler and Eva Braun escaped from the Reich Chancellery bunker to live out the remainder of their lives in seclusion in Argentina. The book claims that on April 28, 1945, one of Hitler's doubles (likely Gustav Weler) and an unknown German actress from Joseph Goebbels' film production studios were "switched" for the real Hitler and Eva Braun in the middle of the night.[9]

Over the next two days, these look-alikes pretended to be Hitler and Braun to the remaining staffers still in the bunker—people who had known the Nazi dictator and his mistress for years, in some cases decades. This is supposed to account for the fact that some of the survivors of the bunker would later insist that Hitler seemed to undergo a dramatic personality change in the final days and "didn't seem like himself." That was because it wasn't the real Hitler!

The real Hitler and Braun, according to Williams and Dunstan, used secret tunnels from the bunker linked to Berlin's subway system to escape, thereby safely bypassing the fierce battle waging on the streets above them. They made their way to a plane waiting for them on nearby Hohenzollerndamm Boulevard. At three in the morning of April 28, the two climbed aboard a Junkers 52 aircraft piloted by a South African–born Luftwaffe pilot named Peter Baumgart—a real figure who stood trial for war crimes in Poland and apparently vanished after being released from a Soviet prison in 1952.[10]

With Soviet tanks and artillery firing just blocks away, the Junkers 52 roared down the deserted street in the darkness and was soon airborne, its engines straining to gain altitude to escape the artillery fire below. After twenty minutes, the plane had reached ten thousand feet. It was only then that one of the passengers removed his helmet and the pilot could see that it was Adolf Hitler himself.

Back in the bunker, Hitler's loyal aides Martin Bormann and Joseph Goebbels waited anxiously for confirmation that Hitler had gotten away safely before putting into action the second part of their diabolical plan. According to the account in *Grey Wolf*, Bormann arranged for the two doubles to pretend to get married and then retire to their quarters, as later witnesses testified they saw them do. But the two actors didn't realize what would happen next. While they were seated on Hitler's sofa, one of the men in on the plot, likely Gestapo chief Heinrich Müller, calmly shot both of the look-alikes dead.

The Hitler look-alike was shot in the head and the gun placed on the floor near his body. After the rest of the bunker staff discovered that the man they thought was Hitler was dead, the bodies of the two stand-ins were then carried out into the Reich Chancellery garden, doused with nearly 200 liters of gasoline, and burned beyond all recognition.

Baumgart flew the Junkers 52 to an airfield outside Tonder, Denmark, where German prisoner-of-war Friedrich Argelotty-Mackensen later told U.S. intelligence interrogators he had seen Hitler three days after he was announced dead on the radio.

Williams and Dunstan hint that Hitler was aided in this escape by a faction of U.S. intelligence and wealthy industrialists—just as Joseph Stalin claimed. Supposedly, this group believed the Soviet Union was a greater threat than Nazi Germany and sought to facilitate the escape of Hitler and thirty thousand other top Nazis in exchange for access to Germany's top secret weapons technology, such as infrared night vision equipment, jets, and rockets.

Earlier, Bormann and other top Nazis had smuggled hundreds of tons of gold and other assets, worth at least $50 billion today, out of Germany, and this fortune was able to buy the cooperation of the Argentine government.

According to Williams and Dunstan, Hitler and Braun made their way by plane from Denmark to Spain. The authors admit that they do not know precisely how the Nazi leader and his new wife traveled to Argentina, but their guess is that they traveled by air to the Canary Islands and from there boarded one of three U-boats from the Nazi submarine fleet still operating in the Atlantic at the end of the war. The subs took more than a month to reach South America.

In late July, the Nazi submarines reached Argentina's Atlantic coastline near the town of Mar del Plata. From there, on July 30, 1945, Hitler and Braun were flown to the town of Neuquen in the Andes, the plane was refueled, and then they continued on to the picturesque town of San Carlos de Bariloche in Patagonia. They stayed for nine months at Estancia San Ramon, a hacienda that had been used as a hideout by Admiral Wilhelm Canaris in 1915. Hitler and Braun were soon joined by a young girl the authors claim was really their secret six-year-old daughter Ursula, widely photographed and identified as the daughter of Eva Braun's sister Gretl and her husband Hermann Fegelein. The little girl had traveled to Argentina from Spain with Fegelein.

Hitler, Braun, and their daughter left the hacienda in San Ramon and traveled north to a luxury hotel on Mar Chiquita lake in the province of Cordoba. Eventually, Hitler and Braun settled in a Bavarian-styled waterfront mansion, Inalco, on an isolated peninsula jutting into Lake

The now-dilapidated Bavarian villa on Lake Nahuel Huapi in Patagonia, Argentina, where the authors of *Grey Wolf* claim Adolf Hitler, Eva Braun, and their two daughters lived between 1947 and 1955. *Wikimedia Commons*[11]

Nahuel Huapi in Patagonia. There, Williams and Dunstan claim, Hitler, Braun, their daughter Ursula, and another daughter born there lived a quiet, idyllic life from June 1947 until October 1955. They would swim in the lake, ski in the nearby Andes mountains, and socialize with some of the thousands of Nazis who had settled in the nearby town of San Carlos de Bariloche. Occasionally, Argentine President Peron would stop by to pay his respects. In 1947, Hitler's trusted aide Martin Bormann left hiding in Europe and, with the assistance of a Vatican-based "clero-fascist"—a clerical supporter of Mussolini—joined hundreds of other Nazi escapees, including Mengele, in making his way to Argentina. He arrived in Buenos Aires, the authors claim, on May 17, 1948, traveling on a Vatican passport and dressed as a Jesuit priest.

Williams and Dunstan conclude their book with the claim that Eva Braun grew tired of her life on the lake with Hitler, then sixty-five years old and in very poor health. Around the year 1954, they claim, Eva left Hitler and took her two daughters to live in Neuquen, 230 miles northeast.

Williams and Dunstan rely upon the reconstructed memories of a German physician, Dr. Otto Lehmann, who claimed he cared for the former Nazi dictator while he was in Argentina. As the authors explain it, Dr. Lehmann wrote down his account of his life as Hitler's doctor in Argentina and gave the texts first to a sea captain named Heinrich Bethe, who, in turn, gave them to another man named Manuel Monasterio.

Unfortunately, Monasterio lost these papers "during many house moves over a long life" but was later able to quote them from memory in his own 1987 book, *Hitler murió en la Argentina (Hitler Died in Argentina)*.[12] According to this account, Hitler moved to La Clara, Columbia, in 1955—echoing a similar report in the recently declassified CIA documents. There Hitler's health deteriorated further. The doctor and Bethe cared for Hitler for the next six years. Finally, on February 13, 1962, at 3:00 p.m., the seventy-two-year-old mass murderer died following a stroke.

Grey Wolf ends abruptly. It claims that both Martin Bormann and Gestapo Chief Heinrich Müller were still living in 1980 in Argentina, but it does not say what happened to Eva Braun or to Hitler's supposed two daughters. (In 2014, a self-published author and Nazi memorabilia enthusiast, Harry Cooper, claimed in his book *Hitler in Argentina* that Eva Braun lived until at least 2012, age ninety, in an assisted living facility in Argentina.)

Grey Wolf is a riveting read. Much of it is a rehash of previously known events— such as the growth of the Nazi Party, the history of World War II, the looting of Europe, the escapes of various top Nazis, and the presence of German refugees and Nazis in Argentina. After all, Dunstan is a military historian. The two authors also fill their chapters with copious details about weapons systems and the sex lives of various historical characters.

Yet when it comes to their central claims about Hitler, the evidence the authors offer for their gripping tale is thin indeed—and more than a little circumstantial.

For example, for their claim that Hitler and Eva Braun were switched with lookalikes during the final days in the bunker, the authors rely upon a facial recognition expert from University College London who claimed that he could prove scientifically that the man who met with Hitler Youth on April 20, 1945, was not the real Adolf Hitler. Even if this were true, and most historians doubt it, all this shows is that Hitler had a look-alike appear at a minor ceremonial event in his place—not that this look-alike was murdered to fake Hitler's own death.

Hunting Hitler

Two more influential entries in the "Hitler escaped" genre are a book titled *Hunting Hitler*—and, as we have seen, a reality TV series with the same name on the History Channel. The book, published in 2014, is by bestselling author Jerome Corsi. Both the book and the TV series investigate the same basic theory we've examined so far, that Hitler and Eva Braun escaped to Argentina, although there are important differences between the two.

Like *Grey Wolf* and the other Hitler conspiracy titles before it, Corsi's *Hunting Hitler* has a lot of background information interesting for someone just dipping into the subject of Hitler's ultimate demise. The first three quarters of the book go over much of the ground covered in *Grey Wolf*—alleged problems with the official story, the lack of forensic evidence, and so forth. Corsi also has an interesting chapter on Allen Dulles and the U.S. spy service known as the OSS (the precursor to the CIA), the Vatican's role in helping Nazis escape, and the underground Nazi escape route known as the "ratline."[13]

One major difference between Corsi's account and that in *Grey Wolf* involves the timeline: the latter has Hitler and Eva Braun escaping from

Berlin at the last minute, on April 28, in a plane piloted by Peter Baumgart. In *Hunting Hitler*, the pair possibly escaped a week earlier, on April 22, perhaps on board a Focke-Achgelis Fa-223 twin-rotor helicopter recently developed by the Nazis.[14] According to this account, they flew to an airfield outside of Linz, Austria, and from there took a fixed-wing Junkers 290 Ag airplane piloted by the Luftwaffe pilot Werner Baumbach to Barcelona, Spain.

As proof, Corsi refers to the uncorroborated claim by the Argentine author Abel Basti that he had "in his archives" a passenger manifest from a plane leaving Linz that lists Hitler and Braun among the passengers.[15] Baumbach was real. In his bestselling postwar book *Inside the Third Reich*, Albert Speer describes how Baumbach had the use of a four-engine seaplane and on April 21 volunteered to whisk Speer and his associates to an isolated bay in Greenland where they could sit out the end of the war.[16]

But like *Grey Wolf*, Corsi's *Hunting Hitler* is very good at asking questions about the "official" story and pointing out minor inconsistencies in some of the eyewitness accounts, but it presents no actual evidence that Hitler was ever in Argentina. Corsi's final chapter, "The Escape to Argentina," is just twenty-three pages long, and twenty of them are primarily about the documented arrival in Argentine waters of two U-boats, U-530 and U-977, in the summer of 1945, with such startling revelations as the fact that U-530 was found to be missing one large rubber life raft when it was boarded by Argentine naval officers.

Corsi dedicates just two pages of this final chapter to the claim that Hitler found refuge at Walter and Ida Eichhorn's Eden Hotel in La Falda and that the Eichhorns built the Bavarian-themed Residencia Inalca on Nahuel Huapi Lake for him. The last sentence of the chapter is simply, "Hitler moved into the residence in June 1947."[17] And yet Corsi offers zero proof for this claim, only citing other "Hitler Escaped" books such as *Grey Wolf*. In other words, *Hunting Hitler* is mostly a summary of the central claims of *Grey Wolf*—without any attempt to buttress these claims with actual evidence.

In 2015, the History Channel launched its three-year reality TV series, also entitled *Hunting Hitler*, investigating the claims found in *Grey Wolf*, Corsi's book, and others. Using the recently declassified FBI files from the mid-1940s as a springboard, a team of supposed specialists—headed by former CIA case officer, author, and documentary film maker Bob Baer—follow various "leads" from the FBI documents to determine "once and for all" what really happened to Adolf Hitler. The stated goal of the series was to determine whether the notorious dictator managed to pull off "one of the world's greatest disappearing acts" and survived the war.

The team Baer assembled for the series included private investigator and self-proclaimed Nazi hunter Steve Rambam, U.S. Army Special Forces and former MMA fighter Tim Kennedy, former investigator for the International War Crimes Tribunal Dr. John Cencich, British World War II historian James Holland, former "Special Forces operator" Mike Simpson, former commander of U.S. Marshals Lenny Depaul, and *Grey Wolf* co-author Gerrard Williams.

Each episode of the series features Baer at a sort of command post in a Los Angeles office building in communication with various "teams" out investigating in the field. For dramatic effect, the episodes generally alternate between one team investigating hot leads in Argentina and another team pursuing different leads in Berlin. The series investigators make use of what appear to be state-of-the-art technological tools, such as CIA-level database search programs, drone cameras, underground sonar scanning equipment, and so forth.

Each episode ends with a cliff-hanger that seems to add another piece to the Hitler conspiracy puzzle, and the momentum builds towards the conclusion that Hitler appears to have escaped Europe in a Nazi submarine and spent the remainder of a long life in the Argentine countryside. The relatively thin material found in the books *Hunting Hitler* and *Grey Wolf* is stretched to fill out twenty-four episodes of forty-two minutes each.

Despite its length, extensive use of video footage, and interviews with the handful of witnesses still alive, such as the ninety-six-year-old former

Hitler SS bodyguard and telephone operator Rochus Misch, the series is merely a rehash of old rumors and conspiracy theories from the 1940s. It breaks no new ground. Like the books, the series does a good job of proving that there were Nazis in Argentina before and after World War II and that German U-boats visited the Argentine coastline. What it never is able to do, however—and this is the reason the series was ultimately canceled—is provide any convincing evidence about Hitler himself, beyond the vague and long-ago-dismissed reports found in the FBI files.

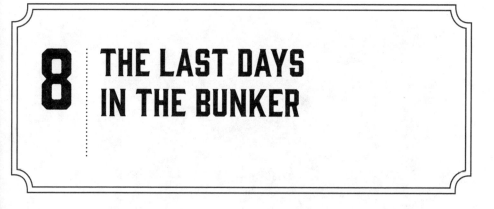

8 THE LAST DAYS IN THE BUNKER

y July 1945, when British historian and intelligence officer Hugh Trevor-Roper began his investigation into what had happened to Adolf Hitler, both British and U.S. intelligence services had already assembled a considerable amount of information—including transcribed statements of many of the German personnel who had been in the Führerbunker until the very end.

Hitler had left the Wolf's Lair in January 1945 and returned to Berlin, staying in the New Reich Chancellery building designed by Albert Speer and built in 1939. It was a new stone office building that abutted the old chancellery building, a small but ornate palace, and that surrounded a large park or garden. The building was a triumph of severe neoclassical architecture, with grand multi-story reception rooms, marble corridors, archways and an enormous office for Hitler. It was destroyed in air raids and demolished in the 1950s.

In the Reich Chancellery park or garden was the two-level air raid bunker that came to be known as the Führerbunker.

In the early 1930s, Albert Speer had designed the original bunker or Vorbunker, located beneath the cellars of the old Reich Chancellery. It

The New Reich Chancellery building, designed by architect Albert Speer and completed in 1939, was located just off Potsdamer Platz in the center of Berlin. It was in the large courtyard behind this building that the underground Führerbunker, where Hitler would spend his final days, was located. *Deutsches Bundesarchiv*[1]

held various storage rooms and kitchens as well as a dining area used by all the inhabitants.

In 1944, just in time for the Allied bombing raids that would destroy most of Berlin, a new, more substantial bunker, the Führerbunker proper, was constructed. It was about thirty feet below ground, protected by fifteen feet of concrete and another twelve feet of soil. The two bunkers were connected by a spiral staircase. Although it had its own generator, electricity, and air filtration system, the entire complex was dark and dank, with low ceilings, poor air circulation, and walls covered with moisture. A staircase at one end led up to an emergency exit to the garden.

Other bunkers in the immediate vicinity, connected by underground tunnels, housed dozens of top Nazi officials and SS security personnel, as many as two hundred people in all. Only the men and women in

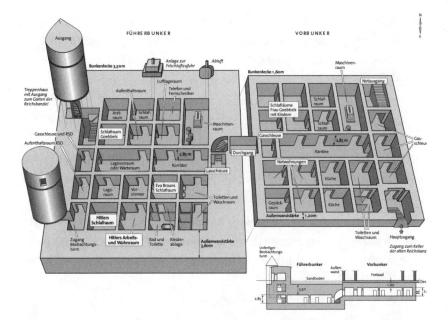

A detailed diagram of the Führerbunker illustrates the warren of small rooms and claustrophobic corridors where Hitler spent his final days. *akg-images/Peter Palm*

Hitler's closest inner circle were in the Führerbunker proper. They included Hitler and his secret longtime mistress, Eva Braun; Hitler's valet Heinz Linge; his SS Adjutant Otto Günsche; two secretaries, Traudl Junge and Gerda Christian; the vegetarian cook Constance Maziarly, and various guards.

Upstairs from the Fürherbunker, in the original air raid shelter or Vorbunker, were Hitler's close aide Martin Bormann; his chauffeur Erich Kempka; General Wilhelm Mohnke; press attaché Heinz Lorenz; Hitler Youth Commandant Artur Axmann; SS bodyguard and telephone operator Rochus Misch; and Joseph Goebbels, his wife Magda, and their six young children.

The Russians captured and severely tortured some of these witnesses before releasing them in the early 1950s, including Misch, Mohnke, Linge, and Günsche. Others, such as Hitler's secretaries Junge and Christian and Albert Speer, were captured by the Americans and interrogated thoroughly. In addition to their statements under interrogation, many of the survivors of the bunkers, including Junge, Misch, Linge and Albert Speer, would go on to write detailed memoirs of Hitler's last hours. Linge's book about Hitler's death, *With Hitler to the End*, was not published until 1980, the year he died.

In addition, Joseph Goebbels's detailed diaries spanning most of his adult life—twenty-nine volumes in the complete German edition—were found by Russian troops. The last entry was made only hours before his own death in the Führerbunker, on May 1. Excerpts were published soon after the war.

There are also the German-language diaries of Count Lutz Schwerin von Krosigk, the Nazi minister of finance who functioned as de facto chancellor in the final month of the war, which Hugh Trevor-Roper quoted at length in his report.

While it may be possible to critique Hugh Trevor-Roper's original account of what happened in the bunkers as rushed or incomplete—though read seventy-five years later, it's remarkably detailed considering the circumstances—the sheer volume of eyewitness testimony and documentary evidence is impossible to ignore.

Over the decades, the participants in the final drama of Hitler's death have told their stories many times. The fact that there is minor disagreement on some details, such as whether Hitler shot himself in the mouth or in the temple, only makes the generally accepted official story more plausible, not less. It is when witnesses agree on every detail that investigators become suspicious that a story is rehearsed.

Moreover, for those conspiracy theorists who claim that the eyewitnesses had a motive, as loyal Nazis, to provide a cover story for Hitler's escape—that might have been true immediately after the war, and even for the first few decades after it ended. But the eyewitnesses persisted in their depictions of the last events of Hitler's life for the rest of their own lives, into the 1990s and beyond, long after a cover story would have served any such purpose. As we have seen, bodyguard Rochus Misch, the last survivor of the bunker, published his account more than

sixty years after the events he described, long after the other participants were dead.

The Beginning of the End: Hitler's Fifty-Sixth Birthday Party

One thing the conspiracy theorists get right is that Hitler's closest
associates wanted him to leave Berlin and live to fight another day. Many
pleaded with him to escape almost to the very end—some, like Magda
Goebbels, begging him on their knees.

This was apparent on the celebration of Hitler's fifty-sixth birthday on April 20, 1945, the last time the Führer was seen or photographed in a public setting.[2] The original plan had been for Hitler to
flee Berlin and move south to his mountain fortress at Obersalzberg,
directing the war from there. Servants and crates of documents had
been dispatched south the week before. But in the week before his
birthday, the military situation had deteriorated to such a degree that
even Hitler now realized it was hopeless. The Soviet army had Berlin
surrounded and was making its way block by block through the outer
suburbs into the city itself.

Despite the danger, most of Hitler's inner circle risked death to make
a pilgrimage back to Berlin from their hiding places throughout Germany
to pay their respects to their leader and urge him to escape. Hermann
Göring, Heinrich Himmler, General Alfred Jodl, Field Marshal Wilhelm
Keitel, Albert Speer, Admiral Dönitz, and Foreign Minister von Ribbentrop all returned on April 20 to Berlin, in some cases braving heavy
anti-aircraft fire from Russian troops.

Hitler met his close associates upstairs in one of the few remaining
rooms of the Reich Chancellery that had not been destroyed by Allied
bombing raids. His old comrades were shocked by what they saw. Now
fifty-six years old, addicted to various drugs, his nerves badly frayed,
Hitler was close to a physical and mental breakdown. He had the physical
appearance of an old man in his seventies. He was stooped, his hands
trembled, and he had to drag his right leg as he walked. There were food

stains on his once-immaculate uniform. When he left the bunker, he could barely walk up the staircase.

After cake and champagne, Hitler made it clear that he had no intention of leaving Berlin. He could not ask his people to fight to the end, he said, if their leader ran away. Hitler's aides could see that he was intent on living out the Wagnerian tragedy, the Götterdämmerung, to the end, even if it meant the total destruction of Germany. Despite this intention, Hitler freed his comrades of their responsibilities and allowed them to leave, knowing they were making plans to escape.

Hitler made his way outside to greet a small group of Hitler Youth, many as young as thirteen, who had "volunteered" to serve in the Volkssturm, the People's Storm, the militia fighting to defend Berlin. No one had actually volunteered. Those who failed to meet a summons were hanged as deserters. Berlin in these days was littered with bodies hanging from trees and lampposts, young people executed by fanatical SS units for not answering a summons to serve. Photographs of Hitler's meeting with the Hitler Youth are sometimes cited by conspiracy theorists who claim they prove that Hitler at this point had been replaced by a body double—an allegation refuted by every eyewitness account from this period.

After greeting his old friends and the Hitler Youth, Hitler returned to the safety of the Führerbunker, where the atmosphere was now utterly without hope. Each day, the entire complex shook as Soviet artillery shells pounded the streets above. Yet Hitler would persist in hoping, almost until the last minute, that a dramatic rescue of some sort might still be in the cards. He seemed to believe that remaining Germany army units, such as the 9th Army, might fend off the Soviet onslaught, buying time. Two days later, at the military briefing held at 3:00 p.m. on April 22, Hitler received word that none of the German units had advanced and that the Russians were now inside the city.[3]

Upon hearing the news, Hitler erupted in rage and berated his generals—a scene memorialized in the German film *Downfall* and later made into hundreds of comic YouTube parodies.

EYEWITNESS ACCOUNT

"As we mechanically took our meals without noticing what we were eating we discussed ways to make sure of dying. 'The best way is to shoot yourself in the mouth. Your skull is shattered and you don't notice anything. Death is instantaneous,' Hitler told us. But we women were horrified at the idea. 'I want to be a beautiful corpse,' said Eva Braun, 'I shall take poison.'"

—*Traudl Junge, Hitler's last secretary*[4]

At this point, Hitler and everyone else in the Führerbunker knew that the end was near. Hitler told everyone that they should make plans to escape but that he intended to die in Berlin. He had already informed two generals, Jodl and Krebs, nearly a week before Mussolini was killed, that he had no intention of allowing his enemies to display his body as a trophy.

On April 23, evacuation efforts for military personnel and their families began in earnest. Hitler's personal physician, Theo Morell, and two of his four secretaries decided to flee, with Hitler's permission. But a surprising number of Führerbunker personnel vowed to stay until the end, including the two women secretaries Junge and Christian.

Joseph and Magda Goebbels, perhaps the most fanatical of all the top Nazi leaders, decided to join Hitler in death rather than save their own lives and those of their six young children. The Goebbels family moved from their nearby home into rooms in the Vorbunker, the small children playing in the corridors—in stark contrast to the evacuation efforts being made for other personnel and their dependents.

From April 23 through April 28, a surreal atmosphere pervaded this claustrophobic underground world. Hitler became increasingly agitated

Hitler's architect Albert Speer, shown here (left) with Karl Dönitz and Alfred Jodl after their arrest by British forces in May 1945, told Hitler in the course of his last visit to the Führer on April 24 that he had disobeyed his "Scorched Earth" order to destroy German industry, but Hitler allowed him to leave anyway. *Imperial War Museum*

as news of the "betrayals" of his most trusted aides reached him, one after the other.

First Göring, in his hideout in the Bavarian Alps, made the mistake of trying to "clarify," via telegram, his position as Hitler's supposedly chosen successor. Göring was meant to take over—so Hitler himself had decreed in 1941—but Hitler did not take his presumption well. Instead of verifying that Göring would indeed be the new leader of Germany, Hitler sacked him.

On that same day, April 23, Heinrich Himmler attempted to negotiate a separate peace with the Western Allies during a series of meetings at the northern German health resort of Hohenlychen with the Swedish diplomat Folke Bernadotte and Norbert Masur, a German Jew who was then the Swedish representative of the World Jewish Congress.

EYEWITNESS ACCOUNT

"Abruptly, Hitler asked me: 'What do you think? Should I stay here or fly to Berchtesgaden? [General] Jodl has told me that tomorrow is the last chance for that.'

"Spontaneously, I advised him to stay in Berlin. What would he do at Obersalzberg? With Berlin gone, the war would be over in any case, I said. 'It seems to me better, if it must be, that you end your life here in the capital as the Führer rather than in your weekend house.'…

"'I too have resolved to stay here. I only wanted to hear your view once more…I don't want my enemies to disgrace my body either. I've given orders that I be cremated. Frau Braun wants to depart this life with me, and I'll shoot Blondi beforehand.'"[6]

—*Albert Speer, Reich Minister of Armaments and War Production, reporting his last conversation with Hitler*

Himmler had been negotiating secretly for weeks with Bernadotte and Masur for the release of concentration camp prisoners, in a scheming and futile effort to lessen his culpability as a war criminal in the eyes of the Allies. He was doing everything in his power to cover up the crimes of the Third Reich, particularly the slaughter at the concentration camps. Himmler had sought out these last-minute meetings at the behest of his personal physician and physical therapist, the mysterious Finnish osteopath Dr. Felix Kersten, who used his position as Himmler's trusted confidant to help rescue an estimated sixty thousand Jews.[5]

The next day, April 24, Hitler's trusted aide, architect and armaments minister Albert Speer, visited Hitler one last time in the bunker.

A month earlier, on March 19, Hitler had issued what became known as the Nero or "Scorched Earth" Decree, an order to destroy all German industrial infrastructure so it could not fall into enemy hands. Appalled by the order, Speer had requested the sole authority to implement the decree—and then made sure it was never put into practice. At this last meeting, Speer confessed what he had done, or rather failed to do, and Hitler let him leave rather than punishing him for his disobedience.

Speer flew first to the small airfield at Gatow, just south of Berlin. He then climbed into a small training plane and, flying low above the streets, landed on the Berlin avenue known as the East-West Axis. "To the surprise of the few drivers on the broad avenue, we landed just in front of the Brandenburg Gate," Speer would write. As Speer recounted in his postwar memoir, *Inside the Third Reich*, Hitler told Speer at this final meeting that he intended to commit suicide and then have his body burned.[7] "I shall not fight personally," Hitler told him. "There is always the danger that I would only be wounded and fall into the hands of the Russians alive. I don't want my enemies to disgrace my body either. I've given orders that I be cremated."[8]

The next day, April 25, Hitler learned that the Soviet army had now completely surrounded Berlin. The only way out was by air—and that, too, was virtually impossible given the presence of substantial Soviet artillery.

Yet as if to demonstrate that the impossible might still be possible, Hitler received a final visitor from outside Berlin. On the night of April 25, Nazi flying ace Ritter von Greim, a distinguished Luftwaffe officer, flew into Berlin with Von Greim's mistress, the famous woman test pilot Hanna Reitsch. They landed at the small Luftwaffe airbase at Gatow, west of central Berlin. Accompanied by forty escort planes, Von Greim and Reitsch flew a Fieseler Storch, bravely dodged ferocious anti-aircraft fire, and somehow landed at the same makeshift airstrip as Speer's plane.

More as a statement of vengeance than anything else, Hitler wanted to appoint Von Greim as Göring's successor as the head of the Luftwaffe. The Führer promoted Von Greim to Field Marshal, but both he and

Reitsch were trapped in the bunker for the next three days, unable to leave because of the heavy Soviet anti-aircraft fire.

During this time, another drama played out that illustrated the monstrous nihilism that had enveloped Hitler's inner circle. It involved Eva Braun's brother-in-law, Hermann Fegelein, the husband of Braun's sister Gretl, who served as Heinrich Himmler's official representative at Führer headquarters. As Ada Petrova and Peter Watson recount in their authoritative 1995 book *The Death of Hitler*, the talk in the bunker increasingly turned to suicide. Both Hitler and Eva Braun said openly that this was their plan. Hermann Fegelein, understandably, wanted no part of it. He had been staying in one of the nearby military bunkers, but as

Hans Georg Otto Hermann Fegelein (1906–1945) was a playboy and officer in the Waffen-SS who married Gretl Braun, the sister of Hitler's longtime mistress and eventual wife Eva Braun. He left the bunker because he did not want to commit suicide with the other members of Hitler's inner circle. Hitler ordered Fegelein shot for desertion. *Deutsches Bundesarchiv*[9]

the talk in the Führerbunker turned more and more to suicide and prussic acid capsules were handed out to all remaining members of Hitler's inner circle, Fegelein decided to quietly slip away from his post. A famous playboy who had only married Braun's sister as a way to advance his career, Fegelein had no desire to end his life with the other hapless denizens of the bunker.

Unfortunately for Fegelein, Hitler, who knew him fairly well—the Nazi dictator had attended a wedding reception for Fegelein and Eva's sister in 1944 at his Berghof residence[10]—summoned his mistress's brother-in-law on April 27. When it was discovered that Fegelein was not at his post, a search party led by one of Hitler's bodyguards, Peter Högl, was sent out, despite the fierce combat raging on the nearby streets. Högl knew where Fegelein had gone because one of the SS guards had driven him to his apartment. Incredibly, the soldiers were able to make it to Fegelein's home in a Berlin neighborhood just west of the Tiergarten and south of the River Spree. According to some accounts, they found him in bed with a woman not his wife and apparently making preparations to escape to Sweden—although how that would be possible, with Berlin now surrounded, is not clear. Fegelein was falling down drunk, and in his possession were documents concerning his boss Himmler's recent attempts to negotiate with the Allies.

Desperate, Fegelein called Eva Braun by phone and managed to get through to the Führerbunker, but she refused to intervene and told him that he had to return. He supposedly told her that she had to leave Hitler and flee, that this was the only way to save her life. The soldiers dragged the intoxicated Fegelein back to the bunker complex, informed him that he was being demoted, and locked him in one of the storage rooms.

The next day, April 28, events occurred that sealed Fegelein's fate. The entire day, Hitler was awaiting word about a last-ditch rescue operation supposedly being conducted by the Wehrmacht 12th Army, commanded by the "boy general" Walther Wenck. Recently reorganized following the American assault across the Elbe River, the 12th Army was supposed to meet up with what was left of the 9th Army and push Soviet forces back enough so that the inhabitants of the Führerbunker could escape. It was not to be. "Where is Wenck?" Hitler demanded to know. "What is happening to the 12th Army?" While waiting for word about a possible rescue, Hitler and his closest aides, Martin Bormann and Joseph Goebbels, discussed their upcoming suicides in detail.

At this time, Hitler gave aviatrix Hanna Reitsch two capsules of poison to use if needed and, according to a once-classified U.S. Army intelligence briefing from after the war, told her, "I do not wish that one of us falls to the Russians alive, nor do I wish that our bodies be found

EYEWITNESS ACCOUNT

"The often-alleged assertions that there was drunken debauchery, indiscipline and 'mutiny' in the Führer-bunker are all nonsense. While Hitler lived, everything proceeded precisely as before. There was a bunker below the New Reich Chancellery containing quarters for everybody not required to live in the Führer-bunker, and what went on there I have no idea. Naturally we took alcohol, but still in moderation."

—*Heinz Linge, Hitler's valet*[12]

by them. Eva and I will have our bodies burned. You will devise your own method."[11]

During the day, Hitler went back above ground and again inspected what was left of his once seemingly impregnable Reich Chancellery building. There is a photograph of him, the last known photograph taken of Hitler, staring out at the ruins.

No word came. Wenck's meagre forces were utterly blocked by the massive Soviet Army that now had Berlin surrounded. The 12th Army got no further than the outer suburb of Potsdam.

Around 9:00 p.m., Hitler's press attaché Heinz Lorenz, who would later write a book about his experiences in the bunker, heard a broadcast from the BBC radio—a report that none other than Heinrich Himmler, the second- or third-most powerful man in the Third Reich, was in negotiations with the Swedish diplomat Count Bernadotte about the surrender of all German forces in the west. Lorenz marched down the long, dark underground corridors until he reached the Führerbunker, where Hitler was in a meeting with the aviators. Lorenz gave a printout of the BBC report to Hitler's valet, Heinz Linge, and Bormann and Goebbels.

For Hitler, the news about Himmler was the last straw, the ultimate betrayal. The Führer exploded in rage—an eruption of fury that went on for hours. Reitsch recalled that his face went from pink to bright crimson. He wanted vengeance.

The hapless Fegelein, Himmler's close aide, was dragged from his makeshift jail cell, still barely able to stand from intoxication, to face Hitler. Gestapo chief Heinrich Müller interrogated Fegelein, and he confessed he had known about Himmler's plans.

Hitler then ordered that Fegelein be court martialed for attempted desertion, and, according to an account by one of Hitler's generals in the 1970s, an ad hoc tribunal made up of Generals Wilhelm Burgdorf and Hans Krebs, SS-Gruppenführer Johann Rattenhuber, and SS-Brigade-führer Wilhelm Mohnke was set up.

According to Hitler's secretary Traudl Junge, Eva Braun begged Hitler to spare Fegelein on account of her sister Gretl, who was then nine months pregnant with Fegelein's child. But he refused.

Hitler conspiracy theorists would later claim that Fegelein's court martial was completely staged—that he had never tried to desert and that he really escaped Berlin along with Hitler and his sister-in-law Eva Braun. Yet Hitler's secretary Junge reported that Fegelein was dragged up the staircase of the bunker to the Reich Chancellery garden and shot in the back of the head with a machine pistol "like a dog."[13] Misch claimed he was shot with a machine pistol in the corridor to the Reich Chancellery.[14] His body was quickly buried outside in the Reich Chancellery garden.

Shortly after Fegelein's brutal execution, Hitler received word that the Russians had already reached Potsdamer Platz, the heart of Berlin, and were just a few blocks from the bunker. Yet miraculously, another plane—a small training aircraft—had somehow managed to thread its way through the anti-aircraft fire and land on the makeshift landing strip in the nearby Tiergarten. This was Von Greim and Reitsch's ride out of Berlin.

At midnight, Hitler met with his new chief of the Luftwaffe, Von Greim, and ordered him to round up whatever was left of the German air force and throw everything he had at the Russians in Berlin. The Luftwaffe was to provide air support for Wenck's supposed rescue operation. The Führer also ordered Von Greim to have Himmler arrested and summarily executed.

While Hitler was giving Von Greim his final instructions, Eva Braun gave Reitsch a letter for her sister Gretl, along with some jewelry. The letter did not mention the execution of Gretl's husband just an hour before, however. Reitsch also took a packet of letters from the other inhabitants of the bunker.

Shortly after midnight Von Greim and Reitsch bade everyone in the bunker farewell and made their way slowly and carefully to the makeshift runway in the Tiergarten near the Brandenburg Gate. It was a wide avenue formerly known as the Charlottenburger Chausée and used for large parades. Early in the morning of April 29, Von Greim and Reitsch were able to take off in a small Arado Ar 96 training aircraft with Reitsch at the controls—the last plane known to have left Berlin at the end of the war.

Soviet soldiers saw the plane take off from the makeshift air strip, assumed it was carrying Adolf Hitler, and tried furiously to shoot it down. But Reitsch was able to gain altitude quickly, and the small plane

German flying ace and test pilot Hanna Reitsch (1912–1979), an ardent Nazi, proposed in 1944 that German pilots adopt the suicide tactics of Japan's kamikazes. The night of April 28, she flew her lover, newly appointed Luftwaffe chief Robert Ritter von Greim (1892–1945), out of Berlin in what is believed to have been the final flight to leave the city at the end of the war. *Deutsches Bundesarchiv*[15]

EYEWITNESS ACCOUNT

"On our second day in the bunker, the 27th of April, I was summoned to Hitler's study. His face was now even paler, and had become flaccid and putty-coloured, like that of a dotard. He gave me two phials of poison so that, as he said, Greim and I should have at all times, 'freedom of choice.' Then he said that if the hope of the relief of Berlin by General Wenck was not realized, he and Eva Braun had freely decided that they would depart out of this life."[16]

—*Hanna Reitsch, Nazi test pilot who flew the last plane out of Berlin*

was soon lost in the clouds. The pilots' escape gave birth to rumors that persist to this day that Hanna Reitsch had flown Hitler out of Berlin on April 29.

Reitsch and Von Greim flew north to the small town of Rechlin, where they landed at three o'clock in the morning. After giving Hitler's orders to the Luftwaffe staff, Von Greim and Reitsch then took off again and flew to Plön, a small town to the north, the headquarters of Admiral Dönitz.

Hitler's Wedding and Last Will and Testament

With the departure of Von Greim and Reitsch, events in the Führerbunker escalated furiously.

In that surreal atmosphere, where there was only artificial light, everyone stayed up all night and slept when they could, usually in their clothes. Shortly after midnight, in the wee hours of Sunday, April 29, Hitler took aside his valet Heinz Linge, the thirty-two-year-old former bricklayer from Bremen, and told him that he would like him to leave the bunker but that before he did, he had a special job for him to do. Hitler needed him to track down at least 200 liters of gasoline.

As Linge recounted in his memoir, Hitler told him that his intention was to commit suicide along with Eva Braun and that, after they did so, Linge was to burn their bodies so they could not be found by the Russians.

"I have another personal job for you," Hitler told Linge. "What I must do now is what I have ordered every commander at every redoubt to do: hold out to the death. This order is also binding on myself, since I feel that I am here as the commandant of Berlin. You should hold in readiness woolen blankets in my bedroom and enough petrol for two cremations. I am going to shoot myself together with Eva Braun. You will wrap our bodies in woolen blankets, carry them up to the garden, and there burn them."

Linge snapped to attention, shouted, "Jawohl, Mein Führer," and left Hitler's bedroom.[17]

Linge immediately called Hitler's chauffeur, Erich Kempka, who was staying in the Vorbunker, and told him what Hitler wanted.

In Kempka's own account, it was Günsche, not Linge, who called him with the request for 200 liters of petrol.

"A mere 200 liters?" Kempka replied, incredulous.

At this stage in the war, gasoline was a rare and precious commodity. Linge or Günsche told the driver that he must not fail. He was to drain whatever gasoline he could find from abandoned vehicles and deliver it all to the bunker's emergency exit in the Reich Chancellery garden. Kempka replied that he would do what he could.[18]

Next, Hitler asked his secretary Traudl Junge to join him in the conference room. He wished to dictate to her his Last Will and Testament—first what he called his "Political Testament" and then his private will. She transcribed Hitler's words by means of shorthand, which she would shortly turn into a typed manuscript.

According to Junge's memoir, Hitler referred to notes as he dictated, leading her to think he had had help from Goebbels in drafting the document. The Political Testament is a long, meandering restatement of Hitler's most insane anti-Semitic beliefs. In it, he claims that he never wanted war in 1939; it had been "provoked entirely by those international statesmen who were either of Jewish origin or who worked in the Jewish interest."

As we have already seen, Hitler also explicitly stated his intention to kill himself. "I do not want to fall into the hands of enemies who need another show, arranged by Jews, for the amusement of their ill-guided masses," he dictated to Junge. "I have therefore resolved to remain in Berlin and there to choose death of my own free will. . . ."

Hitler expelled both Himmler and Göring from the Nazi Party and proceeded to dictate a lengthy list of new government appointments—and to order some of the appointed officials, including Goebbels, not to join him in death but to carry on without him. As the bunker shook violently from artillery barrages on the city streets up above, even the ever-loyal secretary Junge thought the entire exercise absurd. Germany plainly wouldn't have a Nazi government for much longer.

Hitler's private will is much shorter but equally blunt. He gave all of his considerable possessions to the Nazi party or, if it no longer existed, to the German nation. He then again stated his plan to commit suicide. "Myself and my wife choose death to escape the disgrace of being forced to resign or surrender," Hitler dictated. "It is our wish to be cremated immediately at the place where I have done the greater part of my work during the twelve years of service to my people."

With this task completed, Hitler left the conference room for his bedroom as Junge took her shorthand notes and began typing out the documents.[19]

Around 1:00 a.m., Hitler and Eva Braun appeared arm in arm and walked to the map room. Braun was wearing a simple black dress, the traditional wedding color in Germany, with sequins. Her hair had been done by her maid, Liesl Ostertag, one of just five women left in the bunker. Braun had been Hitler's secret mistress for nearly sixteen years, since he first met her, a young girl of seventeen, in 1929 at the Hoffman

Photographic Studio in Munich. Hitler had asked her to keep away from the bunker, but she had returned on April 15, determined to stay with him at all costs. Now Hitler was rewarding Braun's misguided loyalty by finally marrying her.

It was a simple ceremony. Goebbels had arranged for a city magistrate none of them knew, a man named Walther Wagner, to make his way down to the bunker to perform the ceremony. Hitler and Braun sat on one side of the map table, Wagner on the other. Martin Bormann and Goebbels were the witnesses.[20]

Wagner asked some personal details to fill out the official marriage certificate, then took them through the traditional wedding vows. Both Hitler and Braun both swore that they were of "pure Aryan descent and free of any hereditary diseases," and the couple placed gold rings on each other's fingers—rings stolen from the bodies of executed Gestapo prisoners. Hitler and Braun then signed the wedding certificate, which is still

Hitler having lunch with his longtime secret mistress, Eva Braun (1912–1945), in an undated photograph. Hitler married Braun in a civil ceremony at around one o'clock in the morning on April 29. *Shutterstock*

extant—and Braun made a mistake. She first started her last name with a B, then crossed it out and wrote, "Eva Hitler geb Braun." *Geb* is the German word for the French *née*.[21]

After the wedding, the newlyweds proceeded into the main corridor to receive the well wishes of the remaining bunker personnel and then withdrew to their private rooms for a wedding breakfast and reception. They were joined by Hitler's two secretaries, as well as by Bormann and Goebbels. Everyone sat drinking champagne and chatting until about three in the morning.

After a time, Hitler left again with Junge to sign the typescript and copies of his two testaments. She presented Hitler with neat copies, and he signed them, as did three witnesses—Goebbels, Borman, and Nicholas von Bulow. The documents were dated 4:00 a.m., April 29, and were given to three men to smuggle out of Berlin—deputy press attaché Heinz Lorenz, Hitler's army adjutant Willy Johannmeyer, and Bormann's adjutant Wilhelm Zander. All three were soon captured by Allied forces and the documents discovered.

At this point, Hitler decided to go to sleep. But when he left for his room, Goebbels took Junge aside and insisted that he, too, wished to write his own testament, as an appendix to Hitler's. Hitler had ordered Goebbels to flee Berlin to carry out his mission, but this, Goebbels now stated, he could not do. "For this reason, together with my wife, and on behalf of my children, who are too young to speak for themselves, but who would unreservedly agree with this decision if they were old enough, I express an unalterable resolution not to leave the Reich capital, even if it falls," Goebbels dictated, "but rather, at the side of the Führer, to end a life which will have no further value to me if I cannot spend it in the service of the Führer, and by his side." Junge dutifully typed up Goebbels's hideous declaration, thinking of the small children upstairs in the Vorbunker, with whom she had often played.[22]

The rest of Sunday passed slowly. Hitler slept late, as was his custom.

At noon and then again at four in the afternoon, Hitler joined the regular military update conferences attended by his remaining generals,

EYEWITNESS ACCOUNT

"Suddenly Goebbels bursts in. I look at his agitated face, which is white as chalk. Tears are running down his cheeks. He speaks to me because there's no one else around to whom he can pour out his heart. His usually clear voice is stifled by tears and shaking. 'The Führer wants me to leave Berlin, Frau Junge! I am to take up a leading post in the new government. But I can't leave Berlin, I cannot leave the Führer's side. I am Gauleiter of Berlin, and my place is here. If the Führer is dead my life is pointless.'"

—*Traudl Junge*, Hitler's Last Secretary[23]

Bormann, Goebbels, and a few others. By this point, Russians were within a few hundred yards of the bunker. The generals estimated that the Soviets would reach the bunker no later than Tuesday, May 1. Hitler had one day left.

In the afternoon, Hitler decided to test the cyanide capsules they had all been given on his beloved Alsatian dog, Blondi. Even during the bleakest hours in the bunker, Hitler had found time to take Blondi outside in the garden or have someone else do so. Now, one of Hitler's physicians put a cyanide capsule in Blondi's mouth and held her snout closed. The dog struggled and yelped in pain and soon collapsed, dead.

Earlier, as a parting gift, Hitler gave his two female secretaries, Junge and Christian, each one of the same capsules. "I am very sorry that I can't give you a better farewell present," he said.[24]

9 THE DEATH OF ADOLF HITLER

By the time Hitler awoke late Monday morning, April 30, he knew he did not have much time left. The Russians were now in all central Berlin's subway tunnels, even in the tunnels next to the Führerbunker. Despite this knowledge, Hitler appeared calm.

He had lunch at 2:00 p.m. with his secretaries, Junge and Christian, and the cook Constanze Manzialy. It was plain pasta with a cabbage and raisin salad. All non-essential personnel were now ordered to leave the Führerbunker, and the thick main door leading to the outer corridors was locked.

Earlier, during his lunch break upstairs in the New Reich Chancellery building, the SS bodyguard Rochus Misch had spotted the head of the Gestapo, Heinrich Müller. He was nervous that the Gestapo might be planning to eliminate all the surviving witnesses in the bunker, with either explosives or poison gas. Misch started whispering to the Führerbunker's chief engineer, Johannes Hentschell, who had been present during the construction, asking him if the bunker could be wired with explosives. Hentschell shrugged off Misch's concerns.[1]

Allegedly the last picture ever taken of Adolf Hitler (right) as he inspects, along with his adjutant Julius Schaub, the ruins of Albert Speer's New Reich Chancellery building. *akg-images/Ullstein bild*

After lunch, around 2:45 p.m., Eva Braun appeared, wearing another dress, this one dark blue (some said black) with white roses. The remaining staff were once again summoned for a final goodbye.

There were eleven people present: Bormann, Goebbels, Burgdorf, Krebs, Hewel, Naumann, Voss, Rattenhuger, Günsche, Linge, Christian, Junge, Krueger, and Manzialy. The chauffeur, Kempka, would return shortly with five Jerry cans of gasoline, which he placed, as ordered, just outside the emergency exit door in the garden. Magda Goebbels was upstairs in the Vorbunker with her six children.

Eva Braun shook the hand of Hitler's valet, Heinz Linge, thanked him for his loyal service to her husband, and asked him to keep it a secret from her sister how her husband had died. To Junge, Eva Braun said, "'Do your best to get out. It may still be possible. And give Bavaria my love."[2]

After shaking Hitler's quivering hand, the secretary took one last look at Eva Braun and decided to join the Goebbels children upstairs. From the will Goebbels had dictated, she knew what their parents had planned for them.

Goebbels made one last plea for Hitler to escape—knowing that was the only way he, his wife, and his six children could survive. "Mein Führer, it's still possible to escape!" Goebbels told Hitler. "You can oversee the war from Obersalzberg.... Mein Führer, I beg you to consider."

Hitler shook his head. "You know my decision," he said firmly. "I'm not going to change it. You and your family can of course leave Berlin."

Goebbels nodded. "We will stand by you and follow your example, Mein Führer," he replied.

Hitler and Eva then proceeded towards Hitler's study, with Hitler leaning upon Linge's arm for support. At the doorway, he gave his trusted valet his final order.

"I'm going to go now," he said. "You know what you have to do. Ensure that my body is burned and my remaining possessions destroyed."

Linge asked one last question: what should they fight for now?

"For the Coming Man," Hitler replied enigmatically as he walked through the doorway.[3]

Linge shut the door to the study. Suddenly, Magda Goebbels appeared at his side, distraught. She, like her husband, now wanted to make a last-minute appeal for Hitler's life—and the lives of her children. Linge let her inside for a final brief word with Hitler, but she was quickly rebuffed. The valet closed the door for the final time.

Most of the staff left the area. Some went back upstairs to put on records once again.

Outside Hitler's study door stood a handful of Hitler's inner circle—Günsche, Goebbels, Bormann, and Artur Axmann, head of the Hitler Youth.

Around 3:30 p.m., a single gunshot was heard, loud enough that Helmut Goebbels, aged ten, heard it upstairs in the Vorbunker and yelled out, "Bullseye!" He thought it was an artillery shell. Some but not all witnesses heard the shot, depending upon where they were in the bunker.

There is disagreement concerning who entered Hitler's study first. But the best evidence is that it was Hitler's valet Linge, around 3:40 p.m. He first opened the door to the anteroom and then walked slowly to the door to Hitler's study and opened it. Apparently overcome by the smell of gunshot power and poison in the air, Linge backed out quickly, regained his composure after a moment, and then went back into Hitler's study, followed closely by Günsche. After a few moments, Bormann, Goebbels, and Axmann entered as well.[4]

SS bodyguard and telephone operator Misch got up from his station and looked in through the open doors. "I looked for only a few seconds but I have never forgotten what I saw," Misch wrote in his 2013 memoir, *Hitler's Last Witness.*[5]

Hitler and Braun were side by side on the blue sofa—Hitler on the right side, leaning on the right armrest. There was a clearly visible wound of some sort on his right temple. He lay slumped to one side, his head forward on a small table, with copious blood on the arm of the sofa and on the carpet below. Two guns lay at his feet. One was Hitler's pistol, a Walther 7.65. The other was Hitler's backup pistol, a Walther 6.35.[6]

Braun was lying next to Hitler, her bare feet curled up on the sofa. There was no sign of a gunshot wound on her, but next to her was her own Walther 6.35 pistol (for a total of three) and the brass box that contained the cyanide capsules.

"I saw Hitler slumped with his head on the table," recalled Misch, who died in 2013 at the age of ninety-six. "His eyes were open and staring." Braun had her knees drawn tightly up to her chest. She was wearing a dark blue, almost black dress with white frills, but Misch saw no blood.[8] She had a look of intense pain on her face. Hitler had lied when he told her cyanide poisoning is painless.

The surviving eyewitnesses to the corpses—Misch, Günsche, Linge, Axmann, and later Kempka—would later disagree about precisely how

EYEWITNESS ACCOUNT

"I opened the door and went in, Bormann following me. He turned white as chalk and stared at me helplessly. Adolf Hitler and Eva Braun were seated on the sofa. Both were dead. Hitler had shot himself in the right temple with his 7.65-mm pistol. . . . His head was inclined a little towards the wall. Blood had splattered on the carpet near the sofa. To his right beside him sat his wife. She had drawn up her legs on the sofa. Her contorted face betrayed how she had died. Cyanide poisoning."

—*Heinz Linge, Hitler's valet*[7]

they thought Hitler and Braun had killed themselves. None of them had any medical training, and none really examined the bodies closely. Nevertheless, they each had their own opinion. When Russian interrogators would demand to know why the men had not sent for one of the nearby doctors to verify that Hitler was dead, Günsche would reply that it was simply obvious that both Hitler and Braun were dead. The chauffeur, Kempka, thought a physician, Dr. Ludwig Stumpfegger, arrived and certified the death of both Hitler and Braun.[9]

Kempka, who was not in the bunker when the shot was fired but soon arrived on the scene outside Hitler's study, would tell British intelligence officer Trevor-Roper that Hitler had shot himself in the mouth. He had heard this, he said, from Günsche. This became the official account in Trevor-Roper's book, *The Last Days of Hitler*, even though Günsche would later testify that he had told Kempka no such thing, merely that Hitler had shot himself. Apparently Kempka wrongly assumed that Günsche meant that Hitler had shot himself in the mouth. Günsche himself would tell investigators that Hitler shot himself in the

EYEWITNESS ACCOUNT

"We saluted the Führer once more, then he went into his room with Eva and closed the door. Goebbels, Bormann, Axmann, Hewel, Kempka and I stood out in the corridor waiting. It may have been ten minutes, but seemed an eternity to us, before the shot broke the silence. After a few seconds Goebbels opened the door and we went in. The Führer had shot himself in the mouth and bitten on a poison capsule too. His skull was shattered and looked dreadful. Eva Braun hadn't used her pistol, she just took the poison. We wrapped the Führer's head in a blanket, and Goebbels, Axmann and Kempka carried the corpse up all those stairs and into the park. . . . Up in the park we put the two bodies down side by side, a few steps from the entrance to the bunker. We couldn't go far because the firing was so fierce, so we picked a bomb crater quite close. Then Kempka and I poured petrol over the bodies, and I stood in the entrance and threw a burning rag on them. Both bodies went up in flames at once."

—*SS guard Otto Günsche (as quoted by Traudl Junge)*[10]

right temple, while Linge would say the left temple—but then change his story to say it was the right temple.

Most of the eyewitnesses agreed that Braun must have simply swallowed poison because there was no visible wound on her body.

Conspiracy theorists would later claim these minor discrepancies mean that all of the eyewitness accounts about Hitler's death are therefore unreliable. But in fact, homicide investigators routinely have to piece together a plausible narrative of an event based on conflicting eyewitness testimonies.

In the decades to come, a lot of debate revolved around the question of whether Hitler had poisoned or shot himself. The Germans preferred to say Hitler shot himself (supposedly more courageous), while the Russians insisted he likely swallowed poison (considered an easier, more cowardly death).

Later interviews with survivors of the bunkers indicated that Hitler had consulted with his physicians about the best possible method and had been told he should do both—bite down on a cyanide capsule while simultaneously squeezing the trigger of his gun. Many historians now believe this is a likely scenario, but without detailed physical evidence, no one can be sure.

Linge fetched the wool blankets that Hitler had ordered be placed in his study precisely for this purpose. He wrapped Hitler's body in one so that only the legs, with Hitler's distinctive black trousers, were visible. Conspiracy theorists would later make much of the fact that when Hitler's

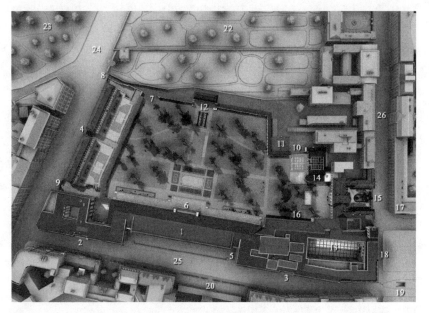

In this diagram of the New Chancellery complex, the exit to the Führerbunker, where Hitler's body was burned, is number 10 is in the diagram. *Wikimedia Commons*[11]

body was taken out of the bunker, his face was not visible. Linge also wrapped Braun's body in a blanket, but not as thoroughly—her head and face could be seen.

Linge, Günsche, Kempka, and SS guard Ewald Lindloff carried Hitler's body down the central corridor to the stairway leading up to the emergency exit. It was a narrow staircase, about three feet wide, thirty-six steps in four flights of nine steps each.

Kempka looked to the side and saw Bormann, whom he despised, carrying the body of Eva Braun, one of his big paw-like hands clutching her breast. "Eva had hated Bormann," Kempka would say later. It infuriated Kempka that Braun was being carried "like a sack of potatoes," and so at the bottom of the staircase he took Braun's body from Bormann and then handed it to Günsche, who was stronger. Günsche carried Braun's body up the long narrow staircase to the exit.[12]

According to a drawing made by eyewitness Erich Mansfeld, an SS guard, and published for the first time only in 2019, the bodies were then placed in a shallow trench just three yards to the left of the bunker's emergency exit and about twenty-five feet from Mansfeld's observation tower.[13]

Günsche, Linge, Kempka, and the SS soldier were followed out of the bunker by the last of Hitler's high command, Goebbels, Bormann, Dr. Stumpfegger, and Generals Krebs and Burgdorf.

Despite the precautions that Hitler's inner circle had taken for secrecy, the disposition of Hitler and Braun's bodies was apparently seen by at least four other eyewitnesses. Besides Erich Mansfeld, the guard on duty in the conical observation tower just a few yards from the entrance, the eyewitnesses were Hermann Karnau, a bunker employee who just happened to be standing near the same observation tower; Harry Mengerschausen, an SS bodyguard patrolling the Reich Chancellery building 600 yards away; and Hilco Poppen, another Reich Chancellery guard, who was only 150 yards away.

Obeying his orders from Hitler, Linge and Kempka quickly took one of the four Jerry cans of gasoline, each holding 20 liters, or about 5.3

EYEWITNESS ACCOUNT

"[SS Major Otto] Günsche and I lay Eva Hitler beside her husband. . . . Tensely we waited for the shelling in our area to die down before pouring petrol over the corpses . . . Alongside me, Günsche and Linge carried out the same duties for Eva. Her dress moved in the wind until finally drenched with fuel. . . . My glance fell on a large piece of rag near the fire brigade hoses at the bunker exit. . . . I set light to the rag and once it was afire lobbed it toward the petrol-soaked corpses. As we watched, in seconds a bright flame flared up, accompanied by billowing black smoke."

—*Erich Kempka, Hitler's chauffeur*[16]

U.S. gallons, and began dousing both of the bodies lying in the shallow trench with gasoline. "I was trembling as I poured the contents over the two bodies, and repeatedly I told myself I could not do it," Kempka would recall, "but I was conscious of it being Hitler's last order and my sense of duty overcame my sensitivity."[14] However, just at the moment Linge and Kempka began pouring the gasoline, the small group came under fire from nearby Russian artillery. Explosions erupted all around them, and the air was filled with dust and acrid black smoke. The artillery fire forced the members of the cremation party to duck repeatedly into the safety of the bunker's concrete exit.

Taking turns, Linge, Kempka, and Günsche ran to where the bodies were lying and poured more gasoline on them. From the doorway, Linge or Goebbels tried to set the bodies on fire with matches Goebbels had brought but failed because of the wind.

Finally either Kempka or Linge[15] took a rag, poured some gasoline on it, lit the rag on fire with Goebbels's matches, and then tossed the burning rag from the bunker entrance onto the two bodies in the shallow trench to the left. The bodies immediately exploded into flames—the Viking funeral that Hitler had wanted.

The members of the tiny group stood at attention for a brief moment, raising their arms in the Nazi salute, before the continuing artillery fire again forced them all to flee to the safety of the concrete bunker.

Right as they did so, bunker employee Hermann Karnau, unable to enter the bunker main exit because the door was locked shut, appeared just as the door closed and the bodies burst into flames. He briefly watched them burn and then also went into the bunker through the emergency exit door. Periodically, SS soldiers returned to the bodies and poured more gasoline on them, keeping the fire going. Karnau was soon ordered to keep watch over the remains for the next two hours.

After dark, when none of the other SS soldiers were around, Karnau and guard Erich Mansfeld walked over to inspect the smoldering bodies. The flesh had been burned away from the legs, and only the bones of Hitler's corpse were visible. The Nazi dictator and his wife were, as Hitler's biographer Ian Kershaw put it, "two charcoaled, shriveled, unrecognizable" bodies.[17] An artillery shell had scored a near direct hit on the trench, further damaging the corpses.

Around 6:00 p.m., Günsche ordered SS guard Ewald Lindloff to bury what was left of the bodies. Lindloff rolled the charred corpses onto a large sheet of canvas and moved them from the place where they had been burned to a deeper bomb crater about ten to fifteen feet in front of the bunker emergency exit, directly abutting the alley Hermann Göring Strasse.

Using a spade, Lindloff proceeded to fill the crater with dirt and smooth it over. He would be killed two days later, on May 2, when a large group of German soldiers and civilians was mowed down by Soviet troops as they attempted to cross the Weidendammer Bridge.

Four or five hours after this, the guard Mansfeld returned to the observation tower and saw, in the light of overhead flares, that the bodies were no longer visible in the sandy trench where they had been burned.

According to eyewitnesses, the bodies of Hitler and Eva Braun were placed in a shallow ditch about six feet from the emergency exit of the Führerbunker (center left, shown in 1947), doused with gasoline, and set on fire. Erich Mansfeld, a guard in the conical tower, watched the events unfold. *Deutsches Bundesarvhiv*[18]

However, he did notice that the bomb crater directly in front of the exit had been filled in with fresh soil. He assumed correctly that the bodies of Hitler and Eva Braun had been moved and buried there.

When the Western Allies investigated Hitler's death, this was the last known account of what happened to Hitler's body. Hugh Trevor-Roper, in his authoritative summary of the final events in the bunker, concluded that Hitler's "bones have never been found." The Western Allies would not learn the truth about what happened to Hitler's body for another twenty-five years.

A complicating factor for Russian investigators looking for Hitler's body was that the entire Reich Chancellery garden was littered with bodies and body parts—German soldiers killed by Soviet troops in the fight for Berlin, executed by the Nazis, or cast outside from the nearby hospital in the Reich Chancellery basement. The Russians were to find no fewer than 166 corpses in this area, many blown to bits by the near-constant artillery fire. All of this would fuel the later rumors of Hitler's escape and survival.

It was now the evening of Monday, April 30. Adolf Hitler was dead by his own hand, his blackened corpse smoldering up above the Führerbunker in the bombed out remains of the Reich Chancellery garden. The few remaining survivors of the Führerbunker, about two dozen men and four women, now had to face their own fates squarely. Soviet soldiers were only a few hundred yards away and would likely burst into the underground fortress at any moment.

The remaining Nazi authorities in the Führerbunker—Goebbels, Bormann and Generals Krebs and Burgdorf—decided to begin negotiating with their Russian counterparts.

Goebbels drafted a letter explaining that Hitler had killed himself the previous day and outlining conditions for a cease-fire and partial surrender. The letter stated that Hitler had passed the authority for the German government to himself, Bormann, and Admiral Dönitz and that the bearer of the letter was authorized to negotiate a truce or cease-fire so long as Admiral Dönitz agreed. Goebbels gave the letter to General Krebs.

Krebs spoke fluent Russian from a stint as military attaché in Moscow years earlier, so, after alerting the Russians via radio, he set off around 10:00 p.m. on April 30, with a white flag flying, to find the Russian command post. He brought with him Colonel Theodor von Dufving, chief-of-staff to General Helmuth Weidling, the last military commander in Berlin, and a Latvian translator. Von Dufving didn't want to rely solely on Krebs's rusty Russian for such important negotiations.

It was a dangerous journey, crossing the dark streets of Berlin, with bullets still flying. Somehow, however, the two German officers and their Latvian translator found their way to the Russian command post.

The contrast between Krebs and his Russian counterpart could not have been greater. General Vasily Chuikov, commander of the Russian force invading Berlin, was a large-boned son of a Russian peasant, a no-nonsense Soviet commander. Krebs was dressed like the Prussian officer he was, his head shaved bald, even sporting a ridiculous monocle. Yet he was scared—and, the Russians would later claim, showed it.

The Russians pretended they already knew everything that Krebs told them—that Hitler was dead and that the new government wanted to negotiate a surrender. In fact, they had known none of it.

Chuikov told Krebs that Hitler's death made no difference. Allied forces would accept unconditional surrender or nothing. The Russians demanded an answer by 4:00 p.m. the following day, May 1, or they would resume their attack.

According to Linge, who heard the story when the negotiators returned to the bunker, the negotiations became quite heated.

"You are the strong party, that we know and you believe it, too," Krebs told Chuikov.

"Naturally, we know that," the Russian general replied. "You will keep fighting in vain and lose people. I ask you, what is the point in your fighting on?"

Krebs looked at his adversary.

"We shall fight to the last man," he said.[19]

Krebs and Von Dufving returned to the bunker around dawn. The two men told Goebbels and Bormann what the Russians had said. As far as the two Nazi leaders were concerned, it meant the end. Hitler had forbidden surrender. For Goebbels, it was a death sentence—not just for himself but for his wife and children as well. He had desperately hoped for a way out at the last minute, a negotiated truce "with honor." But there would be, could be, no honor.

Around 11:00 a.m. and then again at 3:18 p.m. on May 1, Bormann sent telegrams to Dönitz at his headquarters in Plön, informing him that he, Dönitz, was now leader of the Reich. At this point, none of the German people knew Hitler was dead—and German soldiers were still fighting to the death to defend him.

General Weidling, the ranking military commander in Berlin, insisted that a cease-fire must be declared immediately to stop the senseless loss of life. As far as he was concerned, Hitler's suicide was a cowardly act of betrayal, an abandonment of the German people when they needed leadership the most. When he issued a general cease-fire the next day, he told his troops that Hitler, through his suicide, had "abandoned those who had sword him loyalty" and that their oath was therefore no longer in force.[20]

From this point forward, it was the primary aim of the German military commanders, and of Admiral Dönitz and Albert Speer, to do everything they could to save the lives of the surviving troops. That meant maneuvering, as far as was possible, so that most units could surrender to the Western Allies, the Americans and the British, and not to the revenge-minded Soviets. Eisenhower, like the Russians, insisted on unconditional surrender, yet Dönitz's negotiations were able to save 1.8 million German soldiers from being captured by the Russians.

The Death of the Goebbels Family

While most of the denizens of the Führerbunker would eventually try to escape, Joseph Goebbels and his wife Magda—the most fanatical of all Nazis—were determined to follow their leader's example even in death. On April 28, Magda Goebbels had written to her eldest son from an earlier marriage, in a letter carried out of the bunker by the pilot Reitsch, that "life will not be worth living in the world that comes after Hitler and National Socialism."

On Tuesday evening, May 1, around 6:00 p.m., Magda arranged for a Nazi dentist, Dr. Helmut Kunz, to inject all six of the Goebbels young children with morphine in their beds—they were told it was a vaccine—so they would be unconscious. Many blamed Magda for what happened next, but, according to Albert Speer, it was Dr. Goebbels who had

Even hardened Nazis were horrified by the plan of Nazi propaganda minister Joseph Goebbels and his wife Magda (left) to poison all six of their young children. Magda's son from a previous marriage, Harald Quandt (center top), survived the war. *Deutsches Bundesarchiv*[21]

decided in early April that "my wife and children are not to survive me."[22] The master propagandist couldn't bear to think of what the world would say to his children about him after his death.

It is unclear whether it was Magda herself or, more likely, Hitler's personal physician Ludwig Stumpfegger, but one of them then went from bunkbed to bunkbed putting cyanide ampules between the children's teeth and cracking them, killing the children within seconds. In her letter to her eldest son, Magda had written that "a merciful God will understand me when I myself help them to a deliverance (*Erlösung*)."

There is evidence that the eldest child, Helga, aged twelve, may have awoken and resisted her killer. Contrary to what Hitler had told his subordinates, death by cyanide poisoning is, while quick, excruciating, causing intense pain. Even the hardened Nazis in the Führerbunker, who

EYEWITNESS ACCOUNT

"The imploring pleas of the women and some of the staff, who suggested to Frau Goebbels that they would bring the children—Helga, Holde, Hilde, Heide, Hedda and Helmut—out of the bunker and care for them, went unheard. I was thinking about my own wife and children who were in relative safety when Frau Goebbels came at 1800 hours and asked me in a dry, emotional voice to go up with her to the former Führerbunker where a room had been set up for her children. Once there she sank down in an armchair. She did not enter the children's room, but waited nervously until the door opened and Dr. Stumpfegger came out. Their eyes met, Magda Goebbels stood up, silent and trembling. When the SS doctor nodded emotionally without speaking, she collapsed. It was done. The children lay dead in their beds, poisoned with cyanide."[23]

—*Heinz Linge, Hitler's valet*

suspected what would happen to the children, were haunted by their deaths many decades after the war. Some, including Albert Speer, had repeatedly offered to help the children escape, but the Goebbelses had both adamantly refused.

While all this was going on, most of the survivors of the bunker, including Hitler's female secretaries, had begun making preparations for an escape attempt.

Before they left, Joseph Goebbels said a few quick and perfunctory goodbyes, as though they were all about to leave for dinner. The secretary Traudl Junge remembers him walking restlessly up and down, smoking, like a hotel manager waiting for all the guests to leave the bar. He wished Junge good luck. "You may get through," he told her softly.

Most of the remaining inhabitants of the bunker walked down the underground corridor to the big storerooms in the basement of the Reich Chancellery, passing through the hospital area full of dead bodies and surgeons operating. Everyone was changing into simple uniforms without insignia, gathering up what food provisions and weapons as they could.

Traudl Junge and the three other women—Hitler's other secretary Gerda Christian, the cook Manzialy and Martin Bormann's secretary Else Krüger—were given male uniforms, steel helmets, and pistols. They were going to try to pass themselves off as ordinary soldiers, to avoid rape at the hands of the Russians. The survivors sat on the benches that lined the underground corridors, waiting for it to get dark enough for them to leave.

Eyewitness accounts differ on what happened to Joseph and Magda Goebbels and when. Some witnesses said they killed themselves separately inside their rooms in the bunker; others, that they killed themselves together outside in the garden. Their burned bodies were discovered in the garden, but it's possible they were moved there from inside. The consensus is that sometime after 8:30 p.m., both Joseph and Magda walked down the steps from the Vorbunker into the Führerbunker proper, down the long corridor, and then climbed the steps to the emergency exit. They walked out into the Reich Chancellery garden near the bomb crater where Hitler was buried.

Later autopsy results conducted by the Russians suggested that Magda Goebbels first bit down on a cyanide capsule, collapsed on the ground, and was then shot in the back of the head by her husband. He then swallowed poison himself and shot himself in the temple.

Wherever their deaths occurred, the bodies of the Goebbels were quickly doused with what was left of the gasoline from Hitler's cremation and set on fire. However, because there was little gasoline actually left, both of the bodies were clearly recognizable when discovered, unburied, on the next day, May 2, by Russian soldiers.

After the bodies of both of the Goebbelses had been set on fire, an incident occurred that could have killed almost everyone else living in the bunker.

General Mohnke had ordered one of the men who burned the Goebbels' bodies, a Captain Schwaegerman, to take one of the remaining gasoline cans down into the bunker and to set fire to Hitler's study. Linge had already spent much of the day destroying documents and other items from Hitler's safe and office.

The captain did as he was told. He went down to Hitler's study, poured whatever gasoline was left in the can, and then, from the doorway, tossed a light inside and quickly closed the steel door.

Luckily, the Führerbunker engineer had shut off the ventilation shaft into Hitler's quarters or the resulting fire could have sucked all the air out of the bunker, killing everyone left in it. The fire was so hot that it melted the rubber insulation around the door frame, filling the lower bunker with sulphurous smoke. Eventually, because the ventilation had been shut off, the fire slowly burned itself out.

Meanwhile, German radio was making a series of announcements.

It's not clear whether anyone in the bunker was listening at this point, although perhaps some of the remaining survivors still lingering in the Vorbunker may have had their radios turned on.

At 10:00 p.m. on May 1, the announcer said, "Achtung! Achtung! The German broadcasting system is going to give an important German Government announcement for the German people." There followed a slow movement of Bruckner's Seventh Symphony. At 10:25 p.m., the music stopped, there were three dramatic drum rolls, and the announcement of Hitler's death was made: *Der Führer Adolf Hitler ist gefallen.*

It was, as later historians pointed out, another Nazi lie. The announcement said Hitler had "fallen" defending Berlin (when in fact he had killed himself) and that he had died that afternoon and not the day before.

The Escape of Führerbunker Survivors

By this time, most of the remaining Führerbunker personnel were organizing themselves into small groups for a breakout.

The plan was for the small groups to use the subway tunnels to make their way to the main Friedrichstrasse station. They would then come up to the street level and try to meet up with the remaining soldiers under Mohnke's command, then defending the city center. The groups hoped to be able to find a way across the River Spree and head northwest, towards the American lines. Everyone would then scatter and make their way as best they could.

The first group, led by General Mohnke and including Günsche, Hewel, Admiral Voss, Hitler's pilot Hans Baur, and the four women, left around 11:00 p.m. They made it to the Friedrichstrasse station as planned, but when they climbed the steps to the street level, they couldn't believe what they saw. Berlin was in total ruin and burning to the ground. They crossed over the river on a footbridge and made it as far as the famous Charité Hospital. They proceeded a few blocks northwards, but then went back underground. The group sought refuge in a series of cellars, stopping for a little sleep.

The next day, the small group ended up in the courtyard of the Schultheiss-Patzenhofer Brewery on Prinzenallee with a small detachment of SS soldiers. They were soon surrounded by Russian soldiers demanding that they surrender.

Mohnke wrote a final report of events and then ordered the women to take off their military jackets, helmets, and pistols. The men had no chance of escaping, he said, but the women, dressed in civilian clothes, might be able to get through the Russian lines. If they did, they should deliver his final report to Admiral Dönitz. The women agreed to try. They shook hands with all the men.

Incredibly, Mohnke's plan worked.

This particular group of Russian soldiers was actually friendly, passing out cigarettes and schnapps to the Germans, celebrating the end of the war. The four women just walked among the Russian soldiers,

unmolested, as though they were invisible, and simply strolled noncha-
lantly away.[24] Unfortunately, not all of the Russians in Berlin were so
accomodating. The last time Junge saw the cook, Constance Manzialy,
she was being led down into a subway tunnel by two Soviet soldiers. She
was never seen again.

Junge was eventually caught by the Russians and later released to
the British, but Hitler's other secretary, Gerda Christian, somehow made
it to the American lines. Junge, who died in Munich in 2002 at age
eighty-one, would later write a memoir of her time in the Führerbunker,
only published the year she died. It would become the basis of *Downfall*,
the 2004 German film about the last days in the Führerbunker.

The Russians Arrive in the Bunker

Virtually all of the survivors of the bunker made a break for it, with
a few exceptions.

Generals Krebs and Burgdorf and SS Colonel Franz Schädle of Hitler's personal bodyguard had all vowed to shoot themselves rather than
surrender. Krebs and Burgdorf spent their final hours drinking and singing old songs.

General Burgdorf, a round-faced fifty-year-old Army veteran who
had given Rommel poison and sat with him while he drank it, was particularly drunk. Unlike most of the generals, he was determined to obey
Hitler's orders and never surrender.

Earlier that day, he had almost shot a high-ranking German civilian
official, Hans Fritzsche, because Fritzsche had drafted a letter of surrender on behalf of the German people that he intended to send to Russian Marshal Georgy Zhukov. After Goebbels had insisted that the
generals could never surrender, Burgdorf followed Fritzsche to his nearby
office outside of the bunker, where he was writing the letter, and asked
if he intended to surrender in direct violation of Hitler's command. Fritzsche replied that this was precisely what he planned on doing, so Burgdorf raised his pistol to shoot him. Fortunately for Fritzsche, someone

in the office bravely knocked Burgdorf's gun away, so he missed. Burgdorf then left and returned to the bunker.

Now, in a deep baritone, the fanatical general was belting out, in a nonsensical mixture of English and German, a vigorous rendition of the American sea chanty "Johnny Comes Down to Hilo, Poor Old Man," which he may have learned from a phonograph record that some naval officers had brought into the Führerbunker dining hall.

Krebs, the Russian-speaking aristocrat, was more civilized, sporting his absurd monocle, his head shaved "like a Buddhist monk," but an ardent Nazi nonetheless.

Like Burgdorf, Krebs was a career soldier. But for the past month, he had been in the unenviable position of serving as chief of staff of the entire German High Command just as it was losing the greatest war in Germany's history.

Krebs had pulled himself together briefly to say goodbye to Frau Junge and her group when they made their escape, but now he, like Burgdorf, was intoxicated. Around 2:00 in the morning, Krebs and Burgdorf took out their service pistols and shot themselves in the head.

At that point, the last two men left alive in the bunker were the SS bodyguard and telephone operator Rochus Misch, who would live to age ninety-six and die in 2013; and the man responsible for keeping the entire bunker complex running, Johannes Hentschel, the engineer.

As James P. O'Donnell, the *Newsweek* journalist who was among the very first reporters to gain access to the bunker, would point out, Hentschel was in a delicate position.

He knew the Red Army was just hours, perhaps minutes away—and that they could use any number of unpleasant methods to storm and neutralize the bunker. Flame throwers, poison gas, explosives? Hentschel closed most of the bunker's steel doors in case the Russians decided to simply drop some hand grenades down the stairways to clear away potential German die-hards such as himself.

Hentschel worried that Misch, the SS guard, who was armed, might get the crazy idea of fighting it out until the end. Fortunately, Misch was

Hitler's bodyguard, SS Sergeant Rochus Misch (1917–2013), was one of the last two people to flee the Führerbunker as Soviet troops approached and was the last surviving eyewitness of the events there. After publishing his memoirs in 2013, he died at the age of ninety-six. *Wikimedia Commons*[25]

a bit drunk and passed out at his post, mostly from not having any sleep for the past two days.

The SS guard was supposed to have joined one of the breakout groups—indeed, Goebbels himself had ordered him to do so, before he killed himself—but some officer had commanded him at the last minute to remain at his switchboard post, and so he had.[26]

Hentschel need not have worried. Misch had a wife and daughter nearby and was desperate to leave his post to see about their safety.

Hentschel wanted to get rid of the SS guard so he wouldn't accidently bring the full force of the Red Army down on their heads. He woke Misch up and got him dressed in his full battle gear, complete with his rosary beads. Hentschel handed him a letter for his own wife, Greta, in case he didn't survive.

Around 3:30 in the morning, Misch left. The SS soldier went upstairs to the cellar of the Reich Chancellery, where his commander, Führer Body Guard Commander Franz Schädle, had his office, to make his final report.

Misch told his superior that Hitler had released them from their oath. The older man nodded but pointed to the shrapnel wound in his leg that had turned gangrenous. He was in no condition to flee. Schädle advised Misch to try his luck by means of Berlin's subway tunnels—advice that

Misch took. Once Misch left, Schädle took out his pistol and shot himself in the head.

Outside the Reich Chancellery, Misch dashed across the street to the Kaiserhof subway entrance and made his way down into the darkened subway tunnel. He was soon caught by Soviet troops who, by then, knew all about the subway tunnels.

Back in the bunker and now alone, Hentschel suspected that Krebs had killed himself as he had sworn to do—which was horrible luck for Hentschel. He would have liked to have had the Russian-speaking Krebs around to communicate with the Soviet troops when they arrived.

Hentschel spent the next few hours thinking of different scenarios, trying to work out where in the Führerbunker he had the best chance of surviving. He calculated that the Russians would likely only discover one entrance at first, that their sapper squads would enter that way, and that he might be able to simply slip out the other entrance unnoticed when he heard the soldiers coming.

Hentschel had had plenty of opportunities to escape. Two or three times, he had gone up the emergency entrance staircase to the Reich Chancellery garden for some fresh air. The first time, the cold dawn air had chased him back down; the second time, some tracer rounds from a Russian plane flying overhead caused him to flee. He apparently felt safer down in the bunker than making his way through the combat-filled streets of Berlin.

When the Russians finally arrived, around eight in the morning, the enemy was nothing like what Hentschel had expected. He was anticipating Soviet assault troops with flame-throwers. But the Russians who first entered the bunker were about a dozen female personnel, laughing as they made their way into the Führerbunker central corridor.

Hentschel heard them coming, raised his hands to show he was unarmed, and was greeted by a blonde doctor who spoke fluent German with a Berliner accent. She asked him what had happened to Adolf Hitler. When he told her that Hitler was dead, the woman simply nodded and demanded to know where the clothes of Hitler's mistress were kept.

"Herr Hentschel, wo sind die Klamotten?" the blonde officer asked. "Herr Hentschel, where are the clothes?"

The exhausted engineer couldn't quite believe what was happening. The entire scene was surreal.

Hentschel took the women to Eva Braun's bedroom, which was indeed stocked with a considerable supply of elegant outfits. Much to Hentschel's astonishment, the Russian women spent the next hour sifting through Braun's wardrobe.

However, around 9:30 a.m., events took a more serious turn. Two more Russians entered the facility—this time men with drawn pistols in their hands.

Hentschel raised his arms once again but was surprised when six of the female medical personnel all ran by him with their booty, "like women returning from a rummage sale," anxious to get away with the loot before their unsmiling superior officers took it from them.

The other two Russian officers were threatening at first, but then they asked Hentschel where Hitler's body was located. When he told them it was buried in the garden upstairs, they seemed skeptical.

The men then went into the room where the Goebbels children lay dead, saw the horrific spectacle, and quickly left. They asked a few more questions, told Hentschel he would be needed in Moscow, and then were joined by about twenty Russian infantry soldiers who simply helped themselves to what wine was left in the Führerbunker stores.

The Soviet infantry soldiers, laughing and singing and surprisingly friendly, offered Hentschel a drink, just as six more of the medical women rushed by, each with one of Eva Braun's black satin brassieres in her hand.

The final liberation of the Führerbunker was thus something of a farce.

The Russian officers with the pistols were very interested in what had happened to Hitler and Goebbels, but, aside from the women doctors' obsession with Eva Braun's lingerie, they showed little interest in whatever other evidence was still in the bunker, including any documents.

Hentschel showed the intelligence officers the bodies of Joseph and Magda Goebbels in the garden. It was a gruesome sight: the partially burned bodies, with one of Joseph Goebbels's arms at a ninety-degrees angle from his body, would later be displayed for Russian journalists. Soon after that, Hentschel was placed under arrest and marched with other German prisoners to a waiting Soviet Army truck. A Russian soldier stole his rucksack and watches.

As he was driven away, the last survivor of the bunker saw nothing but horror on the streets. Berlin was a smoking ruin, and hanging from lampposts were the bodies of adolescent boys and old men—signs around their necks with the words "Traitor" or "Coward" painted on them. They were victims of the fanatical SS death squads that had appeared on the streets in the final days of the war, murdering anyone they deemed deserters.

Compared to many other survivors of the bunker, Hentschel was relatively lucky.

Because he had prevented some Soviet soldiers from entering Hitler's private study—the room that had been set on fire and was then, he presumed, full of toxic gas—Hentschel was accused of attempted sabotage and sent to a Soviet prison. But he was released from captivity after only four years, in 1949, and died in West Germany in 1982.[27]

10 THE MYSTERY OF HITLER'S MORTAL REMAINS

For decades, what really happened to Hitler's body remained one of the great unsolved mysteries of World War II. The Führer's remains appeared to have been lost in the dust of history.

After V-E Day on May 8, the reports coming from the Russians were often contradictory. At first, the Russians announced that they had found Hitler's body, even displaying it in newsreel footage released to Western reporters. Then they said they had made a mistake. Finally, Stalin told his fellow Allied leaders that Hitler likely escaped alive and might be living in Argentina. There is little wonder that rumors persist to this day.

But over the years, eyewitnesses to the events in early May 1945 slowly came forward. Very gradually, over more than six decades, a fuller picture of what happened emerged—although a few mysteries remain.

Both Hitler's adjutant Otto Günsche and his valet Heinz Linge, two of the three men who claimed to have poured gasoline over the bodies of Hitler and Braun—the other being Hitler's chauffeur, Erich Kempka—were released from Soviet prisons in the early 1950s.

Even before that, U.S. Navy captain Michael Musmanno, one of the presiding judges at the Nuremberg trials, undertook a project to interview as many eyewitnesses to Hitler's final days as he could, including those who claimed to have seen his body. He wanted to prove, once and for all, that Hitler really had died in the bunker.

Beginning in 1948, Musmanno tracked down and interviewed more than a hundred witnesses in Germany and elsewhere. As part of this effort, Musmanno did something unusual for his time: he filmed twenty-two of the interviews on 8mm film with audio. Musmanno sent his interviews to Hollywood, hoping for some kind of movie deal. But by that time, Hollywood had tired of Nazis and World War II. It wanted to concentrate on other things. When he died in 1968, Musmanno's family donated his remarkable but unused film archive to Duquesne University in Pittsburgh.

Ignored for decades, this film archive was only rediscovered in 2007 and finally broadcast for the first time on German television in 2013 and on American television in 2015.[1] It is a good source for in-person interviews with eyewitnesses while their memories were still relatively fresh. One of the interviews was with the guard Hermann Karnau, who had watched the bodies of Hitler and Eva Braun burn for two hours, from about 4:00 to 6:00 p.m. on April 30.

"Hitler was wrapped up in a blanket which had opened up," Karnau told Musmanno. "I saw his face covered with blood. The bodies were still burning and the flesh moved up and down. I touched the burning remains which were lying before me with my feet, and they fell apart. Almost frozen, I remained fixed to the spot and lifted my arm in salute."[2] Virtually every witness Musmanno and others interviewed told a variation on the same story, that the bodies of Hitler and Eva Braun had been incinerated immediately after their deaths.

Still, this was only eyewitness testimony. There was still no physical evidence. Even some of the eyewitnesses, such as Linge, were convinced that the Russians had not truly found the bodies. His reason was simple. Held in a Russian prison until the early 1950s, Linge's Russian interrogators continued to press him on what had happened to Hitler, and they wouldn't have done so had they known all along what had really occurred.

At Last, A Major Breakthrough

Then, in 1968, a major breakthrough occurred.

That year, a Russian journalist and former Red Army soldier, Lev Bezymenski, published a book in West Germany that shed light on what had happened to the mortal remains of Hitler and Eva Braun. The short book, *The Death of Adolf Hitler*, was based on some previously secret documents in the Soviet archives that the Russian authorities had apparently decided to make public.

Bezymenski's account was expanded by further investigations in the 1990s by the Russian journalist Ada Petrova and the British writer Peter Watson in their 1995 book, *The Death of Hitler: The Full Story with New Evidence from Secret Russian Archives.*

According to Petrova and Watson, Soviet Lieutenant-Colonel Ivan Klimenko of the counterintelligence unit SMERSH (a Russian acronym for "Death to Spies"), arrived in the Reich Chancellery garden on May 2 and, aided by a German—likely the engineer Hentschel—viewed the charred but clearly recognizable bodies of Joseph and Magda Goebbels lying near the entrance.

The Russians also discovered the bodies of the Goebbels children below in the Vorbunker.

Soviet photographers took detailed pictures of these bodies in the Reich Chancellery garden and then soldiers took the remains to nearby Plötzensee Prison, where the Russians had set up a command post. The Soviets had just captured Vice Admiral Hans-Erich Voss, a top Nazi who had left the bunker with Mohnke's group but had somehow been separated from it and fallen into Soviet hands. The Russians quickly learned that Voss was part of Admiral Dönitz's staff, so they took him back to the Führerbunker to look for Hitler's body.

Walking through the garden area, Voss saw the body of a man with a short, Hitler-like mustache, and announced that this could be his former leader—but then said he couldn't be certain.

The man did look something like Hitler. He had clearly been shot in the forehead.

In July 1945, a Russian officer shows British and American soldiers the trench outside the Führerbunker where, he said, Soviet intelligence officers dug up the badly burned corpses of Adolf Hitler and his wife, Eva. *akg-images*

Yet Klimenko was not convinced. He returned to the prison, located more captured German officers, and brought them back to the bunker area.

Most of them denied that the dead man was Hitler. Nevertheless, a photograph of this body—later suspected to have been that of Hitler's official body double, Gustav Weler—aired in a newsreel released by the Soviets. For a few days, therefore, there were news reports that the Russians had found Hitler's body.

But Klimenko kept digging, literally and figuratively.

A Russian private told Klimenko that he had found some badly burned corpses buried in a crater near the Führerbunker exit, close to the bodies of Joseph and Madga Goebbels. They were the bodies of a man and a woman.

At the time, Klimenko thought the body of the man shot in the forehead—likely the body double—was Hitler, so he assumed these new bodies were of other people and ordered them reburied.

Eventually, Klimenko was able to reach a former Soviet press attaché at the Berlin Embassy, a man named Andrei Smirnov,[3] who had known Hitler personally. The investigators brought Smirnov to the bunker to inspect the man shot in the forehead. A group of generals all gathered around the corpse, now relocated to the bombed-out remains of the Reich Chancellery. The Soviet press attaché was adamant: that was *not* Adolf Hitler.

Interestingly, the Soviets had by this time located an SS soldier who had been one of Hitler's personal bodyguards and who claimed he had seen precisely where Hitler had been burned and buried. His name was Harry Mengerschausen, and he claimed that he had been guarding the New Chancellery building proper on the evening of April 30 when he saw Günsche and Linge carry the bodies into the garden in front of the emergency exit and set them on fire.

Mengerschausen had watched the whole drama from a considerable distance—about six hundred yards—but he claimed to have seen everything. He also claimed to have watched as the bodies were taken from the original trench where they had been burned to a new grave site, a large bomb crater just a few meters from the exit, and then buried. Mengerschausen supposedly took the Soviet officials directly to the same bomb crater where the Soviet private had found the remains of a man and a woman that had been reburied.

At this point, it's important to point out that the investigation of Hitler's death by the Russians was, from a purely forensic point of view, botched to an almost comical degree. There was no attempt whatsoever to stop looters or secure the premises.

As we saw in the previous chapter, the primary objective of the first Russians inside the bunker—the dozen female doctors and nurses—was to help themselves to Eva Braun's lingerie rather than to investigate a crime scene or preserve evidence for later historians.

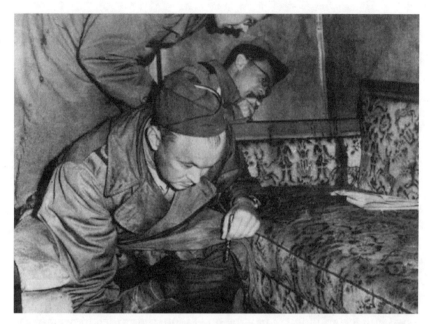

In July 1945, soldiers inspect what is left of Hitler's private study in the badly damaged, partially burned Führerbunker. Blood stains are clearly visible on the right arm of the sofa near where eyewitnesses said Hitler's body was found leaning to the side. *akg-images/Interfoto*

Thousands of valuable historical documents were thus simply left lying around. In the Russians' defense, they had just lost ten million soldiers fighting the Nazis. All they cared about was victory.

When *Newsweek* journalist James O'Donnell visited the Führerbunker on July 4, nearly two months after the war ended, he was able to bribe Russian guards and gain entrance for the price of two packs of American cigarettes.

Once inside, O'Donnell found Hitler's appointment book and other historically invaluable documents just casually tossed to the side. Stalin himself was so unimpressed by the first investigative effort of his intelligence agents that he ordered a second be undertaken a year and a half later, in 1946, so he could be certain that Hitler had not escaped.

Part of Hitler's Skull Allegedly Discovered

It was during this second investigation that the Russians found two charred pieces of a skull in the bomb crater where the bodies were originally discovered—fragments that would be the focus of considerable controversy sixty years later. One of the skull pieces had what looked like a bullet hole in it.

The primary concern of the Russians in the first week of May 1945 was to find out what happened to Hitler's body. Guided by Mengerschausen and the Russian private who had found the remains in the bomb crater, Klimenko returned to the Reich Chancellery garden on May 5.

He ordered that the remains in the bomb crater be dug up once again, and this time, the blackened bones and charred flesh were placed in two large ammunition boxes.

Eventually, in the 1990s, the Russians released grainy, poor-quality photographs of these boxes—adding more fuel to the conspiracy fires. Why were there many crystal-clear, high-resolution photographs of the Goebbels' bodies...yet none of Hitler's remains? Why were there no *autopsy* photos? Some researchers suspect that these photos must still exist, locked deep in the Russian archives, never to be released to the public.

While digging out the bodies, the Russians also found two jerry cans and the bodies of two dogs buried nearby.

The remains found on May 5 were taken to a clinic that had been commandeered by the Russian military in the northern Berlin suburb of Buch. There, on May 8, Russian pathologist Dr. Faust Shkaravski performed a brief autopsy on the alleged remains of Hitler, Eva Braun, the Goebbels family, General Krebs, and the two dogs.

Shkaravski found evidence of cyanide poisoning in all members of the Goebbels family as well as in the dogs. The charred remains supposed to be Hitler and Eva Braun, however, were not the subject of a true autopsy. The organs were not dissected and tissue samples were not analyzed for poisoning.

But the Russians did pay particular attention to the remains of the teeth. They found glass splinters in the mouth and the smell of burnt almonds—a sign of cyanide poisoning. To the Russians, this meant that Hitler had poisoned rather than shot himself. The male jawbone was largely intact, with nine teeth in the upper jaw and a bridge of gold. The lower jaw had fifteen teeth with ten crowns.

To make certain that the remains were those of Hitler, the Russians located Käthe Heusermann, a dental nurse who had helped Hitler's dentist, Dr. Hugo Blaschke, install much of the Führer's bridgework. According to an account first published in English in 2017, a Russian translator named Elena Rzhevskaya carried Hitler's teeth around Berlin in early May 1945, looking for Heusermann.[4] Heusermann claimed that she had held Hitler's bridgework in her hands, and she drew for the Russians, from memory, an illustration of what Hitler's teeth looked like.

The Russians also located the technician who made the gold bridge, Fritz Echtmann, who also drew detailed drawings of Hitler's teeth. Both Heusermann and Echtmann were arrested by the Russians and held prisoner in Russia for nearly a decade, released only in 1956. For her help in identifying Hitler's teeth, Heusermann would spend nearly a decade in Soviet prisons, most of the time in solitary confinement.

The dental nurse's drawing of Hitler's teeth matched the physical teeth held by Rzhevskaya exactly. Hitler had had extensive dental work. His teeth were in such bad shape, according to Rzhevskaya's granddaughter, that the Führer had to have his dentist stay with him in the bunker.

The dentist, who spoke fluent English and trained in the United States, was an ardent Nazi who had helped extract gold from the teeth of Jewish prisoners. He was sentenced to ten years in prison by the Nuremberg tribunal.

The dental examination satisfied the Russian investigators that they had in fact found the remains of Adolf Hitler and Eva Braun.

As a result, the charred bones of Hitler, Braun, and the Goebbels family were taken from the autopsy examination room in Buch to Finow, a small town twenty-five miles northeast of Berlin. They were then reburied in the Brandenburg forest. According to the once-secret Soviet archives, they were placed in new boxes and, on June 3, 1945, buried "along the highway to Sterchow, near the village of Neu Friedrichsdorf."

Less than a year later, however, on February 23, 1946, the Soviets once again dug up the "half-rotten corpses" and reburied them in the courtyard of a house at 36 Westerndstrasse (now Klaussner Strasse 23) in the city of Magdeburg, located about one hundred miles west of Berlin.[5]

The Soviet intelligence unit had a barracks in the town with a garage facility and a deep pit for working on vehicles. The bodies were placed in this large open pit and then covered over with dirt and eventually paved over with asphalt.

And there the bodies remained, in secret, for twenty-five years.

A Closely Guarded Secret

Throughout this time, the Russians kept as a strict state secret the fact that they had Hitler's remains safely buried in Magdeburg. Even as tireless a researcher as James O'Donnell—the *Newsweek* reporter who was in the bunker in July 1945, interviewed more than a hundred eyewitnesses, and wrote one of the best books on the final week of the war, *The Bunker*—had no clue what happened to Hitler's body.

"The possibility that Hitler's ashes were sent to Moscow does exist," he concluded in 1978, "but more likely they were scattered in Buch, where the autopsy took place."[6]

But Hitler's body had not been turned into ashes and scattered in 1945. Instead, it had been buried in the driveway of a military garage.

In 1970, however, the military installation in Magdeburg was going to be transferred from the control of the Russians to that of Communist East Germany.

The Russians worried that the remains of Hitler and Eva Braun might one day be rediscovered and could conceivably become the object of veneration by future neo-Nazis. After all, the body of Vladimir Lenin was on display, embalmed and perfectly preserved, in an ornate glass sarcophagus in the center of Moscow.

As a result, Yuri Andropov, the head of the KGB at the time and later the Russian prime minister, ordered that Hitler's remains, such as they were, be disposed of once and for all. He ordered that the bodies be once again disinterred, burned into dust, and the ashes scattered.

As Petrova and Watson recount, this was no easy feat. Hitler's secret grave had been left undisturbed for a quarter of a century.

Under the code name Operation Archive, the Russians began the elaborate process of digging up the bodies of Hitler, Eva Braun, and the Goebbelses. Andropov selected a KGB officer named Vladimir Gumenyuk to pick a secret final resting place for Hitler's remains and to lead a three-man team in taking the remains there for destruction.

By April 4, 1970, the old Soviet building at 36 Westerndstrasse was surrounded by new high-rise office buildings, and the Russians were afraid that observers might see what they were doing. Gumenyuk's team pitched a large tent over the spot where the remains of Hitler and the Goebbels' family had been buried to prevent observation.

At first, the Russian team, following a set of secret instructions, couldn't find anything. Then they realized that they had counted forty-five meters instead of forty-five paces from a specific coordinate. They put the dirt back, moved the tent, and tried again.

Eventually, they located the wooden boxes that had been buried twenty-five years earlier. Unfortunately, most of the wood had completely disintegrated. The remains of all the buried Nazis and even the dogs were jumbled together in what the Russians called a "jellied mass," mixed with the soil.

"The remains had been lying for a long time in the ground, and I'm generally a squeamish person, so I took rubber gloves, boots, and a special suit of chemical protection," Gumenyuk said in a 2010 interview. "I thought the smell would be terrible, and even took the mask. But when they began to dig, nothing like that happened. Sometimes when digging in the garden, you find a bone—it was the same thing here. We shifted the bones and put the ground back."[7]

Posing as fishermen, Gumenyuk and his team drove to an isolated spot in a nearby forest. There they built two fires, one to cook some soup and another to incinerate the mortal remains of Adolf Hitler. As occurred nearly twenty-five years earlier, the Russians poured gasoline on the bones they had found and then lit them on fire. They waited patiently until only ashes were left, then ground everything into a pile of dust. They scooped up the ashes and placed them in a rucksack.

The Russians then drove to a secret location—revealed later to be the Biederitz River, a tributary of the Ehle just west of the village of Biederitz[8]—and dumped the ashes into the rushing water.

The dénouement of Hitler's reign took only twenty seconds. "It was over in no time at all," Gumenyuk said. "I opened up the rucksack, the wind caught the ashes up in a little brown cloud, and in a second they were gone."[9]

The Truth Is Out There

Yet the final destruction of Hitler and Eva Braun's remains was still a state secret that the Soviets closely guarded. As we saw earlier, in 1968 the Russian journalist Lev A. Bezymenski confirmed for the first time that the Soviets had discovered Hitler's remains in early May 1945 and had even performed an autopsy on what remained of his body.

However, according to Bezymenski, Soviet records indicated that the bodies of Hitler and Eva Braun were thoroughly cremated and their ashes scattered shortly after the autopsies. We now know that this wasn't true. In fact, the bodies of Hitler, Braun, and the Goebbelses were all moved to two different sites and buried in Magdeburg, their burial site undisturbed for almost twenty-five years.

It wasn't until 1992—nearly fifty years after the bodies were first discovered—that the world learned, from Bezymenski, that Hitler's "corpse had been buried and unburied on several occasions before finally being burned in 1978." Other—likely more accurate—accounts say the year was 1970.

Bezymenski also revealed for the first time that Hitler's burial site had been in Magdeburg,[10] and the next year, in 1993, the Soviet government confirmed Bezymenski's account, saying that it had the skull fragment and that the rest of Hitler's remains had been destroyed, without revealing any details as to how.

Bezymenski offered an explanation for the secretive behavior of Soviet intelligence officials and their deliberate deception about what actually happened to Adolf Hitler's body. According to Bezymenski, Stalin knew by the end of May 1945 that Hitler had been killed, but the Soviet dictator believed that one of Hitler's body doubles had escaped. Stalin feared that this body double could someday reappear, claiming to be the Führer and sparking a neo-Nazi movement. The Russians had lost 10 million soldiers defeating the Nazis, and they had no wish to ever have to do so again. As a result, Bezymenski said, Stalin kept the details about what happened to Hitler's body a secret "in case someone might try to slip into the role of the Führer saved by a miracle."

As we have seen, Bezymenski's bombshell report was confirmed by the Soviet government and then greatly expanded upon three years later in Ada Petrova and Peter Watson's 1995 book, *The Death of Hitler*. But it wasn't until the year 2000, nearly a decade after the fall of the Soviet Union, that the Russians finally opened most—but not all—of their Hitler files to Western researchers. Those files revealed that the Soviets had indeed kept a portion of Hitler's remains, namely the jawbone with his teeth intact as well as the two skull fragments that had been discovered in 1946, in the bomb crater.

In April 2000, the Russians put the two skull fragments on public display on black velvet under glass at Russia's State Archives in Moscow. The exhibition was entitled, *The Agony of the Third Reich—Retribution.*

The exhibition included numerous documents taken from the Führerbunker, as well as a portion of Hitler's blood-stained couch. Among the other Nazi artifacts in the exhibit were Hitler's formal jacket with swastika armband, a map of the bunker drawn by Linge for his Russian interrogators, Hitler's Iron Cross medal from the First World War, the diary of propaganda chief Joseph Goebbels, the two small pistols that Goebbels and his wife Magda used to kill themselves, and a portable air-testing device for Hitler's staff to check whether the Soviets were sending sleeping gas into the bunker.

The skull fragments on display were small, with jagged edges and evidence of charring, and they both appeared to be from a single person. One of the pieces had a clearly visible bullet hole—proof, the Russians said, that Hitler had indeed shot himself, as many of the bunker survivors had claimed.

Sergei Mironenko, director of Russia's State Archives, said that the bullet had exited through Hitler's right temple, and that explained the visible cracking seen in the skull fragment—which meant that he shot himself in the left temple even though he was right-handed and his left hand shook from tremors.[11]

The Russians believed that the skull fragments, which had only been discovered more than a year after the original charred remains found in the bomb crater had been taken away, likely fell off the corpse as it was removed. They were found only when Joseph Stalin ordered the second, more thorough investigation in 1946.

The Russians conceded during the Moscow exhibition that they did not have the funds necessary to conduct expensive DNA tests on the skull fragments but expressed hope that interested parties in the West might do so. They were right.

Fuel for the Conspiracy Fires

Very slowly, the Russians allowed Western experts to examine what they had. In 2009, U.S. forensic scientists were given access to the skull fragments (but not the teeth) to perform DNA and other tests.

What they discovered was yet another bombshell—and led to a new series of Hitler conspiracy theories that have continued to the present time.

In 2009, Connecticut archaeologist and bone specialist Nick Bellantoni flew to Moscow to examine the skull fragments and perform DNA tests. He immediately saw things that didn't quite add up. "The bone seemed very thin; male bone tends to be more robust," Bellantoni said in an interview later that year.[12] "And the sutures where the skull plates come together seemed to correspond to someone under 40." What's more, the bullet hole in the fragment would have been at the back of the head, not the side. This meant, according to Bellantoni, that the dead person was shot in the face or in the mouth.

This contradicted what most but not all eyewitnesses of Hitler's corpse had said. Hitler's valet Linge and his SS adjutant Günsche both claimed to have seen wounds in Hitler's temples. Yet as skeptics such as Jerome Corsi like to point out, Hitler's chauffeur Erich Kempka and British historian Trevor-Roper both concluded that Hitler shot himself in the mouth—which could explain an exit wound in the back of the skull.[13]

Despite his doubts that the skull fragments belonged to Hitler, Bellantoni took samples from the material provided by the Russians— including from the blood-stained sofa—for DNA testing in America.

The samples were flown back to Bellantoni's University of Connecticut Lab for Applied Genetics where researchers spent three days conducting tests. The results astonished everyone: the DNA testing supposedly confirmed Bellantoni's suspicions that the skull fragments could not have belonged to Hitler but were those of a woman under forty.

"We used the same routines and controls that would have been used in a crime lab," said Linda Strausbaugh, a forensic scientist.[14]

The samples collected had sufficient viable DNA for analysis in a process known as molecular copying. And according to Strausbaugh, the results were conclusive. The skull fragments were not from Adolf Hitler. They belonged to a young woman, not to a fifty-six-year-old man.[15]

But could they have been of Eva Braun, who was only thirty-three years old when she died?

The researchers said this was possible; there was no way to know for sure. But while the skull fragment definitely had a bullet hole from an exit wound, most eyewitness accounts said that Eva Braun appeared to have died from poisoning, not a pistol shot, because there were no observable wounds on her head or upper body. Also, the Soviet soldiers had found 166 bodies in the Reich Chancellery garden when they arrived in May 1945, many of them blown apart and scattered by the relentless artillery fire that had hit the area. The fragments could have been from one of those bodies.

The announcement of the findings set off an international firestorm. Dr. Bellantoni repeated his findings on a TV documentary broadcast on the History Channel entitled *Hitler's Escape.*

The Russian government simply doubled down, insisting that the American scientists were mistaken, and the skull fragments were Hitler's. But the embarrassing controversy eventually forced the Russian government to come clean about what had actually happened to Hitler's body after the war.

In December 2009, sixty-four years after the events, the head archivist of Russia's Federal Security Service (FSB), the successor to the former Soviet Union's infamous KGB, finally admitted that the Soviets had misled the public when they claimed that Hitler had likely escaped after the war. In an interview with the Russian news service Interfax, General Vasily Khristoforov revealed the timeline of events in the months and years after Hitler's remains were discovered.[16]

He admitted that the Russians had indeed discovered the bodies of Hitler and Eva Braun on May 5 in the bomb crater directly in front of the bunker emergency entrance. After an autopsy, the bodies were buried in a forest near the town of Rathenau, Germany, and then, eight months later, on February 21, 1946, secretly reburied in the Soviet Army's garrison in Magdeburg.

Khristoforov added that the remains had been disinterred on April 4, 1970, "burnt on a bonfire outside the town of Shoenebeck, 11 kilometers away from Magdeburg, then ground into ashes, collected and thrown into the Biederitz River."

The Soviets had done this, the general explained, because the Communist Party leadership feared that Hitler's burial site could become a "place of worship" for Hitler supporters or proponents of fascist ideas.

As incredible as it may seem, it was thus only in 2009 that the world finally got *official* confirmation of how Adolf Hitler's life ended.

Despite this, some people were *still* not convinced—or they saw an opportunity to make a sensational claim. The revelation that the skull fragments the Soviets had recovered from the bomb crater in 1946 might not belong Hitler but to a young woman naturally gave new life to the suspicions that Hitler had escaped.

This is one reason why there was a sudden explosion in books and articles reviving the "Hitler escaped" theory.

As we saw earlier, *Grey Wolf: The Escape of Adolf Hitler* appeared in 2011. Peter Levenda's *Ratline: Soviet Spies, Nazi Priests, and the Disappearance of Adolf Hitler* came out in 2012. And Jerome R. Corsi's *Hunting Hitler: New Scientific Evidence That Hitler Escaped Nazi Germany* was published in 2014.

After all, the Russians had claimed for years that they had Hitler's skull in their archives. Now scientific tests revealed that this might not be correct. What else in the "official story" might not be true?

As a result, pressure began building on the Russians to allow an international team of researchers to physically examine the other, and the last, major piece of forensic evidence in the Russian archives: Hitler's teeth.

11 THE FINAL WORD: HITLER'S VERY BAD TEETH

ussian paranoia created the confusion about what happened to Adolf Hitler at the end of the war, and Russian secretiveness continued to sow confusion right up into the 2000s.

For one thing, the policy of dribbling out information one tiny piece at a time—releasing a little information to the Russian journalist Bezymenski in 1968, a little more to Ada Petrova and British writer Peter Watson in their 1995 book *The Death of Hitler*—only guaranteed that the story would generate numerous conflicting theories. This same dynamic of partial information release was seen with the final and most definitive piece of forensic evidence of Hitler's death, his teeth.

During the autopsy they conducted May 8, 1945, in the Berlin suburb of Buch, the Russians took detailed photographs of dental remains from the two corpses they believed were Adolf Hitler and Eva Braun. They also took photographs of the drawings made from memory by the dental assistant Käthe Heusermann and Fritz Echtmann, the dental technician who fashioned Hitler's metal bridge work. (Many researchers suspect that the Russians still have not released all of the photos in their archives and that equally detailed autopsy photographs of the bodies exist but are still being kept secret.)

The Russians allowed the journalist Bezymenski to have access to the dental photos for his 1968 book but did not share information about Hitler's actual dental records or about X-ray films of his skull that were taken in 1944 as part of a medical examination after the Stauffenberg assassination attempt.

Once again, the Russians dribbled out information one piece at a time.

In 1971, outside dental experts were allowed to view Soviet records—but, significantly, not the actual physical remains—to confirm that the dental remains in Soviet hands were actually Hitler's. Dr. Ferdinand Strøm from Oslo and Dr. Reidar Sognnaes, former dean of the dental school at the University of California, Los Angeles, were given permission to view records at the national archives in Moscow. For the first time, these were compared with X-ray films taken of Hitler's skull after the Stauffenberg attempt in 1944 that are in the possession of the United States. As a result of this research, the two doctors published "The Odontological Identification of Adolf Hitler" in the February 1973 issue of *Acta Odontologica Scandinavica*, confirming that the Russians had Hitler's teeth.

At first, the two experts were much more skeptical about the dental remains claimed to be Eva Braun's. There were no official dental records of Eva Braun's teeth, only the drawings made from memory by Echtmann and Heusermann. Interestingly, Eva Braun was scheduled to have a bridge inserted on April 19, 1945, but the dentist had to flee Berlin before he could complete the work. The Russians found the bridge in the dental clinic in the cellar of the Reich Chancellery. After further examination of the dental records in Soviet files, Strøm and Sognnaes decided that the dental remains the Russians had in their possession and which they claimed came from Eva Braun's corpse were, in fact, hers. All of these findings were reviewed in a 2014 article, "Dental Identification of Adolf Hitler and Eva Braun," in the *Journal of Dental Problems and Solutions*.[1]

But the Russians were still reluctant to allow outside experts to perform detailed forensic testing on the dental remains. In the 1990s and then again in 2003, they allowed a few experts to see the actual teeth but did not permit any forensic testing on them. Perhaps the Russians feared that their most prized trophy of the war—proof that they had succeeded in capturing what was left of Adolf Hitler—might turn out to be a fake.

Western researchers, such as the forensic expert Mark Benecke from Cologne, who examined both the skull fragments and teeth for a 2003 National Geographic documentary, were shocked by the casual manner with which the Russians stored these valuable historical artifacts. As late as the early 2000s, Hitler's alleged skull fragments were stored in a plastic floppy-disc box from the 1980s—because, Benecke remarked, it had a clear-plastic lid and a little lock on the front. The dental remains were stored in an old cigar box inside of a "large overseas travel suitcase" along with the original files from the investigation into Hitler's death.

The Russians Finally Relent

However, the bombshell 2009 claim that the Russians *didn't* have Hitler's skull after all—with the suggestion that there was perhaps less proof of Hitler's suicide than previously believed—finally forced the secretive Russians to show more of their cards. In 2016, more than seventy years after the Soviet Army dug up the bodies of Adolf Hitler and Eva Braun in the bomb crater outside the Führerbunker, the Russian government finally permitted another investigative team to examine its files and examine the physical evidence in its possession.

Beginning in April 2016, two journalists—the French reporter and author Jean-Christophe Brisard and the Russian documentary filmmaker Lana Parshina—set out on a quest to determine once and for all whether or not the Russian government had the physical remains of Adolf Hitler in its possession. If it did, this would finally prove, beyond a shadow of a doubt, that the German dictator died in April 1945 as eyewitnesses claimed and did not escape to live a life of ease in South America.

As part of their two-year investigation, Brisard and Parshina had to do battle with seventy years of Soviet and then Russian deception and cover-ups—exacerbated by the hyper-secrecy that permeates all levels of the Russian government and by inter-departmental rivalries that persist to this day. As they recount in their definitive 2018 book, *The Death of Hitler: The Final Word*, the two investigators were constantly stymied by bureaucratic runarounds and one-upmanship. Letters and emails would go unanswered for months on end. Meetings and appointments would be canceled at the last minute.

Yet a handful of helpful, sympathetic Russians in the top levels of the government came to their aid, getting them permission to examine physical evidence and to see top secret files to which no Westerner had ever been given access.

In the end, Brisard and Parshina were able to secure permission for the first ever detailed forensic examination, in July 2017, of the teeth in the Russian government's possession. This was the first time the teeth had been subjected to close-up inspection since the botched Soviet autopsy on May 8, 1945. Previous physical examinations of the teeth had been done by non-experts. Up until then, the only expert examination, done by Strøm and Sognnaes in 1971, was solely of records and photographs, not of the teeth themselves. The Russian-French team received permission to examine the teeth microscopically.

During the physical examination of the teeth, small fragments of tartar broke off on the gloves and underlying paper on which the teeth were placed, allowing for later chemical and microscopic analysis that the Russians only begrudgingly and belatedly authorized. The team was also given permission to examine, but not test, the skull fragments.

On March 28, 2017, the French paleopathologist and coroner Dr. Philippe Charlier, aged forty, flew from Paris to Moscow's Sheremetyevo Airport.

Renowned for his work in identifying the remains of famous historical figures, including Richard the Lionheart and Henry IV, Charlier had been given just two days to conduct a forensic analysis of the skull fragments held in the State Archives of the Russian Federation (known by the Russian acronym GARF for *Gosudartstennyy Arkhiv Rossyskov Federatsii*).

Brisard and Parshina had been shown the fragments the year before by archivists, but they lacked the necessary scientific training to evaluate them.

French paleopathologist and coroner Dr. Philippe Charlier has finally settled scientifically the question of whether Adolf Hitler escaped from Berlin or died in the Führerbunker, as eyewitnesses claimed. *Wikimedia Commons*[2]

It was precisely these skull fragments that the American archaeologist Nick Bellantoni had declared back in 2009 were not Hitler's, based on the space between the skull sutures and later DNA analysis of bone scrapings. Bellantoni's blockbuster report had traumatized the Russians for a decade. It had called into question their great trophy of World War II, proof that Hitler was actually dead. As a result, the Russians wouldn't let a foreign scientist near their holdings. It took Brisard and Parshina months of begging and pleading to arrange for another examination.

Dr. Bellantoni had insisted that the fragments were too thin to be a man's and that the space between the sutures—the "joints" binding the pieces of a skull together—meant that the skull belonged to someone under age forty and that the thinness of the fragments suggested it was a woman. Bone samples taken from the skull pieces and subjected to DNA analysis had supposedly confirmed Dr. Bellantoni's judgement.

It was immediately clear to the new team that Bellantoni's research, which was never published in a scientific journal but broadcast around the world, had only reaffirmed the Russians' distrust of foreign scientists.

The Russians claimed that whatever bone samples Bellantoni had were acquired surreptitiously without their permission and could not be trusted.

So Charlier's visit to the Russian archives was accompanied by a certain amount of paranoia and by bureaucratic games—last-minute announcements that the inspections might be canceled and so forth. Eventually, however, Charlier was given two hours, from 6:00 to 8:00 p.m. on March 29, 2017, to examine the skull fragments purported to be those of Hitler. He was not allowed to touch the fragments, even with gloves, but only to look at them through the plastic lid of the floppy disc box in which they are (still!) held.

Despite the constraints, Charlier immediately disputed Bellantoni's certitudes. He said that you cannot identify the sex of a skeleton without the pelvis and that skulls are far too variable to permit the determination of sex based on simply the size or "thinness" of the bone. The same was true of the sutures: while it is often true, Charlier said, that the joints of the skull close up as people age, it's by no means an absolute.

What's more, an examination of the X-rays of Hitler's skull taken in 1944 and in the possession of the American archives clearly shows that Hitler's skull sutures specifically had gaps between them. "In those x-rays, you can see the sutures at the top of Hitler's skull," Charlier told Brisard and Parshina. "These sutures are quite wide apart. That is the proof that you can't claim that because sutures are open they belong to a young individual. It's an argument that doesn't hold water."[3]

What's more, Charlier insisted that the carbonization of the skull fragments indicated the body from which the skull had come "was burnt at a very high temperature."[4] As for the bullet hole, Charlier agreed with

Bellantoni that it was definitely as exit wound—the outward splaying showed that—but he disagreed with Bellantoni about the likely direction of the shot fired. Because the bone fragments came from the left parietal bone—the lower left back of the skull—Bellantoni had claimed the subject was shot in the face. But Charlier disagreed, insisting that if the subject fired into the right temple, "the exit of the bullet through the left parietal seems logical." This would seem to be particularly likely to be true if the gun was held at a slight angle back towards the center of the head and not flush with the temple.

This seemingly technical issue is important because one of the mysteries of Hitler's suicide is the manner in which he killed himself. The earliest reconstruction, that of Trevor-Roper for British Intelligence, based on hearsay that was later contradicted, was that Hitler "had shot himself through the mouth."[5] This dramatic detail came from the interrogation of Hitler's chauffeur Erich Kempka after the war. Kempka claimed he heard it from Hitler's adjutant Günsche; Günsche, however, later disputed in a German courtroom that he ever told Kempka any detail beyond the fact that Hitler had shot himself. Kempka had simply embellished the story, as he had been accused of doing on other occasions, or had simply assumed that Hitler shot himself in the mouth.

It's important to remember, though, that even the two best eyewitnesses to the events around Hitler's death—SS Adjutant Günsche and valet Linge—disagreed dramatically on certain key details. As Brisard and Parshina point out, Günsche claimed emphatically that he found Hitler dead in an *armchair* facing the door of the study, not on the sofa; Linge and other witnesses, such as SS guard Rochus Misch, said Hitler was found slumped to the side of the sofa next to Eva Braun. Photographs of the sofa taken in 1945, with blood visible on the sofa's right armrest, seem to support Linge's version.

Because of disputes such as these, Dr. Charlier had high hopes that forensic science might be able to help settle the issue of how Hitler killed himself once and for all. The two issues he hoped would be resolved were: (1) whether there was any evidence of cyanide poison in the teeth claimed to be Hitler's, and (2) whether there was any evidence of a gunshot in the teeth, such as gun powder or certain metals.

As far as the skull fragments are concerned, the forensic scientist remained restrained and unwilling to issue a definitive decree. Dr. Charlier would not commit himself to whether the fragments belonged to Hitler or not. They were from the burned body of an adult who had suffered a gunshot wound in the head. That was as much as he believed science could say with certitude.[6]

This was why the teeth held in the Russians' possession—and never physically examined by an expert—were so important. Because of the fingerprint-like quality of dental records and dental evidence, an examination of the teeth might allow for more definitive judgments.

The Definitive Analysis of the Dental Remains

As a result, Dr. Charlier returned to Moscow in July 2017 for another wrestling match with Russian archivists reluctant to allow any foreign scientist near their precious historical artifacts and records. On July 12, 2017, Dr. Charlier went with Brisard and Parshina to the massive beige fortress of the Lubyanka Building a few hundred yards from Red Square—once the offices of the dreaded KGB and now the home of the Russian Security Services or FSB. It is here that the most important records, photographs, and artifacts of Adolf Hitler are kept, including what the Russians insist are the remains of his teeth.

Although he would not be allowed to perform any chemical or other tests on the teeth, the Russians had consented to allow Dr. Charlier to bring with him a powerful microscope that included within it a digital camera. The investigators took an elevator up to the third floor of the dreaded building, walked down a windowless corridor, and entered a small office where the inspection of the teeth would take place. Five Russian men and one woman would watch the team's every move. They brought into the office the exhibits that the Russians have hidden from

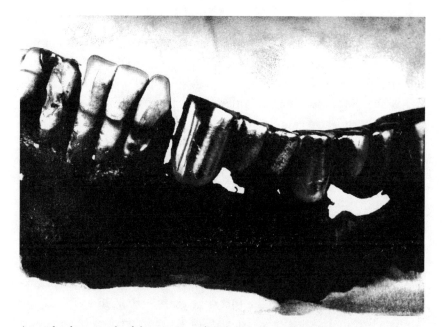

An early photograph of the remains of Hitler's lower jaw, held in the secret archives of Russia's intelligence services since it was first discovered in May 1945. *akg-images/Interfoto*

the world for more than seventy years, still preserved, incredibly, in an old cigar box.

The Russians allowed Dr. Charlier to touch the dental specimens—he wore surgical clothes, of course—and to examine them under his powerful microscope. To avoid contamination, he placed each of the dental specimens on brand-new sheets of sterile paper.

The first thing that Dr. Charlier wanted to establish was that the teeth were genuine and not Russian-made fakes. That the teeth were real human teeth was immediately evident, he said, from the presence of organic matter (such as carbonized mucus membranes) and, specifically, tartar on the teeth.

By all accounts, including that of his dentist and dental hygienist, Hitler had horrible teeth. He had chronic gingivitis and parodontopathy that had resulted in the exposure of the roots of his teeth. By the time of his death, the powerful German dictator had only four of his natural teeth left. All the rest were crowns or dentures, held together by elaborate bridgework.

When the plane carrying Hitler's actual dental records went down near Salzburg, Austria, in late April 1945, they were lost—yet another fact beloved of the conspiracy theorists! But as we have seen, the Nazi dictator's dentist, Dr. Hugo Blaschke, and others who worked on his teeth survived the war and drew detailed reconstructions of the Führer's teeth.

Based on these records, the transcribed interrogations of Blaschke and the others, and the five crystal-clear x-rays of Hitler's skull in American archives, Charlier had no hesitation in declaring that the teeth he was examining definitely belonged to Adolf Hitler. He was thus concurring with the judgement made forty-six years earlier, in 1971, by the dentists Strøm and Sognnaes, based solely upon written records and photographs.

But Charlier's powerful microscope did pick up one peculiarity: the presence of bright blue spots on the teeth and the metal bridge. That color is important. The reason the poison known as cyanide has this name is because of the dark blue color called cyan. The chemical, discovered by German chemists in the eighteenth century, is the same dark blue color associated with Prussia. For this reason it is sometimes called Prussian blue—and the poison is also known as prussic acid.

The presence of these dark blue spots on the teeth might support the notion that Hitler followed the advice of his doctor and tried the double method for suicide, biting down on a cyanide glass capsule while simultaneously squeezing the trigger of his Walther pistol.

To find out, chemical tests would be necessary—tests that the Russians absolutely forbade. Frustrated but compliant, Charlier completed his visual inspections of the teeth and then packed up all of his equipment—carefully taking off his gloves and putting them with the sheets of paper on which he had placed the dental artifacts.

After completing their forensic investigation of the teeth, taking hundreds of high-resolution photographs with Charlier's microscope, and positively identifying the teeth as belonging to Adolf Hitler, the team left the Lubyanka complex.

But then, Charlier, Brisard, and Parshina had a piece of unexpected luck.

Back in his laboratory in Paris, Charlier examined the latex gloves he had used—and, much to his shock, he found that "some tiny pieces of tartar from Hitler's teeth had come away during the examination."[8] It wasn't much: just two or three crumbs. But with modern electron microscopes and

In his laboratory in Paris, Dr. Philippe Charlier examined residues from Hitler's dental remains under an electron microscope. *Wikimedia Commons*[7]

other scientific tools, it was actually a forensic goldmine.

The problem was, Charlier, Brisard and Parshina didn't want a repeat of the Bellantoni fiasco—with the Russians enraged, denying the validity of the tests, and so on. What's more, they wanted to publish their findings in a peer-reviewed scientific journal, not broadcast them on the conspiracy-promoting History Channel. As a result, before they could proceed, the team needed to get permission from the Russian authorities to test the tartar.

It could cause another international incident. Like Bellantoni, the French team had somehow accidentally acquired physical specimens that the Russians had categorically forbidden them to take. Unsurprisingly, it took months before the Russian authorities even responded, much less granted permission.

Yet because the French team had already supported the validity of the Russian claim to have Hitler's teeth in their possession, the risk of another major embarrassment, like that of Bellantoni's claims, seemed minimal. As a result, the Russians agreed to allow Dr. Charlier to test the tartar deposits he had acquired.

With the aid of the powerful electron microscope at the Solid State Physics Laboratory at the University of Paris-South, Dr. Charlier and a colleague, Raphaël Weil, subjected Hitler's dental tartar to a host of tests, examining it molecule by molecule. The results were interesting but inconclusive on one of the two questions most driving Dr. Charlier.

The tartar showed no evidence of meat fibers, consistent with the fact that Hitler was a vegetarian in the last years of his life, and also no evidence of metals that are usually found when a gunshot is fired into a mouth. This means that the analysis of Hitler's teeth suggested that Hitler did not commit suicide by firing into his mouth.

But on the crucial issue of whether Hitler also swallowed poison at the same time, the tests were inconclusive. The chemical cyanide dissipates within hours and leaves few traces—one reason why it's popular with assassins and spies. Even current toxicological testing can only detect cyanide poisoning for up to two days. Researchers typically rely upon biomarkers such as the distinct smell of almonds that the poison leaves in its wake—the very smell that some of Hitler's associates claimed to have smelled when they entered his study after his death.

Thus the blue traces that Charlier found on Hitler's teeth were interesting but did not settle this final question. It might be possible to ascertain whether cyanide was present with further chemical analysis of the teeth in Moscow, but that will likely be years in the future, if ever.

The Final Results

In the end, Dr. Charlier and his colleagues published the scientific results in the peer-reviewed journal, the *European Journal of Internal Medicine*, in May 2018.

Entitled "The Remains of Adolf Hitler: A Biomedical Analysis and Definitive Identification," the study closes once and for all one of the greatest mysteries of the past century: whether Adolf Hitler committed suicide in Berlin on April 30, 1945, as he asserted he would do in his last will and testament and as all the surviving members of the Führerbunker claimed he did for decades afterwards—or, alternatively, the suicide story was an elaborate hoax perpetrated by the Nazis to cover up Hitler's escape.

Along with the clearest full-color photographs of Hitler's teeth ever published, the study asserts categorically that Hitler died in 1945. The dental remains, autopsy reports found in Russian archives, and X-rays found in U.S. archives provide, it says, "sufficient pieces of evidence in the definitive identification of the remains of the former Nazi leader Adolf Hitler."

Of course, such proof still may not satisfy conspiracy theorists.

After all, the skeptics will continue to point out that no one has Hitler's actual dental records (they were lost in a mysterious plane crash) but only the *drawings* of his teeth made from memory by loyal, confirmed Nazis, such as his dentist.

They will also claim, rightly, that there were ways Hitler might have been able to evade capture by using secret tunnels and that Hitler's supporters were planning for his escape by plane up until the very last days of the war. Hitler's personal pilot, Hans Baur, had a plane standing by that could have theoretically whisked Hitler and Eva Braun away as late as the last week of April—as the successful aerial escape of Ritter von Greim and Hanna Reitsch on April 29 proves.

It's also true that the Nazis were able to sneak billions of dollars in cash and other valuables out of the Reich at the very end of the war—and that some top Nazis managed to escape justice and flee Europe. (The existence of an organized escape organization known as Odessa, however, has now largely been debunked.) There was a large community of expat Germans in South America, including many open supporters of the Nazi regime, and at least two Nazi submarines fled to Argentina after the war rather than surrender to the Allies. All of this is true.

Yet these inconclusive facts must be balanced by the overwhelming evidence that Hitler chose not to escape but to die, as he insisted he must, in Berlin. His personal will and his so-called political testament both contain assertions that he intended to commit suicide rather than fall into enemy hands. Three copies of these documents were all signed, witnessed, and dated and still exist.

The intelligence officers of both the Western Allies and the Russians repeatedly interrogated all of the surviving inhabitants of the Führerbunker—those held by the Russians, under torture—and these testimonies agree about what happened to a remarkable degree, while differing about minor details. What's more, the eyewitnesses repeated their testimonies over the years in innumerable interviews and then in memoirs published thirty, forty, fifty, even sixty years or more after the war.

For example, Joseph Goebbels's secretary Brunhilde Pomsel refused all requests for interviews or to write her memoirs for sixty years, only agreeing to be interviewed about what she knew in 2011, when she was one hundred years old.[9] Even if the survivors all agreed to stick to a specific story to aid their beloved leader, the need to do so would have disappeared after so prolonged a period. Hitler would have died of natural causes long before.

While the evidence that Hitler died in Berlin is overwhelming, the evidence that he escaped is literally nonexistent—nothing more than scraps of hearsay contained in FBI and British intelligence files. These are claims made by often anonymous sources repeated to others and then sent in a letter, often years or decades later, to a government office.

As noted earlier, the History Channel's three-year reality series *Hunting Hitler* begins with a report in recently declassified FBI files that a source had heard from someone that this someone had met Adolf Hitler on a beach in Argentina in July 1945. When you look up this report, however, you discover that it was actually from a *Los Angeles Examiner* reporter who met someone in a bar one night and, while drinking, was told this story.

The reporter did not have the source's name and never saw him again, despite returning to the bar every day for more than a week. The claim in the preeminent "Hitler escaped" book *Grey Wolf* that Hitler was cared for by a German physician in Argentina comes from a man who said he read the physician's memoirs but then lost them when he moved houses. All of the "Hitler escaped" books, documentaries, and TV series rely upon unconfirmed reports like these. They end up being investigations into facts no one disputes—the existence of a large German expat community in Argentina, the layout of subway tunnels in Berlin—but they provide no credible, corroborated evidence of their central claim: that Hitler escaped.

Finally, and most significantly, the opening up of once Top Secret Soviet-era files about the Nazi era proves conclusively that the Soviet leadership, from Stalin on down, deliberately spread the lie that Hitler escaped to further their own agendas.

Stalin lied to Truman's face when he claimed that the Russians had no idea what had happened to Adolf Hitler. Stalin had already read the autopsy report that stated conclusively what had happened to Hitler: that what was left of his charred remains had been pulled from a shallow grave just a few feet in front of the Führerbunker's emergency exit, taken to a military hospital in the nearby suburb of Buch, and positively identified by means of his elaborate and quite distinctive dental work.

Much of this information was exposed in 1968 by the Russian journalist Lev A. Bezymenski, then published again in 1995 by Ada Petrova and Peter Watson and finally, in 2018, by Jean-Cristophe Brisard and Lana Parshina in *The Death of Hitler: The Final Word.*

Yet it has taken decades for the full story to be pieced together due to the decision by the Soviet leadership, in 1945, to launch a deliberate disinformation campaign and then, later, its refusal to release all of the evidence held in its archives. However, despite this deliberate

EYEWITNESS ACCOUNT

"I don't know what would have happened if the assassination had succeeded. All I see is millions of soldiers now lying buried, gone forever, who have instead come home again, their guns silent and the skies quieter once more. The war would have been over."

—*Traudl Junge,* Hitler's Last Secretary[10]

obstruction, the true story of what really happened when Adolf Hitler died has gradually been pieced together over many decades.

There are still many unsolved mysteries in our past, events about which people still legitimately disagree. But the death of Adolf Hitler is no longer one of them.

Between 3:30 and 4:00 p.m. on Monday, April 30, 1945, Adolf Hitler shot himself in the right temple with a Walther pistol while also likely swallowing a small but lethal dose of hydrogen cyanide liquid. His wife of one day, Eva Braun, died next to him after also biting down on a glass vial of cyanide.

The bodies of Hitler and his wife were then taken immediately outside to a shallow trench just six feet to the left of the Führerbunker emergency entrance, doused with gallons of gasoline, set on fire, and allowed to burn for several hours.

Their charred remains were then moved, during the evening, to a larger, deeper bomb crater and covered with dirt.

These remains were discovered four days later, on May 5, by Russian intelligence soldiers. They were then removed and taken for an autopsy on May 8 in the Berlin suburb of Buch.

After removing part of the jaw from Hitler's now-blackened body, the Russians took the remains, buried them for less than a year in the Brandenburg forest, then dug them up and moved them to a parking area in a Soviet intelligence building in Magdeburg, where they remained in secret for twenty-five years. Fearful that the remains might one day be discovered by neo-Nazis, in 1970 Soviet authorities ordered that the remains of Hitler, Eva Braun, and the Goebbels family all be once again exhumed, cremated until nothing but dust remained, and scattered in a nearby river.

In the end, despite innumerable books, documentaries, and even full-blown reality TV series that speculate about Hitler's alleged escape, that is what really happened to Adolf Hitler.

EPILOGUE

The war in Europe officially ended on May 8, 1945, just over one week after Hitler and his bride of one day committed suicide in the Berlin bunker. At two in the morning on May 7, at the Supreme Headquarters Allied Expeditionary Force (SHAEF) in Reims, France, the chief-of-staff of the German Armed Forces High Command, General Alfred Jodl, signed a document of unconditional surrender for all German forces. The next day, May 8, Field Marshal Wilhelm Keitel and other top German officials signed again, this time in Berlin in the presence of Soviet Marshal Georgi Zhukov and representatives of SHAEF.

While V-E Day was a time of celebration throughout the world, the suffering that had been unleashed by Hitler and the Nazi Party continued. Germany's major cities were now piles of rubble, its industrial infrastructure largely destroyed. In the midst of the carnage, some of the architects of this wanton destruction followed their leader's example and committed suicide. Others tried to escape and were caught. A tiny few, such as Gestapo chief Heinrich Müller, vanished without a trace.

Heinrich Himmler, the head of the SS and the second or third most powerful man in Germany until Hitler sacked him on April 28, had tried to negotiate with the Allied leadership. But a week after Hitler's death, on May 6, Hitler's successor, Admiral Karl Dönitz, personally handed Himmler a letter of dismissal. Himmler realized the time had come to flee. He put on a disguise that included a patch over one eye, shaved off his mustache, and assumed the fake name of Sergeant Heinrich Hitzinger.

Traveling with a caravan of four cars, Himmler led a small group of similarly disguised SS officers south from Admiral Dönitz's headquarters in Flensburg, near the border with Denmark, to the mouth of the Elbe River, northwest of Hamburg. There they abandoned their vehicles, were ferried across the wide river by a fisherman, and continued south on foot until they reached the small town of Bremervörde.[1] But then, on May 22, Himmler's luck ran out. He was detained at a checkpoint by a British patrol, then turned over to interrogators. After admitting who he was, Himmler was examined by a British doctor who attempted to peer into Himmler's mouth. The Nazi leader jerked his head away, bit down on a cyanide capsule he was secretly holding in his cheek, and was dead in fifteen minutes.

Perhaps the biggest war criminal the Allies were able to claim was Hermann Göring, the head of the Luftwaffe and, until he made the mistake of pressing the matter in late April, Adolf Hitler's designated successor as Führer. Like Himmler, Göring had the delusional belief that he would be able to negotiate a separate peace agreement with the Western Allies, in particular with General Dwight Eisenhower himself.

By early May, Göring was being held under a kind of house arrest by SS soldiers at his own Mauterndorf Castle, near Salzburg, Austria. Before the war had officially ended, on May 6, a U.S. Army unit was dispatched to pick Göring up. Much to Göring's shock, he was not treated like a defeated political leader but as a common criminal, sent to a prisoner of war camp, put on a strict diet, and gradually weaned off his morphine habit.

Six months later, in November, Göring would stand trial at Nuremberg for war crimes and crimes against humanity, including the genocide of six million Jews. The court convicted Göring on all counts and sentenced him to death on October 1, 1946. The night before his execution, on October 15, Göring managed to swallow a cyanide capsule that had likely been retrieved from his confiscated personal effects and smuggled into his cell. Allied soldiers put his corpse on display at the execution grounds and then cremated the remains, throwing the ashes into a nearby river.

Other top Nazis sentenced at the war crimes tribunal and executed on October 16, 1946, included Hans Frank, who had overseen much of the carnage in Poland; Wilhelm Frick, the architect of the Reich's racial laws; Alfred Jodl, the Nazi general who had signed the declaration of surrender and who ordered the executions of Allied prisoners and Russian commissars; the top SS official Ernst Kaltenbrunner, in charge of the Nazi death squads, the Einsatzgruppen, which had murdered millions in Eastern Europe; Wilhelm Keitel, the loyal Nazi general who ordered numerous executions of prisoners; Joachim von Ribbentrop, Nazi Germany's foremost diplomat and foreign minister; Alfred Rosenberg, the Nazi Party's chief ideological thinker; Fritz Sauckel, who oversaw the slave labor program in the East; Arthur Seyss-Inquart, the Reich's governor of the Netherlands; and Julius Streicher, publisher of the anti-Semitic Nazi newspaper *Der Stürmer.*

Some Nazi leaders were able to escape the hangman's noose, however. Admiral Dönitz, head of the German navy and appointed by Hitler to be his successor, successfully argued at Nuremberg that the United States had used the same lethal submarine tactics he had. Dönitz was released after ten years in prison and died in 1980. Albert Speer, Hitler's friend, favorite architect, and Reich minister of armaments, was sentenced to twenty years in prison and released from Spandau Prison in 1966. After his release, Speer wrote his detailed account of Hitler's rise and fall, *Inside the Third Reich*, which became an international bestseller when it was published in 1970. In recent years, historians have challenged Speer's portrayal of himself as the "good Nazi," the technocrat who had no real knowledge of the Holocaust. Another top Nazi, Rudolf Hess, Hitler's deputy Führer and the editor of *Mein Kampf,* who had flown to

Britain in 1941 on a bizarre "peace mission," was sentenced by the Nuremburg tribunal to life in prison for helping to plan a war of aggression. Hess spent the rest of his life in Spandau Prison, in West Berlin. In August 1987, at age ninety-three, Hess hanged himself in a reading room in the prison.

Martin Bormann, Hitler's close aide and probably the most powerful man in Germany in the final days of the Third Reich, was an interesting case. He seemingly vanished in the chaos of the final day at the Führerbunker. Bormann was tried in absentia by the Nuremburg tribunal and sentenced to death, but what became of him was something of a mystery. Some of those who claimed that Hitler had escaped from the bunker, such as the authors of *Grey Wolf*, also claimed the same about Bormann. In fact, by some accounts Bormann was the chief architect of Hitler's flight to Argentina and joined him there after the war. In the early 1960s, the West German government even offered a reward for his capture.

Eyewitnesses in the Führerbunker claimed to have spotted Bormann during one of the "breakouts" from the bunker that occurred on May 1, 1945. Bormann was in the group that included Hitler Youth chief Artur Axmann, the SS doctor Ludwig Stumpfegger (who helped murder the Goebbels children), and Hitler's personal pilot Hans Bauer. The group had taken a subway tunnel to Berlin's Friedrichstrasse station, which still exists today, and then came up to street level. At around two in the morning on May 2, they were attempting to cross the Spree River at the Weidendammer Bridge near the Reichstag, hiding behind a tank when the tank was hit by artillery fire.[2] Later, the group apparently managed to make it across the river, but then Axmann became separated for a time. When forced to double back due to the presence of Soviet troops, Axmann saw two bodies on a bridge, one of which he believed was Bormann's.

The mystery of what became of Bormann was finally solved in December 1972 when construction workers, digging near the railway bridge close to the Lehrter station in Communist East Berlin, found the skeletal remains of two individuals dating back to the 1940s. Autopsy tests and reconstructed dental records, drawings made from memory by the same dentist who had worked on Hitler's teeth, indicated that the bodies were likely those of Bormann and Stumpfegger. The examiners found glass splinters in the teeth, evidence that the pair probably committed suicide by cyanide as they were about to be captured by Soviet troops. But that fact was not conclusive. Then, in 1998, sophisticated DNA tests on skull fragments and samples provided by Bormann's relatives proved that one of the two bodies was indeed that of Bormann. Nevertheless, those who believed Hitler escaped refused to accept the DNA results.

Strangely, most of the other denizens of the Führerbunker survived the war. Hitler's two female secretaries, Traudl Junge and Gerda Christian, were at first captured by Soviet troops but both were released and managed to escape to the west. Junge would go on to write a memoir of her time in the Führerbunker that would become the basis, at least partly, for the 2004 German film *Downfall*. (Another longtime Hitler secretary who was not in the bunker, Christa Schroeder, also wrote a postwar memoir that was far less contrite than Junge's.)

Hitler's loyal aides in his final days—his valet Heinz Linge, chauffeur Erich Kempka, SS bodyguard and telephone operator Rochus Misch, SS adjutant Otto Günsche and chief engineer Johannes Hentschel—were all captured by Soviet troops. Linge, Günsche, and Misch were tortured severely and imprisoned in Soviet prisons for many years. Misch was released in 1954, Linge in 1955, and Günsche in 1956.

Kempka and Hentschel were luckier. If a Yugoslav partisan had not helped him, and he had been discovered by Soviet troops, Kempka would have likely met the same fate as Günsche, Linge, and Misch. The woman introduced Kempka, by then dressed in civilian clothes, as her husband, and Kempka and the Soviet troops drank vodka together and toasted the fall of Berlin.[3] Later Kempka would be captured by American soldiers and become the first Nazi to tell what had become of Hitler. He was released in 1947. Hentschel, too, was released by the Soviets early, in

1947. Both Kempka and Linge wrote books about their time in the Führerbunker. Günsche, who refused all requests to talk about his years as Hitler's adjutant, lived quietly near the Rhine River until 2003, when he died at age eighty-six.

As for the Führerbunker itself, that is an interesting story in its own right. As we saw earlier, the Soviets, who had lost between eight and ten million soldiers defeating Adolf Hitler, were more interested in destroying Berlin than in preserving buildings and artifacts for history. Their initial investigation of the Führerbunker was at first dominated by the search for Eva Braun's lingerie, not Hitler's top secret papers. Eventually, the Soviets did remove artifacts and papers for storage in the KGB's secret archives, but not before looters of all stripes and nationalities had descended upon the building.

In the first years after the war, the Soviets spent considerable time and effort demolishing the monuments and buildings of the Third Reich. Albert Speer's imposing New Reich Chancellery building, located just northeast of Potsdamer Platz along Voßstraße, was leveled.

The bunker itself remained, although the conical ventilation tower and emergency exit were toppled by 1947. When the Berlin Wall was built in 1961, the site of the Führerbunker was located in the no-man's-land between East and West Berlin and therefore left undisturbed for nearly four decades. But in 1988 the East German government began excavating the site to prepare the foundation for a series of new apartment blocks. The buried Führerbunker, partially flooded, was exposed for the first time since the end of the war.

An East German photographer named Robert Conrad risked jail by sneaking down into the bunker thirty times disguised as a construction worker. He took hundreds of photographs showing the bunker walls and furnishings damaged but largely intact. Yet by the time the excavation was completed, the concrete roof of the Führerbunker would be torn off and what remained of the interior filled with rubble, sand, and gravel. The site was then smoothed over and turned into a parking lot, which it remains to this day. In 2006, Berlin municipal authorities relented and put up a small sign marking the location.

For history buffs, however, the street plan of this part of Berlin remains largely unchanged since 1945. To the south, running east to west, there is the street along which Albert Speer built his New Reich Chancellery, Voßstraße. In its place stands a modern seven-story apartment building. North and east of this street is Wilhelmstrasse; north and west, Ebert Strasse (formerly Hermann Göring Strasse). In the lower third of the rectangle formed by these streets is the location of the Führerbunker, at the intersection of two quiet side streets, Gertrude-Kolmar-Strasse and In den Ministergärten. It's a favorite pastime of tourists to imagine precisely where the emergency entrance to the bunker was located and thus where Hitler was temporarily buried. Eerily enough, one strong possibility is that the large concrete cube that housed the bunker's emergency exit extended out into what is now the current intersection. This would place Hitler's temporary grave beneath a corner sidewalk across the street from a parking lot near a children's playground.

Many of the other macabre remnants of Hitler's evil empire are not as difficult to locate. The Bendlerblock office complex, almost entirely unchanged, is still found where it was in Stauffenberg's time, just off the street now named Stauffenbergstrasse, south of the Tiergarten park. Stauffenberg's old home in the south Berlin suburb of Wannsee, at Tristanstrasse 8, is also still there, marked by a simple plaque. The Wannsee Villa where the Final Solution was discussed in January 1942 is only ten minutes away, on the lakeshore. Tempelhof Airport, where Stauffenberg likely landed after his failed attempt to kill Hitler, is still there but now abandoned, used by locals for weekend barbecues and games of soccer. The Reichstag building, where a fire helped Hitler seize absolute control of the government in 1933, has been restored to its former glory and is now once again, after more than eighty years, the home of Germany's democratic parliament.

Just south of the Reichstag lies Berlin's large central park, the Tiergarten. At the east end of the park stands the famous Brandenburger Tor (Brandenburg Gate), topped by the golden Goddess of Victory in her chariot. At the other end towers the Victory Column, also topped by a golden goddess of victory. The column was once located near the Reichstag but was moved to its current location and raised in height by Hitler's architect, Albert Speer. Between these two monuments is the long avenue that the Nazis called the East-West Axis, from which daredevil pilots such as Hanna Reitsch flew out of Berlin in the final days of the war. Today it has been renamed the Straße des 17 Juni in remembrance of the day in 1953 when the Red Army opened fire on protesting workers.

Past the Brandenburg Gate, this road becomes the famous avenue known as the Unter den Linden, leading past the enormous exhibition hall and former military museum, the Zeughaus, where a general named Rudolf von Gersdorff tried to blow up Hitler in 1943 by becoming a suicide bomber. The Zeughaus now houses the Museum of German History. Just a few steps away, on the bank of the River Spree, is the ornate Berlin Cathedral, run by the Evangelical Church, where Hermann Göring was married in 1935 and Hitler was the best man. Closed during the forty years of communist rule, the cathedral was restored and reopened in 1993.

Tourists get caught up visiting these sites, if only because they remind them of what really happened not so long ago. The July 20 plotters who tried to kill Hitler and take over the government in a coup were tried, as we have seen, in the so-called People's Court, housed in the neoclassical school building at Bellevuestrasse 15, in Potsdamer Platz. That building was destroyed, along with the chief judge, in an Allied air raid in 1945. Today the location is the site of Sony Corp's German headquarters, the Sony Center, a futuristic glass skyscraper.

Yet the prison where the July 20 plotters were executed still stands. Plötzensee Prison, built in 1879, is still a working prison, the entrance located on Friedrich Olbricht Damm just south of Berlin's Tegel Airport. But the Plötzensee Memorial, the brick shed where the July 20 plotters were hanged, is around the back, down a dark alley and somewhat difficult to find. It is perhaps the most chilling of all the Nazi sites in Berlin, surrounded, as it is, with towering brick walls and guard towers.

More than three-quarters of a century ago, a handful of very brave men and women risked their lives, and the lives of their families, in a desperate attempt to overthrow an evil regime and stop a world war. Many would pay for their failure, in this dank shed, with their lives. In the end, surrounded by the world's armies, Hitler did to himself what no one else could. He ended his own life, and, as soon as he did so, the killing stopped. The greatest genocide in history was finally over.

SELECT BIBLIOGRAPHY

Allen, William Sheridan. *The Nazi Seizure of Power.* New York: Franklin Watts, 1965.

Beevor, Antony. *The Fall of Berlin 1945.* New York: Penguin Books, 2002.

Behrens, Petra and Johannes Tuchel. *"Our True Identity Was to Be Destroyed": The Children Consigned to Bad Sachsa after July 20, 1944.* Berlin: German Resistance Memorial Center, 2017.

Brisard, Jean-Christophe and Lana Parshina. *The Death of Hitler.* New York: Da Capo Press, 2018.

Corsi, Jerome R. *Hunting Hitler: New Scientific Evidence That Hitler Escaped Nazi Germany.* New York: Skyhorse Publishing, 2014, 2017.

Daly-Groves, Luke. *Hitler's Death: The Case against Conspiracy.* Oxford: Osprey Publishing, 2019.

Duffy, James P. and Vincent L. Ricci. *Target Hitler: The Plots to Kill Adolf Hitler.* Westport, CT: Praeger, 1992.

Fest, Joachim. *Plotting Hitler's Death: The German Resistance to Hitler, 1933–1945*. Translated by Bruce Little. London: Phoenix Books, 1996.

———. *Inside Hitler's Bunker: The Last Days of the Third Reich*. Translated by Margot Bettauer Dembo. New York: Farrar, Straus and Giroux, 2004.

Galante, Pierre. *Operation Valkyrie: The German Generals' Plot against Hitler*. New York: Harper & Row, 1981.

German Resistance Memorial Center, *Georg Elser and the Assassination Attempt of November 8, 1939*. Berlin: German Resistance Memorial Center, undated.

Gisevius, Hans B. *To the Bitter End: An Insider's Account of the Plot to Kill Hitler, 1933–1944*. Translated by Richard and Clara Winston. New York: Da Capo Press, 1947.

Hanfstaengl, Ernst. *Hitler: The Memoir of a Nazi Insider Who Turned against the Führer*. Translated by John Willard Toland. New York: Arcade Publishing, 1957.

Haupt, Michael, editor. *The Wannsee Conference and the Genocide of the European Jews*. Berlin: House of the Wannsee Conference Educational and Memorial Site, 2018

Hawes, James. *The Shortest History of Germany*. London: Old Street, 2017.

Hoffmann, Peter. *Stauffenberg: A Family History, 1905–1944*. Cambridge: Cambridge University Press, 1995.

———. *The History of the German Resistance, 1944–1945*. Translated by Richard Barry. Cambridge, MA: MIT Press, 1977.

Jones, Nigel. *Countdown to Valkyrie: The July Plot to Assassinate Hitler*. London: Frontline Books, 2008.

Junge, Traudl. *Hitler's Last Secretary: A Firsthand Account of Life with Hitler*. Translated by Anthea Bell. New York: Arcade Publishing, 2003, 2011.

Kempka, Erich. *I Was Hitler's Chauffeur: The Memoir of Erich Kempka*. Translated by Geoffrey Brooks. London: Frontline Books, 2010.

Kershaw, Ian. *Hitler: 1936–1945 Nemesis.* New York: W. W. Norton & Company, 2000.

———. *The End: The Defiance and Destruction of Hitler's Germany, 1944–1945.* New York: Penguin Press, 2011.

Kubizek, August. *The Young Hitler I Knew.* Translated by Geoffrey Brooks. London: Greenhill Books, 2006.

Linge, Heinz. *With Hitler to the End: The Memoirs of Adolf Hitler's Valet.* Translated by Geoffrey Brooks. London: Frontline Books, 2009.

Mayo, Jonathan and Emma Craigie. *Hitler's Last Day: Minute by Minute.* London: Short Books, 2015.

Misch, Rochus. *Hitler's Last Witness: The Memoirs of Hitler's Bodyguard.* London: Frontline Books, 2014.

Nagorski, Andrew. *Hitlerland: American Eyewitnesses to the Nazi Rise to Power.* New York: Simon & Schuster, 2012.

O'Donnell, James P. *The Bunker: The History of the Reich Chancellery Group.* New York: Da Capo Press, 1978.

Petrova, Ada and Peter Watson. *The Death of Hitler: The Full Story with New Evidence from Secret Russian Archives.* New York: W. W. Norton & Company, 1995.

Shirer, William L. *Berlin Diary: The Journal of a Foreign Correspondent, 1934–1941.* New York: Alfred Knopf, 1941.

Speer, Albert. *Inside the Third Reich.* Translated by Richard and Clara Winston. New York: Macmillan, 1970.

Toland, John. *Adolf Hitler,* Vol. 2. New York: Doubleday, 1976.

Trevor-Roper, Hugh. *The Last Days of Hitler,* 6th Edition. Chicago: University of Chicago Press, 1987.

Ullrich, Volker. *Hitler: Ascent, 1989–1939.* Translated by Jefferson Chase. New York: Vintage, 2016.

Williams, Gerrard and Simon Dunstan. *Grey Wolf: The Escape of Adolf Hitler.* New York: Sterling Publishing, 2011.

NOTES

Introduction

1. "Adolf Hitler: Doenitz Announces Hitler's Death," Jewish Virtual Library, https://www.jewishvirtuallibrary.org/doenitz-announces-hitler-s-death-may-1945. For a recording of the announcement see Various Artists—Topic, "Death of Hitler: German Announcement, 8 May 1945," YouTube, November 10, 2014, https://www.youtube.com/watch?v=C6U_5cCoZvM.

2. Mark Abadi, "Hitler Died 73 Years Ago Today—Here's How Newspapers around the World Reacted," *Business Insider*, April 30, 2018, https://www.businessinsider.com/hitler-death-newspapers-2018-4#heres-what-shaef-a-newspaper-for-displaced-allied-military-members-in-europe-had-to-say-13.

3. Lucy Ash, "The Rape of Berlin," BBC News, May 1, 2015, https://www.bbc.com/news/magazine-32529679.

4. Robert Philpot, "'Hitler Lived': Scholar Explores the Conspiracies That Just Won't Die," *Times of Israel*, May 2, 2019, https://www.timesofisrael.com/hitler-lived-scholar-explores-the-conspiracies-that-just-wont-die/.

5. Declassified document part 01 of 04 on Hitler in "FBI Records: The Vault," Federal Bureau of Investigation, https://vault.fbi.gov/adolf-hitler/adolf-hitler-part-01-of-04/view.

6. "Russian Writes of Hitler's Death," *New York Times*, February 22, 1964, https://www.nytimes.com/1964/02/22/archives/russian-writes-of-hitler-death-chuikov-states-his-troops-found-body.html.
7. Uki Goñi, "Tests on Skull Fragment Cast Doubt on Adolf Hitler Suicide Story," *The Guardian*, September 26, 2009.
8. "Fresh Doubts over Hitler's Death after Tests on Bullet Hole Skull Reveal It Belonged to a Woman," *Daily Mail*, September 28, 2009.

Chapter 1: Plotting the Death of Hitler

1. Peter Hoffmann, ed., *Behind Valkyrie: German Resistance to Hitler, Documents* (Montreal: McGill-Queen's University Press, 2011), 337.
2. Hans B. Gisevius, *To the Bitter End: An Insider's Account of the Plot to Kill Hitler: 1933–1944*, trans. Richard and Clara Winston (New York: Da Capo Press, 1998), 484.
3. A new German biography of Stauffenberg by historian Thomas Karlauf strives to chart a middle ground between those who see Stauffenberg as a moral hero and those who claim he only acted to save Germany from military defeat. See Thomas Karlauf, *Porträt eines Attentäters* (Berlin: Karl Blessing Verlap, 2019), not yet available in English.
4. For most of the details of Stauffenberg's life, I rely upon Peter Hoffmann's excellent and authoritative biography. See Peter Hoffmann, *Stauffenberg: A Family History, 1905–1944* (Cambridge: Cambridge University Press, 1995).
5. Courtesy of Stippe, https://commons.wikimedia.org/wiki/File:Staufenberg_Berlin_Wannsee_(2).JPG.
6. James P. Duffy and Vincent L. Ricci, *Target Hitler: The Plots to Kill Adolf Hitler* (Westport, Connecticut: Praeger Publishers, 1992), 162.
7. Or 2.5 square miles. For this and more information about Hitler's Wolf's Lair, see http://www.wolfsschanze.pl/historia.html, the official website of Wilczy Szaniec/Wolfsschanze/Wolf's Lair, the historical site now managed by the Srokowo Forest District of the Republic of Poland.
8. Joachim Fest, *Plotting Hitler's Death: The German Resistance to Hitler 1933–1945*, trans. Bruce Little (London: Weidenfeld & Nicolson, 1996), 255.
9. See U.S. Holocaust Museum, "Documenting the Number of Victims of the Holocaust and Nazi Persecution," https://encyclopedia.ushmm.

org/content/en/article/documenting-numbers-of-victims-of-the-holocaust-and-nazi-persecution.

10. Alan Axelrod, *Encyclopedia of World War II, Volume 1* (New York: Facts on File, 2007), 213.

11. August Kubizek, *The Young Hitler I Knew*, trans. Geoffrey Brooks (London: Greenhill Books, 2006), 93–94.

12. Ibid.

13. Adolf Hitler, *Mein Kampf*, trans. Ralph Manheim (Boston: Houghton Mifflin, 1943, renewed 1972), 21.

14. Volker Ullrich, *Hitler: A Biography, vol. 1: The Ascent (1889–1939)*, trans. Jefferson Chase (London: Vintage, 2016), 44.

15. Courtesy of Deutsches Bundesarchiv, https://commons.wikimedia.org/wiki/File:Bundesarchiv_Bild_146-1974-082-44,_Adolf_Hitler_im_Ersten_Weltkrieg_retouched.jpg.

16. https://commons.wikimedia.org/wiki/File:February_1919_US_News_coverage_of_unrest_in_Germany.png.

17. Hitler's official DAP membership card listed him as member number 555. But the party officials had purposely added an additional 500 to the number of members in order to make the tiny party look bigger than it actually was.

18. Courtesy of Deutsches Bundesarchiv, https://commons.wikimedia.org/wiki/File:Bundesarchiv_Bild_119-1486,_Hitler-Putsch,_M%C3%BCnchen,_Marienplatz.jpg.

19. Courtesy of Bildarchiv Preußischer Kulturbesitz, https://commons.wikimedia.org/wiki/File:Hitler,_Maurice,_Kriebel,_Hess,_Weber,_prison_de_Landsberg_en_1924.jpg.

20. Ernst Hanfstaengl, *Hitler: The Memoir of a Nazi Insider Who Turned against the Führer* (New York: Arcade Publishing, 1957), 107.

Chapter 2: Saving Germany from the Nazis

1. Courtesy of Deutsches Bundesarchiv, https://commons.wikimedia.org/wiki/File:Bundesarchiv_Bild_183-S38324,_Tag_von_Potsdam,_Adolf_Hitler,_Paul_v._Hindenburg.jpg.

2. Hans B. Gisevius, *To the Bitter End: An Insider's Account of the Plot to Kill Hitler: 1933–1944*, trans. Richard and Clara Winston (New York: Da Capo Press, 1998), 84.

3. Courtesy of Deutsches Bundesarchiv, https://commons.wikimedia. org/wiki/File:Bundesarchiv_Bild_119-1486,_Hitler-Putsch,_M% C3%BCnchen,_Marienplatz.jpg.

4. August Kubizek, *The Young Hitler I Knew*, trans. Geoffrey Brooks (London: Greenhill Books, 2006), 94,155.

5. Ian Kershaw, *Hitler: 1936–45: Nemesis* (New York: W. W. Norton & Company, 2000), 151.

6. From "The Right of Emergency Defense," chapter 15 of volume II of *Mein Kampf*, 679, quoted in Leni Yahil, *The Holocaust: The Fate of European Jewry, 1932–1945* (Oxford: Oxford University Press, 1991), 51.

7. From "A Reckoning," chapter 12 of volume I of *Mein Kampf*, 338, quoted in Yahil, *The Holocaust*.

8. Courtesy of Yad Vashem, https://commons.wikimedia.org/wiki/ File:Selection_on_the_ramp_at_Auschwitz-Birkenau,_1944_ (Auschwitz_Album)_1c.jpg.

9. Gisevius, *To the Bitter End*, 461.

10. Courtesy of Deutsches Bundesarchiv, https://commons.wikimedia. org/wiki/File:Bundesarchiv_Bild_146-1980-033-04,_Ludwig_Beck. jpg.

11. James P. Duffy and Vincent L. Ricci, *Target Hitler: The Plots to Kill Adolf Hitler* (Westport, Connecticut: Praeger Publishers, 1992), 63.

12. Roger Moorhouse, *Killing Hitler: The Plots, the Assassins, and the Dictator Who Cheated Death* (New York: Bantam, 2007), 2. Moorhouse cites the German historian Willi Berthold's book, *Die 42 Attentate auf Hitler* (Munich: Goldmann Allgemeine Reihe, 1981). James P. Duffy and Vincent L. Ricci discuss fourteen attempts by civilians to kill Hitler and another seven by German military officers, leaving off some of the minor efforts that Moorhouse highlights. See their book, *Target Hitler: The Plots to Kill Adolf Hitler* (Westport, Connecticut: Praeger, 1992).

13. Courtesy of Narodowe Archiwum Cyfrowe, https://commons. wikimedia.org/wiki/File:Georg_Elser_2-12179.jpg.

14. Gisevius, *To the Bitter End*, 407.

15. Courtesy of Deutsches Bundesarchiv, https://commons.wikimedia. org/wiki/File:Bundesarchiv_Bild_183-E12329,_M%C3%BCnchen,_ B%C3%BCrgerbr%C3%A4ukeller,_Sprengstoffanschlag.jpg.

16. In *Target Hitler*, James P. Duffy and Vincent L. Ricci relate the details of the various theories surrounding the Munich bombing attempt.

They conclude that Himmler was likely behind the plot in an effort to replace Hitler as leader of Germany. But other historians believe that Elser acted alone. See Kershaw, *Hitler*, 274.

Chapter 3: Showing the World

1. Albert Speer, *Inside the Third Reich*, trans. Richard and Clara Winston (New York: Simon & Schuster, 1970), 322. Originally published in German, Albert Speer, *Erinnerungen* (Verlag Ullstein, 1969).
2. Courtesy of Deutsches Bundesarchiv, https://commons.wikimedia. org/wiki/File:Bundesarchiv_Bild_146-1976-130-53,_Henning_v._ Tresckow.jpg.
3. Peter Hoffmann, *The History of the German Resistance, 1933–1945*, trans. Richard Barry (Montreal: McGill-Queen's University Press, 1996), 256.
4. William L. Shirer, *The Rise and Fall of the Third Reich* (New York: Simon & Schuster, 1960), 830. See also Ian Kershaw, *Hitler: 1936–45: Nemesis* (New York: W.W. Norton & Company, 2000), 356.
5. Ibid.
6. "Directives for the Treatment of Political Commissars [Commissar Order] (June 6, 1941)," U.S. National Archives and Records Administration, College Park, Maryland, Nuremberg Trial, National Archives Record Group 238m, Entry 175, Box 27, NOKW-1076. See also Paul R. Bartrop and Michael Dickerman, *The Holocaust: An Encyclopedia and Document Collection*, Vol. 1 (Santa Barbara, CA: ABC-Clio, LLC, 2017), 1229.
7. Kershaw, *Hitler*, 359.
8. Courtesy of Deutsches Bundesarchiv, https://commons.wikimedia. org/wiki/File:Bundesarchiv_Bild_146-1976-130-51,_Rudolf-Christoph_v._Gersdorff.jpg.
9. In 1940, the exchange rate was roughly 2.50 Reichmarks to one U.S. dollar. Accounting for inflation, a 1940 U.S. dollar would be the equivalent of $18 in 2020 dollars. Thus 500,000 RM from 1940 would be the equivalent of $3.6 million today. See DollarTimes.com for inflation calculators.
10. Kershaw, *Hitler*, 660.
11. Ibid.

12. Courtesy of Deutsches Bundesarchiv, https://commons.wikimedia. org/wiki/File:Bundesarchiv_Bild_146-1981-072-61,_Friedrich_ Olbricht.jpg.

13. Hans B. Gisevius, *To the Bitter End: An Insider's Account of the Plot to Kill Hitler: 1933–1944*, trans. Richard and Clara Winston (New York: Da Capo Press, 1998), 519.

14. Jeremy Noakes, ed., *Nazism, 1919–1945, Vol. 4: The German Home Front in World War II* (Exeter, United Kingdom: University of Exeter Press, 1998), 621. The original German text is available in Hans-Adolf Jacobsen, *Opposition gegen Hitler und der Staatsstreich von 20. Juli 1944. Geheime Dokumente aus dem ehemaligen Reichssicherheitsamt* (Stuttgart: Seewald Verlag, 1984), vol. 1, 24–25, online at: http://germanhistorydocs.ghi-dc.org.

15. Courtesy of Morgan Hauser, https://commons.wikimedia.org/wiki/ File:Europe_under_Nazi_domination.png.

16. Kershaw, *Hitler*, 663.

17. Joachim Fest, *Plotting Hitler's Death: The German Resistance to Hitler 1933–1945*, trans. Bruce Little (London: Weidenfeld & Nicolson, 1996), 217.

18. Ibid., 219.

19. Courtesy of Deutsches Bundesarchiv, https://commons.wikimedia. org/wiki/File:Bundesarchiv_Bild_146-1994-022-32A,_Axel_ Freiherr_von_dem_Bussche-Streithorst.jpg.

20. Peter Hoffmann, ed., *Behind Valkyrie: German Resistance to Hitler Documents* (Montreal: McGill-Queen's University Press, 2011), 338.

21. Kershaw, *Hitler*, 670.

22. Gisevius, *To the Bitter End*, 507–8.

23. Kershaw, *Hitler*, 670.

24. Courtesy of Deutsches Bundesarchiv, https://commons.wikimedia. org/wiki/File:Bundesarchiv_Bild_146-1984-079-02,_F%C3%BChrerhauptquartier,_Stauffenberg,_Hitler,_Keitel_ crop.jpg.

25. Fabian von Schlabrendorff, *They Almost Killed Hitler* (New York: Macmillan, 1947), 37.

26. Peter Hoffmann, *The History of the German Resistance, 1933–1945*, trans. Richard Barry (Cambridge, Massachusetts: MIT Press, 1977), 265.

27. Ibid., 266–67.

28. Ibid., 265.

29. Fest, *Plotting Hitler's Death*, 257.
30. John Toland, *Adolf Hitler* (New York: Doubleday, 1976), vol. 2, 904; Shirer, *The Rise and Fall of the Third Reich*, 29.
31. Shirer, *The Rise and Fall of the Third Reich*, 29; Toland, *Adolf Hitler*, vol. 2, 904.
32. Hoffmann, *Stauffenberg*, 266.

Chapter 4: The Luck of the Devil

1. John Toland, *Adolf Hitler*, vol. 2 (New York: Doubleday, 1976), 905.
2. Heinz Linge, *With Hitler to the End: The Memoirs of Adolf Hitler's Valet*, trans. Roger Moorhouse (London: Frontline Books, 2009), 156.
3. Ian Kershaw, *Hitler: 1936–45: Nemesis* (New York: W. W. Norton & Company, 2000), 673.
4. Courtesy of Deutsches Bundesarchiv, https://commons.wikimedia. org/wiki/File:Bundesarchiv_Bild_146-1972-025-10,_Hitler-Attentat,_20._Juli_1944.jpg.
5. Traudl Junge, *Hitler's Last Secretary*, trans. Anthea Bell (New York: Arcade Publishing, 2003), 132–33.
6. Courtesy of Deutsches Bundesarchiv, https://commons.wikimedia. org/wiki/File:Bundesarchiv_Bild_146-1972-025-64,_Hitler-Attentat,_20._Juli_1944.jpg.
7. Toland, *Adolf Hitler*, vol. 2, 906–7.
8. Courtesy of Jörg Zägel, https://commons.wikimedia.org/wiki/File:Berlin,_Tiergarten,_Reichpietschufer,_Bendler-Block_02.jpg.
9. Courtesy of Deutsches Bundesarchiv, https://commons.wikimedia. org/wiki/File:Bundesarchiv_Bild_146-1969-168-07,_Friedrich_Fromm.jpg.
10. This dialogue is taken from the transcripts of the war crimes trial of Fromm, quoted in Hans B. Gisevius, *To the Bitter End: An Insider's Account of the Plot to Kill Hitler, 1933–1944*, trans. Richard and Clara Winston (New York: Da Capo Press, 1998), 546–47.
11. Ibid.
12. Courtesy of Deutsches Bundesarchiv, https://commons.wikimedia. org/wiki/File:Otto_Ernst_Remer_portrait.JPG.
13. Joachim Fest, *Plotting Hitler's Death: The German Resistance to Hitler 1933–1945*, trans. Bruce Little (London: Weidenfeld & Nicolson, 1996), 271.

14. Courtesy of Deutsches Bundesarchiv, https://commons.wikimedia. org/wiki/File:Bundesarchiv_Bild_146-1978-043-13,_Erwin_v._ Witzleben.jpg.

15. Courtesy of MisterBee1966, https://commons.wikimedia.org/wiki/ File:Stauffenberg%27s_office.JPG.

16. Fest, *Plotting Hitler's Death*, 277.

17. Courtesy of C. Seiberl, https://commons.wikimedia.org/wiki/ File:Berlin_Mitte_Bendlerblock_Innenhof.jpg.

18. John Toland, *Adolf Hitler*, vol. 2 (New York: Doubleday, 1976), 919.

19. Quoted in ibid.

20. The text is available in *The Guardian*'s archives, "Hitler's Six-Minute Broadcast," July 21, 1944, https://www.theguardian.com/ theguardian/1944/jul/21/fromthearchive.

21. Courtesy of Deutsches Bundesarchiv, https://commons.wikimedia. org/wiki/File:Bundesarchiv_Bild_183-R63893,_Carl_Heinrich_von_ St%C3%BClpnagel.jpg.

22. Fest, *Plotting Hitler's Death*, 281.

23. Ibid.

Chapter 5: The Aftermath

1. Ian Kershaw, *Hitler: 1936–45: Nemesis* (New York: W. W. Norton & Company, 2000), 693.

2. Heinz Linge, *With Hitler to the End: The Memoirs of Adolf Hitler's Valet*, trans. Roger Moorhouse (London: Frontline Books, 2009), 161.

3. Joachim Fest, *Plotting Hitler's Death: The German Resistance to Hitler 1933–1945*, trans. Bruce Little (London: Weidenfeld & Nicolson, 1996), 292.

4. Matthew Wagner, "Chabad: Make Nazi Commander a 'Righteous Gentile,'" *Jerusalem Post*, August 4, 2009, https://www.jpost.com/ Jewish-World/Jewish-News/ Chabad-Make-Nazi-commander-a-righteous-gentile.

5. Kershaw, *Hitler*, 1004.

6. Paul Callan, "The Day My Dad Tried to Kill Hitler," *Daily Express*, October 1, 2014, https://www.express.co.uk/news/history/58191/ The-day-my-dad-tried-to-kill-Hitler.

7. John Toland, *Adolf Hitler*, vol. 2 (New York: Doubleday, 1976), 926.

8. Peter Hoffmann, *The History of the German Resistance, 1933–1945*, trans. Richard Barry (Montreal: McGill-Queen's University Press, 1996), 280.

9. Courtesy of Deutsches Bundesarchiv, https://commons.wikimedia.org/wiki/File:Bundesarchiv_Bild_151-39-23,_Volksgerichtshof,_Reinecke,_Freisler,_Lautz.jpg.

10. Fabian Von Schlabrendorff, *They Almost Killed Hitler: Based on the Personal Account of Fabian Von Schlabrendorff* (Whitefish, MT: Kessinger Publishing, LLC, 2010), 139.

11. Courtesy of MisterBee1966, https://commons.wikimedia.org/wiki/File:Pl%C3%B6tzensee_Prison_01.JPG.

12. Fest, *Plotting Hitler's Death*, 303

13. Albert Speer, *Inside the Third Reich*, trans. Richard and Clara Winston (New York: Simon & Schuster, 1970), 504. Originally published in German, Albert Speer, *Erinnerungen* (Verlag Ullstein, 1969).

14. Kershaw, *Hitler*, 692.

15. Fest, *Plotting Hitler's Death*, 296.

16. Courtesy of Deutsches Bundesarchiv, https://commons.wikimedia.org/wiki/File:Bundesarchiv_Bild_146-1987-074-16,_Dietrich_Bonhoeffer.jpg.

17. Courtesy of Deutsches Bundesarchiv, https://commons.wikimedia.org/wiki/File:Bundesarchiv_Bild_146-1977-018-13A,_Erwin_Rommel(brighter).jpg.

18. Douglas Martin, "Manfred Rommel, Son of German Field Marshal, Dies at 84," *New York Times*, November 9, 2013, https://www.nytimes.com/2013/11/11/world/europe/manfred-rommel-son-of-german-field-marshal-dies-at-84.html.

19. Courtesy of SchorSch, https://commons.wikimedia.org/wiki/File:Herrlingen_Villa_Lindenhof.jpg.

20. "The Forced Suicide of Field Marshal Rommel, 1944," EyeWitness to History, 2002, http://www.eyewitnesstohistory.com/rommel.htm.

21. Erwin Rommel, *The Rommel Papers*, ed. Basil Henry Liddell Hart, Lucia-Maria Rommel, Manfred Rommel, and Fritz Bayerlein (New York: Harcourt Brace, 1953), 504–5.

22. Jonathan Mayo and Emma Craigie, *Hitler's Last Day* (London: Short Books, 2015), 26.

Chapter 6: The Beginning of the End

1. Traudl Junge, *Hitler's Last Secretary*, trans. Anthea Bell (New York: Arcade Publishing, 2003), 140.
2. Ian Kershaw, *Hitler: 1936–45: Nemesis* (New York: W. W. Norton & Company, 2000), 702.
3. "Bombing, States and Peoples in Western Europe 1940–1945," Centre for the Study of War, State and Society, Exeter University, https://humanities.exeter.ac.uk/history/research/centres/warstateandsociety/projects/bombing/germany/.
4. Courtesy of A. Savin, https://en.wikipedia.org/wiki/Wannsee_Conference#/media/File:Haus_der_Wannsee-Konferenz_02-2014.jpg.
5. House of the Wannsee Conference, *The Wannsee Conference and the Genocide of European Jews* (Berlin: House of the Wanssee Conference, 2018), 129. The text quotes from the "Trial of Adolf Eichmann," Record of Proceedings in the District Court of Jerusalem, ed., State of Israel, Ministry of Justice (Jerusalem: 1992–1999).
6. Minutes of Wannsee Conference, January, 20, 1942, NG-2586, "Trial of War Criminals before the Nuremberg Military Tribunals," XIII (Washington, D.C., 1952), 212–13.
7. Laura Geggel, "1.32 Million Jews Were Killed in Just Three Months during the Holocaust," Live Science, January 4, 2019, https://www.livescience.com/64420-holocaust-jewish-deaths.html.
8. Hitler's "Scorched Earth" Decree (Nero Decree) (March 19, 1945), in United States Chief Counsel for the Prosecution of Axis Criminality, Nazi Conspiracy and Aggression. Supplement B. (Washington, D.C.: United States Government Printing Office, 1948). Speer Document 27, 950–51. English translation edited by GHI staff. See Speer, *Inside the Third Reich*, 562–82.
9. See J. Robert Lilly, *Taken by Force: Rape and American GIs in Europe during World War II* (London, Palgrave, 2007), 26. Lilly estimates the number of rapes by American soldiers was about eleven thousand, compared to up to two million for the Soviet Army, including a hundred thousand in Berlin alone.
10. Albert Speer, *Inside the Third Reich*, trans. Richard and Clara Winston (New York: Simon & Schuster, 1970), 557. Original published in German, Albert Speer, *Erinnerungen* (Verlag Ullstein, 1969).

Chapter 7: Rumors of Hitler's Escape

1. "FBI Records on Adolf Hitler," The Vault, 75, https://vault.fbi.gov/adolf-hitler/adolf-hitler-part-01-of-04/view.
2. *National Police Gazette,* https://stuffnobodycaresabout.com/wp-content/uploads/2015/12/Police-Gazette-Hitler-December-1960.jpg.
3. A photocopy of the original CIA memo is available online on the CIA's website at https://www.cia.gov/library/readingroom/docs/HITLER%2C%20ADOLF_0005.pdf.
4. Confidential Routing and Record Sheet, https://www.cia.gov/library/readingroom/docs/HITLER%2C%20ADOLF_0005.pdf.
5. See Robert Valencia, "CIA Investigated Whether Hitler Survived World War II and Moved to Colombia," *Newsweek*, October 30, 2017, https://www.newsweek.com/cia-investigated-whether-hitler-survived-world-war-ii-and-moved-colombia-696847, and the photocopy of the original CIA memo on the CIA website, https://www.cia.gov/library/readingroom/docs/HITLER%2C%20ADOLF_0003.pdf.
6. See the obituary of Douglas Martin Carto, "Willis Carto, Far-Right Figure and Holocaust Denier, Dies at 89," *New York Times*, November 1, 2015, https://www.nytimes.com/2015/11/02/us/willis-carto-far-right-figure-and-holocaust-denier-dies-at-89.html.
7. Simon Dunstan and Gerrard Williams, *Grey Wolf: The Escape of Adolf Hitler* (New York: Sterling, 2011).
8. Vanessa Thorpe, "Hitler Lived until 1962? That's My Story, Claims Argentinian Writer," *The Guardian*, October 26, 2013, https://www.theguardian.com/world/2013/oct/27/hitler-lived-1962-argentina-plagiarism.
9. Dunstan and Williams, *Grey Wolf.*
10. Ibid., chapters 15 and 16.
11. Courtesy of Janitoalevic, https://commons.wikimedia.org/wiki/File:Casa_Inalco.jpg.
12. Dunstan and Williams, *Grey Wolf,* chapter 23ff.
13. Jerome R. Corsi, *Hunting Hitler* (New York: Skyhorse Publishing, 2014), 78–101
14. Ibid., 109.
15. Ibid., 110.
16. Albert Speer, *Inside the Third Reich*, trans. Richard and Clara Winston (New York: Simon & Schuster, 1970), 622. Originally

published in German, Albert Speer, *Erinnerungen* (Verlag Ullstein, 1969).

17. Corsi, *Hunting Hitler*, 126.

Chapter 8: The Last Days in the Bunker

1. Courtesy of Deutsches Bundesarchiv, https://commons.wikimedia. org/wiki/File:Bundesarchiv_Bild_146-1988-092-32,_Berlin,_Neue_ Reichskanzlei.jpg.

2. As noted in an earlier chapter, some of those authors who believe Hitler escaped also insist that the Hitler photographed on April 20 was merely a body double, not the real Hitler. However, their evidence for this is purely conjectural, based on dubious photographic analyses. The surviving witnesses, such as Speer, insisted to their dying day that the man they met that day was Adolf Hitler.

3. Ian Kershaw, *Hitler: 1936–45: Nemesis* (New York: W. W. Norton & Company, 2000), 803.

4. Traudl Junge, *Hitler's Last Secretary*, trans. Anthea Bell (New York: Arcade Publishing, 2003), 177.

5. Hugh Trevor-Roper, "The Strange Case of Himmler's Doctor Felix Kersten and Count Bernadotte," *Commentary*, April 1957, https:// www.commentarymagazine.com/articles/the-strange-case-of-himmlers-doctorfelix-kersten-and-count-bernadotte/.

6. Albert Speer, *Inside the Third Reich*, trans. Richard and Clara Winston (New York: Simon & Schuster, 1970), 605. Originally published in German, Albert Speer, *Erinnerungen* (Verlag Ullstein, 1969).

7. Speer would subsequently claim that he had a plan to assassinate Hitler during this final meeting by dropping poison down a ventilation shaft but that his plans were foiled by the installation of new filtration equipment. Speer's claim was met with widespread skepticism by historians.

8. Speer, *Inside the Third Reich*, 605.

9. Courtesy of Deutsches Bundesarchiv, https://commons.wikimedia. org/wiki/File:Hermann_Fegelein.jpg.

10. There is even video of the event on YouTube.

11. "Adolf Hitler: The Last Days in Hitler's Air Raid Shelter: Hanna Reitsch Interrogation," BACM Research, Paperless Archives, http://www. paperlessarchives.com/FreeTitles/HitlerLastDaysHannaReitsch.pdf.

12. Heinz Linge, *With Hitler to the End: The Memoirs of Adolf Hitler's Valet*, trans. Roger Moorhouse (London: Frontline Books, 2009), 193.
13. Junge, *Hitler's Last Secretary*, 180–81.
14. Rochus Misch, *Hitler's Last Witness: The Memoirs of Hitler's Bodyguard* (New York: Frontline Books, 2014), 164–5.
15. Courtesy of Deutsches Bundesarchiv, https://commons.wikimedia.org/wiki/File:Bundesarchiv_Bild_183-B02092,_Hanna_Reitsch.jpg.
16. Hanna Reitsch, *The Sky My Kingdom: Memoirs of the Famous German World War II Test Pilot*, trans. Lawrence Wilson (Philadelphia: Casemate, 2009).
17. Linge, *With Hitler to the End*, 192.
18. Erich Kempka, *I Was Hitler's Chauffeur*, trans. Geoffrey Brooks (Yorkshire: Frontline Books, 2010), 76.
19. Junge, *Hitler's Last Secretary*, 183.
20. Linge, *With Hitler to the End*, 194.
21. Mayo and Craigie, *Hitler's Last Day*, 55–56. See also Junge, *Hitler's Last Secretary*, 184.
22. Junge, *Hitler's Last Secretary*, 185.
23. Ibid., 184.
24. Ibid., 177.

Chapter 9: The Death of Adolf Hitler

1. Rochus Misch, *Hitler's Last Witness* (London: Frontline Books, 2013), 18.
2. Jonathan Mayo and Emma Craigie, "Hitler's Last 24 Hours: 'Bullseye!' Shouted Goebbels' Little Boy as Hitler Shot Himself in the Head," *Daily Mail*, April 13, 2015, https://www.dailymail.co.uk/news/article-3037701/Hitler-s-24-hours-Bullseye-shouted-Goebbels-little-boy-Hitler-shot-head.html.
3. Heinz Linge, *With Hitler to the End: The Memoirs of Adolf Hitler's Valet*, trans. Roger Moorhouse (London: Frontline Books, 2009), 199.
4. Ibid. See also Ada Petrova and Peter Watson, *The Death of Hitler: The Full Story with New Evidence from Secret Russian Archives* (New York: W. W. Norton & Company, 1995), 68.
5. Misch, *Hitler's Last Witness*, 172.
6. Linge, *With Hitler to the End*, 199.

7. Ibid., 199.
8. "Last Hitler Bodyguard Rochus Misch Dies," BBC News, September 6, 2013, https://www.bbc.com/news/world-europe-23989454.
9. Erich Kempka, *I Was Hitler's Chauffeur*, trans. Geoffrey Brooks (London: 2010), 77.
10. Traudl Junge, *Hitler's Last Secretary*, trans. Anthea Bell (New York: Arcade Publishing, 2003), LOC 3168.
11. Courtesy of Christopher Neubauer, https://commons.wikimedia.org/wiki/File:Karte-reichskanzlei.jpg.
12. Kempka, *I Was Hitler's Chauffeur*, 78.
13. Luke Daly-Groves, *Hitler's Death: The Case Against Conspiracy* (Oxford: Osprey Publishing, 2019), 143.
14. Kempka, *I Was Hitler's Chauffeur*, 39.
15. Both would take credit for this final act. See Linge, *With Hitler to the End*, 200, and Kempka, *I Was Hitler's Chauffeur*, 80.
16. Kempka, *I Was Hitler's Chauffeur*, 80.
17. Ian Kershaw, *Hitler: 1936–45: Nemesis* (New York: W. W. Norton & Company, 2000), epilogue.
18. Courtesy of Deutsches Bundesarchiv, https://commons.wikimedia.org/wiki/File:Bundesarchiv_Bild_183-V04744,_Berlin,_Garten_der_zerst%C3%B6rte_Reichskanzlei.jpg.
19. Linge, *With Hitler to the End*, 204.
20. Kershaw, *Hitler*, 832.
21. Courtesy of Deutsches Bundesarchiv, https://commons.wikimedia.org/wiki/File:Bundesarchiv_Bild_146-1978-086-03,_Joseph_Goebbels_mit_Familie.jpg.
22. Albert Speer, *Inside the Third Reich*, trans. Richard and Clara Winston (New York: Simon & Schuster, 1970), 588.
23. Linge, *With Hitler to the End*, 207.
24. Junge, *Hitler's Last Secretary*, 194.
25. https://commons.wikimedia.org/wiki/File:MISCH-Rochus.jpg.
26. James P. O'Donnell, *The Bunker: The History of the Reich Chancellery Group* (New York: Da Capo Press, 1978), 342–48.
27. Joachimsthaler Anton, *The Last Days of Hitler: The Legends, the Evidence, the Truth*, trans. Helmut Bögler (London: Brockhampton Press, 1999).

Chapter 10: The Mystery of Hitler's Mortal Remains

1. Marlow Stern, "Hitler's Final Days Revealed: Eyewitnesses Recount the Nazi's Death in Unearthed Footage," *Daily Beast*, April 13, 2017, https://www.thedailybeast.com/hitlers-final-days-revealed-eyewitnesses-recount-the-nazis-death-in-unearthed-footage.

2. Red Baron, "The Day Hitler Died," YouTube, May 17, 2017, https://www.youtube.com/watch?v=cNxcCEGTxkM.

3. Steven Erlanger, "Historian Asserts Soviet Soldiers Found Hitler's Charred Remains," *New York Times*, September 18, 1992, https://www.nytimes.com/1992/09/18/world/historian-asserts-soviet-soldiers-found-hitler-s-charred-remains.html.

4. Julie Masis et al., "The Woman Who Carried Hitler's Teeth on V-Day," *The Times of Israel*, September 6, 2017, www.timesofisrael.com/the-woman-who-carried-hitlers-teeth-on-v-day/.

5. Ada Petrova and Peter Watson, *The Death of Hitler: The Full Story with New Evidence from Secret Russian Archives* (New York: W. W. Norton & Company, 1995), 88.

6. James Preston O'Donnell, *The Bunker: The History of the Reich Chancellery Group* (Boston: Houghton Mifflin, 1978), 369.

7. Will Stewart, "Russian Who 'Cremated' Hitler Refuses to Reveal Where He Scattered His Ashes," *Daily Mail*, April 30, 2010, https://www.dailymail.co.uk/news/article-1270108/Russian-cremated-Adolf-Hitler-refuses-reveal-scattered-ashes.html.

8. "Wo Hitlers Asche Verstreut Werde," Berlin Story, May 26, 2016, https://www.berlinstory.de/blog/wo-hitlers-asche-verstreut-wurde/.

9. Stewart, "Russian who 'Cremated' Hitler."

10. Steven Erlanger, "Historian Asserts Soviet Soldiers Found Hitler's Charred Remains," *New York Times*, September 18, 1992, https://www.nytimes.com/1992/09/18/world/historian-asserts-soviet-soldiers-found-hitler-s-charred-remains.html.

11. Maura Reynolds, "Moscow Display on Hitler May End Mystery," *Los Angeles Times*, April 28, 2000, https://www.latimes.com/archives/la-xpm-2000-apr-28-mn-24481-story.html.

12. Uki Goñi, "Tests on Skull Fragment Cast Doubts on Hitler Suicide Story," *The Guardian*, September 26, 2009, https://www.theguardian.com/world/2009/sep/27/adolf-hitler-suicide-skull-fragment.

13. Jerome R. Corsi, *Hunting Hitler* (New York: Skyhorse Publishing, 2014), 45.

14. Goñi, "Tests on Skull Fragment."

15. For interviews with both Bellatoni and Strausbaugh, see UConn, "The Hitler Project—Nick Bellatoni," YouTube, June 15, 2011, https://www.youtube.com/watch?v=ZqrrjzfnsVY.

16. Maxim Tkachenko, "Official: KGB Chief Ordered Hitler's Remains Destroyed," CNN, December 11, 2009, http://www.cnn.com/2009/ WORLD/europe/12/11/russia.hitler.remains/index.html.

Chapter 11: The Final Word: Hitler's Very Bad Teeth

1. Xavier Riaud, "Dental Identification of Adolf Hitler and Eva Braun," *Journal of Dental Problems and Solutions*, October 27, 2014, https:// www.peertechz.com/Dental-Problems-Solutions/JDPS-1-103.php.

2. Courtesy of Anne Jea, https://commons.wikimedia.org/wiki/ File:Philippe_Charlier.jpg.

3. Jean-Christophe Brisard and Lana Parshina, *The Death of Hitler: The Final Word* (Boston: Da Capo Press, 2018), 305.

4. Ibid., 231.

5. Trevor-Roper, *The Last Days of Hitler,* 230.

6. Ibid., 305.

7. Courtesy of Tiberi77, https://commons.wikimedia.org/wiki/File: PhilippeCharlier.jpg.

8. Trevor-Roper, *The Last Days of Hitler*, 284.

9. Allan Hall, "'He Got Away Lightly with Suicide': Goebbels' Secretary, 100, Breaks Vow of Silence to Reveal Secrets of Hitler's Propaganda Minister," *Daily Mail*, August 29, 2011, https://www. dailymail.co.uk/news/article-2031365/Goebbels-secretary-100- breaks-silence-cold-distant-monster-Germans-hate-Jews.html.

10. Traudl Junge, *Hitler's Last Secretary*, trans. Anthea Bell (New York: Arcade Publishing, 2003). LOC 2215.

11. See "Should We Be Glad the Plot to Kill Hitler Failed?" *BBC History Magazine*, January 2017, https://www.historyextra.com/magazine- issue/january-2017/.

Epilogue

1. Roger Manvell and Heinrich Fraenkel, *Heinrich Himmler: The Sinister Life of the Head of the SS and Gestapo* (London: Skyhorse Publishing, 2007), 244–45.

2. Linge, *With Hitler to the End*, 210; see also Erich Kempka, *I Was Hitler's Chauffeur* (London: Frontline Books, 2010), 94.

3. Ibid., 99.

INDEX

ABOUT THE AUTHOR

Robert J. Hutchinson is an award-winning travel and religion writer and the author of numerous books of popular history, including *What Really Happened: TheLincoln Assassination* (Regnery History), *The Dawn of Christianity* (Harper Collins), *Searching for Jesus: New Discoveries in the Quest for Jesus of Nazareth* (Harper Collins), *The Politically Incorrect Guide to the Bible* (Regnery), *When in Rome: A Journal of Life in Vatican City* (Doubleday) and, as editor, *The Book of Vices: A Collection of Classic Immoral Tales* (Putnam). He has presented seminars and public lectures for groups in the U.S., Germany, and France.

Raised in the Pacific Northwest, Hutchinson attended a Jesuit high school and university, earned an undergraduate degree in philosophy, moved to Israel in his early twenties to learn Hebrew, and earned a graduate degree in New Testament studies.

For the past thirty years, Hutchinson has worked full-time as a professional writer. He has won numerous writing awards, and contributes essays and columns to such outlets as Fox News, The Blaze, Catholic Vote, MercatorNet, Catholic Exchange, Human Events, Christianity Today, and many more.

An avid traveler, Hutchinson is also the former managing editor of *Hawaii Magazine* and the former Hawaii bureau chief for *The Hollywood Reporter*. He lives with his wife and children in a small seaside village.

STAY IN TOUCH

For more information about Robert Hutchinson and his upcoming books and presentations, visit his website, www.RobertHutchinson.com. You'll find free resources that include these and more:

- Book excerpts
- Exclusive features
- Downloads of audio and video presentations
- Special reports
- Free e-mail updates